New Europe

plays from the continent

New Europe

plays from the continent

EDITED BY
Bonnie Marranca and Małgorzata Semil

New York, New York

New Europe: plays from the continent is published by PAJ Publications, P.O. Box 532, Village Station, New York, NY 10014.

PAJ Publications is distributed to the trade by Consortium Book Sales and Distribution: www.cbsd.com
Publisher of PAJ Publications: Bonnie Marranca

This publication is made possible with public funds from the New York State Council on the Arts, a state agency.

New Europe: plays from the continent / edited by Bonnie Marranca and Małgorzata Semil. – 1st ed.
p. cm.
ISBN 978-1-55554-085-2
1. Drama—Collections. 2. European drama—Translations into English. I. Marranca, Bonnie. II. Semil, Małgorzata.
PN6112.N46 2009
808.82'994—dc22

2009032024

Contents

Preface

Days of August

Bonnie Marranca

Today is August 19, 2009, and the Chancellor of a united Germany, Angela Merkel, is in a little Hungarian town called Sopron to celebrate the twentieth anniversary of the "pan-European picnic," the day when the country's borders with Austria were opened to a flood of East Germans, paving the way for the fall of the Berlin Wall a few months later, in November. That same summer day in 1989, the people of Estonia, Lithuania, and Latvia forged a human chain of two million, stretching four hundred miles, to declare their opposition to Soviet control of the Baltics. By June Solidarity had emerged victorious from a national election in Poland. Vaclav Havel, so recently having been jailed, led the Velvet Revolution all the way to the palace when he became president of Czechoslovakia by the end of the year. Gorbachev spoke of "our common European home" and Francis Fukuyama of the "end of history." An era of "anti-politics" and spiritual authority had already been envisioned by György Konrad as an antidote to power relations and ideology as the basis of society. In the White House, George H. W. Bush was laying the groundwork for a new world order in which the triumph of capitalism would be the centerpiece.

The *pax Europa* was not to last. Before long the old ethnic feuds and territorial disputes surfaced after decades, in some cases centuries, of suppression, as communists, democrats, and far-right officials would switch sides in their respective governments for years to come while the old Europe gave way to the new or the new to the old, depending on how you viewed things. Before long the deadly forces of ethnic cleansing were on the prowl in Yugoslavia, a country that had always prided itself on being the very model of multiculturalism, facing West instead of East. When war broke out in that country, the horror of genocide descended again on a continent that still had not laid to rest the torment of the Second World War, and even now Europeans are preparing to mark the seventy years since it began with the German and Soviet attack on Poland, in September 1939. Surveying the last half-century of Europe's recovery in his monumental study, *Postwar*, Tony Judt unequivocally affirms his belief in the power of history while also allowing that "some measure of neglect and forgetting is the necessary condition for civic health."

By the time these historic events of 1989 occurred PAJ Publications had already begun the DramaContemporary series of plays in translation, organized by country or region, and featuring such titles as *DramaContemporary: Czechoslovakia* and *DramaContemporary: Hungary*. The post-war landscape of Europe was still held in check by an Iron Curtain, with East and West Berlin and the two Germanies the most profound symbol of a divided continent. Western and Eastern Europe, represented by NATO and the Soviet bloc, were locked in a fierce Cold War struggle delineated by the Oder-Niesse line. What a different world that was.

Now after German unification the city of Berlin is the cultural capital of Europe, so calm this summer that its inhabitants seem to care more about the international games in its famous (rebuilt) Olympic Stadium than the upcoming election. The expansion of the twenty-seven member European Union, working towards the common currency of the Euro and open borders from Britain to the Balkans, including eight former communist countries, has put into place a map of Europe representing five-hundred million people and twenty-five per cent of the world's wealth. Its Charter of Fundamental Rights includes the right to free education, the right to health care and social services, the right to parental leave, the right of care for children and the elderly and disabled, and the promise of environmental and consumer protection. The ideal of this transnational model of interdependence and cultural exchange is encapsulated in its motto: "United in Diversity." A sculpture of Europa atop a bull stands watch outside one of the European Parliament buildings to remind everyone that it traces a founding, albeit violent, myth all the way to antiquity and across linguistic and cultural divides as a symbol of pan-Europeanism. Jürgen Habermas and Jacques Derrida had once proposed turning the EU into the "avant-gardist core" of political cultures on the continent. Alas, nowadays ministers and businessmen hold more power in the affairs of state than intellectuals.

PAJ Publications still retains its commitment to European dramatic literature, if not to Europe's former borders. For this reason, *New Europe*, the start of what I hope will be an ongoing series, includes plays from across the continent. Even though not all of the authors represented live in countries that are part of the European Union, the intention is to consider Europe as a cultural, geographic, political, and economic entity, envisioned as far back as 1950 by Jean Monnet when he wrote the manifesto for a devastated continent that would eventually bring into existence the EU. There remain plenty of Euroskeptics on both sides of the Atlantic and English Channel to challenge the Eurocentrics. Nonetheless, for those countries whose borders, histories, and elites were erased by totalitarian regimes, the idea of Europe has always been a fervent dream. Europe is a place, a state of mind, an idea, a symbol, a way of life.

The authors in this volume, all of them born after the Second World War—in the fifties and sixties—represent new generations of Europeans who cross boundaries of countries, languages, and genres with ease. Their biographical facts reflect European history and its many transformations while generationally they are freer than older Europeans to move beyond it. Igor Bauersima was born in Prague a few years before the Soviet and Warsaw Pact tanks drove into his city, and grew up in Switzerland. Goran Stefanovski left his home in Macedonia during the Yugoslav War that set ethnic group against ethnic group, and started a career in England. Juan Mayorga spent his early years under the fascism of Franco's Spain. A few years after Małgorzata Sikorska-Miszczuk was born, the long, persistent resistance against Polish communist rule began to grow. Roland Schimmelpfennig was born in a divided Germany and Petr Zelenka in a country still called Czechoslovakia. Jon Fosse was born in Norway less than a decade after the Marshall Plan helped to rebuild its fishing industries. Their histories typify the European of the post-war generation, whose lives are grounded in the great historic events of their individual countries. All of the plays in *New Europe* have been first produced since 2000, foregrounding in their multiplicity of concerns an evolving continent experiencing numerous social changes in the post-1989 era.

The plays represent both the Europe that offers a cradle-to-grave security blanket through a strong government role in the well-being of its citizens, side by side with the Europe undergoing social, political, and economic instability while newer countries in its expanded community of nations build democratic infrastructures and institutions with scant resources. Their authors are writing a new history of mentalities in Europe, in a vernacular language that has now moved away from the earlier, more literary dramatic language of European drama. Unrestricted to any one form, they write plays, films, essays, poetry, and novels. In particular, the plays are often more influenced by popular culture and independent cinema and media. One of the intriguing aspects of the plays is the distinctive use of the pause or the dash, often signifying the silence, tentativeness, and estrangement of contemporary speech, with its calculated fears and breakdown of communication.

What is the news of their day? Iceland has had a financial meltdown. The president of France decided that one cannot swim with a "burqini." Berlusconi is trifling with young women in Rome. Switzerland is making public the names in secret accounts of tax evaders. Britain has just buried its last veteran of the First World War. Pirates have returned to European waters for the first time in centuries.

In August many citizens of the wealthier European capitals are nowhere to be found as they are on the long holidays their generous social welfare systems provide, while those in the poorer countries to the east are trapped in evolving capitalist economies burdened by debt, lack of new technologies, the destruction of rural culture, and emigration of their compatriots to other countries in search of work. Beneath the veneer of security and wellbeing promoted as the continental social model, the European way of life is full of contradictions and exclusions and looming dangers. Europe today includes the most progressive social model in the Nordic countries as well as its only dictator in Belarus, with diverse political conditions in between.

War and poverty have brought a continuous stream of refugees and migrants, over land and sea, to the gates of European countries, several of which have no desire to welcome them as eventual citizens, even though they are eager for their cheap labor. Earlier this month Italy has gone so far as to criminalize illegal immigration, making it possible for citizen patrols to report undocumented persons living among them. In many parts of Europe, conservative Muslim populations are in conflict with liberal European societies, the most disturbing examples of this tension being the violent protests that erupted when newspaper cartoons featuring the face of Mohammed, published in a small town in Denmark, set off protests in the Middle East, and the earlier assassination on an Amsterdam street of a Dutch filmmaker for his documentary on Muslim women. Whether Turkey is able to gain entry to the European Union in the next decade will be determined by Europe's ability to cope with its rising Muslim population, as much as 15% in Oslo and 10% in Paris. Christianity and Islam are now the dominant faiths on a continent more secular than religious.

The new Euro economies of emerging democracies in eastern Europe have triggered high unemployment, social unrest, and contemporary dystopias, while criminal rings from former communist countries and Russia have spread their sex and porno trade across the continent, often ensnaring young women who have sought to emigrate from their poorer homelands. Basque separatists continue to wage their violent campaign inside a progressive contemporary Spain still coming to terms with the legacy of the Spanish Civil War. Nationalist movements and far-right parties have moved foreigners and the Roma population, still prey to attack and murder, to the forefront of any discussion of cultural identity, one of the main issues on a continent prone to confusing history and myth. Youth facing high unemployment and outmoded institutions riddled with corruption, are provoked to violent riots by confrontations with institutional power, as the Athens demonstrators proved last year, even mounting on the Acropolis, the very symbol of Western democracy, a banner calling for "resistance."

A panoramic play occurring in multiple spaces, such as Goran Stefanovski's *Hotel Europa*, demonstrates all of the tragedy and comedy in the tensions of "old Europe" with its burnished charm, nationalist myth, and blood feuds as well as the "new Europe" of humiliated exiles and refugees, criminals and consumers. Here heartbreaking honesty mingled with the poetry of broken dreams delineates the bittersweet lives of each wandering soul's definition of "Europeanness." In Petr Zelenka's *Tales of Ordinary Madness*, a family coming apart, their neighbors, and friends create an absurdist enclave in a post-communist world defined by the old Marxist-tinged newspeak, sexual perversity, and a peculiar strain of mental disjunction. Terse short sentences and half-formed words circulate in the silent undertow of Jon Fosse's portrait of a family whose members gather around a dying mother in an intense psychological drama of imploding pauses and rigorous self-control. This is family drama *in extremis* in an aging Europe.

Words take on another meaning in Igor Bauersima's *norway.today*, based on an actual incident, whose characters meet in a chat room where a young woman is looking for someone to commit suicide with her. She, and the teenager who answers, are the children of affluent Europe, who endlessly analyze their empty lives staring into the abyss, but not before videotaping and reimagining themselves in the dialogue and images of movies and literary texts. Also a view of contemporary life, *Push Up 1–3* moves into the new global world of young corporate executives who are ruthless and competitive, and so little differentiated that they often speak the same dialogue, usually revolving around success, clothes, shopping, food, and sex. Take a leap from *Mad Men* to the new capitalist marketplace.

The inclusion of children and young people is characteristic of contemporary European drama, surely linked to concern for the future of the human race in the face of so much social and environmental devastation worldwide. There has also been a marked rise in child pornography, sex slavery, kidnapping, and murder of children in Europe. Juan Mayorga has given "The Pied Piper" a new twist in *Hamlyn* to reveal the sexual and economic exploitation of young boys, compounded by the corruption of state power. Complicity and obfuscation protect the guilty and destroy the innocent.

The violent assault on the German state was the mission of the Baader-Meinhof gang, an ongoing subject of films, dance, visual art, and literature since their rampages in the late sixties and seventies. On the European continent utopia and revolution are central themes in social philosophy, and so it is not surprising that there are German intellectuals who continue to support the basic premises of Andreas Baader, Ulricke Meinhof, and the other notorious RAF member, Gudrun Ensslin. However, from her contemporary vantage point, Małgorzata Sikorska-Miszczuk views them as burlesque figures whose radical political program can only have led to death and destruction and, in their case, hanging themselves in a jail cell once their situation became hopeless. This disenchantment with ideological extremes, along with the cognizance of their attraction, can be measured in the decades separating Ulrike Meinhof's tragic-comic role in *The Death of the Squirrel-Man* and Heiner Müller's glorification of the feminist terrorist in *Hamletmachine*.

Those were tumultuous days when the utopian ideals of revolution and social transformation were alive so soon after Europe's experience of '68. Whether your country was locked down or opened up depended on which side of Prague you faced, for it was that year, on August 21, that the Soviet Union's brutal entry into the city in the middle of the night cast an icy shadow over Europe that was not fully lifted until the fall of the Berlin Wall twenty-one years later. A few months before that momentous event, on an August day in 1989, Poland, land of the Pope who had been looking after Europe from the Holy See, elected its first non-communist prime minister, the Catholic Tadeusz Mazowiecki.

Today is August 25, 2009. Fires are raging in the ancient Greek villages near Boeotia where Europa's brother Cadmus came looking for his sister, who had been abducted by Zeus (or Jupiter, if you were a Roman) appearing in the form of a seductive bull and carried to other lands. He traveled on to Delphi to ask about her. Who knows what the Oracle is thinking these days while the hot winds blow this way and that?

norway.today

Igor Bauersima

Translated from German by Anna Köhler

norway.today premiered at Schauspielhaus Düsseldorf, Germany, in November 2000. It was directed by the author.

CHARACTERS

JULIE

AUGUST

The air resonates with "I'll See You in Another World" by Nurse with Wound, and with silence. White noise. Enter Julie. *She is wearing a T-shirt with the slogan julie@home.shirt.*

Julie: Hi, I'm Julie. This is the first time I'm communicating at this location. So I apologize if what I'm saying is not appropriate. Because my message is only intended for people who wish to commit suicide. Therefore I am asking those who don't intend to do away with themselves to please disregard this and maybe leave this chat room for a little while.

I am going to, and this is not a rash decision, commit suicide, soon. I've thought about it for a long time. But my decision is made. And it might sound a little strange to some, but I would like to do it with someone else. So here's my question: Would someone like to step over that threshold with me? You don't need to respond right away. I understand completely if there's nobody who wishes to admit publicly that they're fed up with it all. You might be sitting next to your significant other, and he might be totally okay with staying and continuing to rob the Earth of its resources for a while longer, and to wait for cancer or some other epidemic to scratch him from the surface of this planet. But I don't want to be a bummer. Smiley face. What I'm trying to say is normally there are still quite a few ties between the one who wishes to get out and the others. There are not too many who comprehend the most supreme act of life's execution, and so are able to understand what it means to the dignity of a human being, "to do away with oneself." As a rule you wish to be alive until you notice that everyone else is gone and that you're alone, and always have been. I mean, one of us here will outlive all the others. And that you can be dead sure about. But I don't want to spread discord here either—on the contrary. Because the ones who are still serious about it all, they are still the norm. I mean, most people are caught up in some sense-producing, life-preserving brain constructs. Emotional ties. A sense of responsibility, right? Obsession with success, reproductive instinct, the craving for pleasure, and other reactionary needs. Okay. But you're all here because you want to kill yourselves sooner or later. If you didn't feel fucked with by what I just said, then we're together on this. Right. Yeah. Well.

Yeah. Well as I said, all serious replies are welcome. You can also mail me and we can arrange it all. Smiley face.

Because, guys, you might have already caught on to the fact that I don't fit in with people, not even with the suicidal ones. It's a sad truth, but it's the truth. If I'm uncomfortable socializing, it's less because others—but more because *I*—don't show myself in a way that I like. The need to act a part and an inner aversion against having to do that make it annoying to socialize, and I can only be happy with my own company, because only there am I allowed to be genuine. You can't be that among people, and so nobody is …

Please don't take this the wrong way. But I'm now going to pretend you're not here.

Enter AUGUST. *He is wearing a T-shirt with the slogan august@home.shirt.*

AUGUST: Well, if nobody's going to say anything right now, then I will say something. Because … well my name is August and … please don't ask why. I don't know. I had nothing to do with it.

… Actually, I never anticipated having anything to do with life. Just in general. I don't know if others feel the same way. But most of what goes down in life is just so weird, so weird … I don't mean funny, I just mean weird. It has its moments. For example, when I'm alone, running, I can hear my breathing and the steps; and the blood is pumping in my ears pretty loudly. But I don't run all the time, after all. Not possible, unfortunately, to run all the time. The goal is to almost not be there. So to be nowhere. To be absent from everywhere. That is being alive. That way, my presence being almost non-existent, it would be bearable for a little while longer. You can talk about being alive, meaning you're very much in it. But don't say you're full of life. I mean, if somebody says that they're "full of life," I am damn sure that they are full of it, and a fake shitface.

But the thing is, most of the time everything is standing still. And I'm standing still, and can't hear a sound.

Only this indefinable noise. Like I said, I don't know if others feel the same way. No idea. Maybe I'm sick. But I don't want to hear that either. "You're sick, my boy." I mean, if a really weird character walks up to you with a really screwed up smile on and says, "You have to get better first, and then you will see…"—that makes me go right to sleep. Who are those totally bizarre people that think they can tell you, "Whatever you think is going on, isn't. What is really going on is what we think." You know what I mean? I mean, that what's going on is not what I think; that, I can figure out by myself. But where does anybody get off thinking that what's going on is what they think? We have the most gigantic lie here. It's totally hypocritical. They all pretend to be someone, and all the while they're not even someone else. And so how does anybody think they know what's going on? Nothing's going on. The truest feeling I can feel is feeling nothing. If I take this chair here, for example, and go up with it, like that … then it does that. Okay. It goes up. But there's nevertheless a strange sense of uncertainty. I don't know, did it go up for real, or did it just pretend? Is real even real? When I let it come down, then it … maybe … yes, it comes down. Although—and that's the point—it probably only pretends to come down to put us at ease. It's all fake. I mean you can see it everywhere, this nothingness. Well sometimes here in this chat room somebody will speak up against that, but in vain. But most users are chilling out there as lurkers, and sometimes they pinch themselves just to give themselves the feeling of being alive. Because most of them are too scared to make their exit. They prefer to hang on for another round. Maybe something real will happen. Here nothing real happens. I mean, just imagine, we could take the plunge now with Julie. All of us. That would be real! We could all cut each other's wrists.

I mean, you're all here because you've had enough of it all. There's potential there. That could be a good beginning. That could start off something.

It was high time for someone to "come out" here. That Julie says, "I'm going," I think that's great.

Julie: Thanks.

August. I'm not just saying that.

Julie: Cool.

August: It's a sign of life.

Julie: Okay.

Were you being ironic?

August: About what?

Julie: Sign of life.

August: No. Yes. No! All I mean to say is that otherwise nothing would be going on here.

Julie: Yeah. Maybe.

August: It's even hard to know who actually is here, really. In all this silence. Only when someone says "I'm going now" can I imagine that they were here before.

Julie: Users come, users go.

I'm still here.

August: Yeah.

Julie: And obviously you are too.

August: Oh yeah. So you want to die?

Julie: I'm going to die. Yes.

August: So am I.

Julie: Yeah?

August: Yeah.

Julie: You mean, pretty soon?

August: Yeah.

Julie: Seriously?

August: What?

Julie: I mean, for real?

August: For real?

Julie: Cut off the connection, you know.

August: The connection?

Julie: To, like, life and all that.

August: Yeah, sure. Like I said, there isn't that much that needs to be disconnected, in my case.

Julie: Right.

August: It's easy for me to quit this "fake" here. Even tonight, if necessary.

Julie: But this here is not real. I'm talking about being gone for real.

August: Yeah, sure.

Julie: Gone, gone.

August: No logging off or dozing off or whatever.

Julie: Exactly.

August: That's my plan.

JULIE: Are you, like, sick?

AUGUST: No. Yes. Don't know. As I'm saying ...

JULIE: I'm not sick.

AUGUST: Oh, right. Yeah well.

JULIE: Hey listen, I don't want to keep show-chatting here. Like I said, I'm in a hurry.

AUGUST: Tell me, what do you look like?

JULIE: What do you mean, what do I look like?

AUGUST: Tell me what you look like.

JULIE: Like Natalie Wood. Like Natalie Wood before she drowned.

AUGUST: Who's Natalie Wood?

JULIE: Some actress. She drowned.

AUGUST: Oh, right.

Tell me, what did she look like?

JULIE: Dark hair.

AUGUST: I like that.

JULIE: Ninety percent of all humankind has dark hair.

AUGUST: Yeah? Yeah, I like that.

JULIE: The Wood woman before drowning, that is being in a psychic state. She was in *Rebel Without a Cause*. And nobody has a cause to know anything more about all that, and even less what she looked like before she drowned. And if there were someone who knew, then he helped her do it and I can say here whatever I like. Natalie Wood is a fucking star and her death is a mystery.

AUGUST: I am sure she looked great, just before she drowned. I imagine she had a shitty life, being an actress. It's all totally fake. Fake walls, fake floors, fake people, nothing's real, and somebody is constantly telling you what to do. Nobody can handle that. It can squeeze the breath right out of you. I believe that when she realized she was about to drown, she was relieved. Being an actress and all. I mean ... no, seriously, there is something freeing in that.

Julie: Yeah.

August: Yeah. But I wouldn't go for drowning.

Julie: No, not my thing either.

August: How would you like to do it?

Julie: Together with someone.

August: But how?

Julie: I can't talk about that here. Only "in the event of." Here there are some bleeding hearts for sure, who like nothing more than saving something or somebody. All I can say is that it is dead sure. One-way ticket.

August: So take me with you.

Julie: How old are you?

August: That doesn't matter, right?

Julie: Yeah.

August: So there.

Julie: Well, how old?

August: Nineteen.

Julie: Forget about it.

August: What do you mean?

Julie: I don't want to drag any beginners into this.

August: I'm not a beginner.

Julie: Have you ever killed yourself? I mean, have you ever tried?

August: No. Yes. Sure.

Julie: And?

August: And it hasn't worked yet.

Julie: So you're a beginner.

August: Hold on. Aren't you still alive?

Julie: Yeah. But I haven't tried it yet. I'm not going to try it, I'll do it. People who just try a little and then get into the pity thing, that's not my thing.

August: Hold on. I made some real attempts. I have a scar on my face. I fell out of bed, right after I was born. I'd thrown myself on the floor. My first reflex. Ever since I can remember I've been thinking of killing myself. Seriously. I was gonna crash into the pillar of a bridge with a motorbike, for example. So it would look like an accident and nobody would have to worry.

Julie: And?

August: And what?

Julie: What happened with the pillar?

August: That was theory. That was one possibility. Don't know. Anyway, I don't have a driver's license.

Julie: This is for real.

August: Yeah. I know. That's what I sensed from you.

Julie: What?

August: That this is for real.

Julie: For real?

August: For real.

Hello?

Julie: Yeah. Do you have a picture of yourself.

August: A picture? A picture like what?

Julie: A picture. To look at.

August: Yeah.

Julie: Let's see.

That's you?

August: Yeah.

Julie: Just what I was afraid of.

August: What?

Julie: You're cute.

August: Excuse me?

Julie: Total heartthrob.

August: That's bullshit. Let me see one of you.

Julie: There.

August: For real?

Julie: What?

August: Like, it looks totally okay.

Julie: Thanks.

August: I'd like to go with you.

Julie: Hold on. I have a question. If you answer it correctly, I'll think about it.

August: You're serious?

Julie: I mean, I don't know you. You could be, like, some kind of pervert.

August: Right. Smiley face.

Julie: Well, are you?

August: Nope. Smiley face.

Julie: Okay, if all of you out there would like to take a guess too, go right ahead. Well, ready? Reason. What is that?

August: What?

Julie: Yeah.

August: Yeah?

Julie: That is the question. Take your time.

August: Reason? What is reason? Reason is sick. Everybody knows that.

JULIE: That's all?

AUGUST: Don't know.

JULIE: Anybody else know? Not a clue? Yeah? No. Reason?

AUGUST: Yeah. I don't know. It's different for everybody. Well, for example, for me it seems reasonable to kill myself, but not for somebody else. There was that philosopher, well, he didn't kill himself, but he discovered that we have eyes in order not to see, and ears in order not to hear. What was his name again? Anyway he says that reason relies on eyes that can't see and ears that can't hear. And that's why reason is an unreasonable concept. Really quite world-famous. Pretty much one of the Greats. Can't remember … his name was something like …

JULIE: If you want, I'll take you with me …

What's the matter?

AUGUST: Yes.

JULIE: Yes, you're in? We'll do it together?

AUGUST: Yes!

JULIE: No. I mean, I wanna know.

AUGUST: Yes.

JULIE: I wasn't ready for that. So fast. You're serious about that …

AUGUST: Yes.

JULIE: You're dead serious. No bullshit.

AUGUST: Sure.

JULIE: You're serious.

AUGUST: Shitfuckingdeadserious.

JULIE: Am I, like, really happy now?

AUGUST: I don't know.

JULIE: I am probably really happy just now.

Now you must promise me something.

August: What?

Julie: You have to promise you won't tell anybody about it. What we're going to do, you must not tell anybody about it. Not your parents, not your friends, not your girlfriend, nobody. We'll go away, and we won't tell anybody where. Absolutely nobody.

August: No.

Julie: Swear! Swear you won't tell anybody.

August: Sure.

Julie: Say: "I swear I won't tell anybody."

August: I swear I won't tell anybody.

Julie: "May I rot in life forever if I can't keep my mouth shut."

August: May I rot in life forever, if I can't keep my mouth shut.

Julie: "Long live death!"

August: Long live death!

Julie: "Amen."

August: Amen.

Julie: We need a tent.

August: A tent?

Julie: And some food.

August: Food?

Julie: Beer.

August: Shall I fix some sandwiches?

Julie: And warm clothing. At night it's I don't know how much below zero. Very low, at any rate.

August: Where are we going?

Julie: Into the snow.

AUGUST: Freeze to death?

JULIE: Track me down. After you get to my homepage, wait a minute, to see that nobody followed you. Then I will come and pick you up. Smiley face! people.

AUGUST: Smiley face.

SCENE CHANGE. Accompanied by "Wouldn't It Be Nice" by the Beach Boys. Day, continuous snowfall, stage cuts off into a void. The edge of the world. Loaded with heavy backpacks, the two arrive on the plateau. They stand for a long time looking out over the diffused white panorama. Finally they take off their packs and put them in the snow. AUGUST ventures some steps towards the drop, he slips and falls and comes back.

AUGUST: It's slippery.

It's beautiful here.

JULIE: You think so?

AUGUST: That river.

JULIE: That's a fjord.

AUGUST: It's awesome. Where does all that water come from?

What?

JULIE: That's a fjord. That's ocean water. That's the ocean.

AUGUST: Still. Something's going on.

JULIE: What?

AUGUST: What's going on?

JULIE: Why should something be going on?

AUGUST: You're not saying anything.

Something's going on.

JULIE: No.

AUGUST: I'm saying how beautiful it is here, and you don't say anything. Something's going on.

JULIE: Oh.

August: You can tell me what's going on.

Julie: Nothing–is–going–on.

August: Are you afraid or something?

Julie: What?

August: I don't know. Could be.

Where does it go, this fjord! Docs it go anywhere?

I think it's beautiful here.

Julie: Can't you be silent, for once?

August: Why?

Julie: Because you're not really saying anything, the whole time.

August: I say: "It's beautiful here."

Julie: That is nothing. Nothing at all.

August: Oh.

How long do you want to be silent?

Julie: Forever. I want to be silent forever.

August: Already now?

Julie: Including now.

August: Forever?

Julie: Yeah.

August: I think I'm too freezing for that.

In this cold you can't be silent forever. Not for very long, at any rate.

Julie: You're, like, a little Joker, aren't you.

August: Excuse me?

Julie: Were you the class clown? August, the comedian?

August: No.

Julie: So you're trying to catch up right now?

August: You are really annoying.

Julie: Is your name really August? What's your real name?

August: August.

Julie: That's not your real name.

August: Yes. I got it. For my birthday.

Julie: You said your name was August in the chat room, because my name is Julie.

August: Julie … July, I hadn't even noticed. No, not at all. How dumb is that. July. You're a little cold though, for July.

Julie: Alright, whatever. At any rate, I don't believe it's your name. Never.

August: Tell me, why didn't you want to do it on your own?

You didn't say a word in the cab. And nothing before that either. I don't know.

Julie: I–don't–need–to–talk–all–the–time. Do you understand? Or don't you?

August: Yes, I understand. I don't need to talk all the time either. Except I feel like it right now. I sense that something's going on. Why aren't you telling me what's going on?

Julie: What's going on? Here we are, on the edge of the abyss. There is the abyss. That's the back country, that's where little people live and worry about things. There is the middle. That's the edge, then there's nothing for quite some time and then there's the ocean. And there are fish in it, and they are hungry. That's it.

August: If you prefer, we can be silent. Nothing's better than being silent with somebody. Except to be silent by yourself, maybe. I mean I would have killed myself by myself anyway, but what you said, about not fitting in with people. That you can only be yourself when you're by yourself—that, I liked. Same thing is going on with me.

Julie: You didn't tell anybody about us being here?

August: No. Why?

Julie: I just wanna make sure.

AUGUST: Nobody has any idea anyway where this is, where we are. I said: I'm going to stay with a friend for a couple of days. They are only gonna start looking for me the day after tomorrow. But definitely not here. And you?

JULIE: No one is looking for me.

AUGUST: I don't know. I can imagine someone looking for you.

JULIE: What is that supposed to mean?

AUGUST: Well. Look at you. It makes sense. I can't actually imagine that nobody would be looking for you. Somebody like you—thousands, ten thousand people would be looking for.

JULIE: Would they, really?

AUGUST: No, seriously. Millions are looking for someone like that. Someone a little sad, a little gone wrong.

I can barely look down.

JULIE: Then don't look.

AUGUST: I always feel that I'll jump any minute in a spot like this. Always been that way. You feel like that too?

JULIE: Yeah.

AUGUST: But I've never been up this high.

JULIE: 2000 feet.

AUGUST: I looked it up on the net. The average speed of a fully clothed person free falling is between 118 and 127 miles per hour; that's about 180 feet per second. So it comes … two thousand … you factor in the acceleration, you fall for about ten seconds.

JULIE: Just about.

AUGUST: You've calculated that already, haven't you? What do you do in those ten seconds?

JULIE: Fall.

AUGUST: Really.

JULIE: And be dead.

AUGUST: That's all?

JULIE: Ten seconds to be dead. Yeah. I'll just let go and then there is nothing more, it's all there, but nothing exists anymore. There is not a single thing, not a single event in this world, nothing that concerns me. You have given up everything: your sadness, your joy, your hatred, your love, your lousy character, the responsibility to recycle. Simply everything. It leaves you completely cold. Our continent produces forty-million tons of shit every day, and it's absolutely not your problem. All thoughts are redundant. All action impossible. It's all behind you now. You have no obligations, you don't even have to breathe. You're absolutely free to do nothing at all. Absolute, unlimited freedom. You are God, and God does nothing. You perceive it all, for a few seconds, but there's no turning back, no pros and cons.

And then you're gone.

AUGUST: And your memory. What about your memory? You can't just simply forget everything.

JULIE: Sure. You have to find closure with everything, beforehand.

AUGUST: Find closure.

JULIE: Yeah. You have to focus on the moment.

AUGUST: The moment, yeah?

JULIE: Unless you want to die without being aware of it. But to live your whole life looking forward to that moment, and then miss it, is the dumbest thing I can imagine.

AUGUST: I always hoped that I wouldn't miss that brief moment of real life, should it occur.

JULIE: They're both the same.

AUGUST counts to ten.

AUGUST: Before I thought I would only think one thing while falling: This is it. This is it. This is it. This is it. I thought, that will be my last thought. "This" and "is" and "it." A thought void of anything. It doesn't mean anything. It's completely void of anything and somehow appropriate. But I'm afraid now that it won't be enough to fill ten seconds, and that shortly before impact I will suddenly be thinking about something unnecessary and inappropriate, like, "you're thinking 'this is it' because you planned to, and all the while your father did buy you that lemon ice, in the amusement park, when you were four." Crash.

JULIE: Lemon ice?

AUGUST: I just made that up.

JULIE: Your father didn't buy you lemon ice?

AUGUST: He did, I think. He did, I'm sure. I'm sure I won't be able to think: "this is it" for ten seconds straight. Never. Now I'm sure that I will waste a tenth of a second on lemon ice. I won't even go through the most unique, most alive moment of my life without losing focus. I can't take anything seriously for very long.

JULIE: If you don't take things seriously, you have to lie all the time.

AUGUST: Yeah. They all lie. All the time. Even "this is it" sounds like a lie, the more I think about it. So why should I focus on anything for longer? The only thing that lasts is boredom. That I can take seriously. Boredom.

JULIE: I can't stand boredom.

AUGUST: You have to take it seriously though. It's everywhere. The entire universe is bored to death. Everything's slowing down. DJs, music, cars, planets, electrons. It's all chilling. Total chill out. One day the Moon is going to crash into Earth, I heard. Because of gravity. Because the earth is sucking on it and the moon is losing momentum. My father also lost momentum. Because he revolves around my mom. Everything's sucking on something. The universe is sucking and disintegrating and ends up uniform and boring and cold and dead. Chill out. I read this, somewhere: "Big bang was a tap on the forehead of stupidity. The universe was created out of the realization of its own incompetence." I memorized that. I don't know what it means, for real, but it sounds absolutely right on, I think. The tone of it. I mean, falling for ten seconds straight is too long, so boredom will occur. Even if nothing concerns you anymore, memories keep flashing through your mind of the most meaningless things that happened. And you remember a cool afternoon by the lake and the sun shining on the moss, and the smells in the summer rental, and when you had a toothache, and the kid with the epileptic fits, and your bicycle in the basement, and the escalator where you kissed for the first time, and you realize how dumb you were, and hypocritical, and small, and miserable, how you never managed to do anything with what you had, and you are overcome by boundless boredom. It's an eternity, ten seconds. I wonder if we shouldn't jump from further below.

JULIE: Do you have a girlfriend?

AUGUST: No.

JULIE: I'm not surprised.

AUGUST: Really?

JULIE: I get depressed when I listen to you awhile.

AUGUST: But aren't you depressed anyway?

JULIE: No.

AUGUST: No?

JULIE: What?

AUGUST: You're not depressed?

JULIE: No.

AUGUST: So what are you?

JULIE: Normal. I'm happy.

AUGUST: Now you're putting on an act for me, aren't you?

JULIE: No.

AUGUST: I don't get it.

JULIE: I tend to lean towards happiness.

AUGUST: Yeah. Okay, that's normal.

JULIE: That's what I said.

AUGUST: I mean the tendency is normal. But not if you're suicidal. Then you tend to lean over precipices and such. And towards fear and horror.

JULIE: Yeah.

AUGUST: I don't get it.

JULIE: It's pointless to be depressed. It's stupid, it holds you back, and it's no fun. It doesn't do anything. Absolutely nothing. Even if you're suicidal it doesn't do anything. Depressed suicide candidates are weak.

AUGUST: But why are you killing yourself then?

JULIE: Are you a complete moron, or what?

AUGUST: What?

JULIE: You're killing me with all these questions! I told you I simply had enough. I've had it all. I'm stuffed. It's enough. I don't feel like starting over again.

AUGUST: You don't need to scream like that. You could wake up some animals that are hibernating around here. Are there actually bears around here?

JULIE: Yeah.

AUGUST: Shit ...

You still haven't told me why you didn't want to do it by yourself.

JULIE: Because ... on the input-output scale it doesn't balance right. It has to pay off. I want my life to fulfill itself all the way till the end. Living alone is pathetic; dying alone is too. I don't want to miserably waste away in a corner. Also, by myself I might not do it all.

AUGUST: What do you mean by that, "pay off"?

JULIE: I want to get something out of it. I want to know how somebody acts who is about to die. I've seen people getting shot on TV, in slow motion and all that. But TV is fake. And slow motion doesn't let you see more, it shows you more of what you can't see.

AUGUST: You want to watch somebody die.

JULIE: Yeah.

AUGUST: Like, how I die.

JULIE: Yeah.

AUGUST: You're totally fucked up. I mean, that's totally sick. You're really out of it.

JULIE: Really.

AUGUST: Are you high or something?

JULIE: You cross half of Europe to hang around here with me in this whiteness. And that's not sick? Look at yourself. You think you're normal? At least I know what I'm doing. Do you know what you're doing? Where you are? Why you are where you are?

AUGUST: No idea.

JULIE: You're on the edge of the abyss. You have arrived at the other end of your unlived life, dude.

AUGUST: Maybe I'm not here to kill myself, honey.

JULIE: What do I know about why you're here.

AUGUST: Yes, what do you know about why I'm here?

JULIE: Now you're being, like, all secretive, right?

AUGUST: What if I told you I won't do it? Simply because I wasn't going to in the first place? That I just came out of curiosity?

JULIE: Do you know why that's a lie? Because you are shitting your pants. Because in the taxi just now you were trembling. I was afraid you were gonna give us away. The driver kept looking down at your hands. I saw that. You are scared.

AUGUST: I was cold. I'm still freezing. And ever since I've been standing here listening to you, I feel even more freezing.

JULIE: You're scared.

AUGUST: I don't know you. I don't know who you are or whatever.

JULIE: That really doesn't matter. I'm no different from any other girl you know. You may project on me whatever you want. I even brought some make-up to make it easier.

AUGUST: Project on you?

JULIE: Yeah. Just imagine, like, I'm your mother. Whatever your hang up is.

AUGUST: You're totally screwed up. What am I doing here?

JULIE: You're getting weak. We only just arrived. This is no picnic. I didn't pay for your flight just for you to get weak.

August: I'm not getting weak, goddammit. I don't know you.

Julie: Who cares—we both want the same thing. We want to kill ourselves here. That's what counts.

August: I don't trust you. I don't believe anything you say. I don't get you. You're not even depressed, goddammit. Why do you want to kill yourself? I don't know. You won't talk to me. At least not honestly. Are we here on some show or something? Why don't you talk normally with me? Why do you keep pretending? I'm not pretending anything.

Julie: If I sound slightly fake then it's because I'm forcing myself to talk to keep you in good spirits ... That's what's going on.

August: Yeah, why don't we come out with what's going on. I can dig that.

Julie: Because you're forcing me to pretend to be, like, talkative.

August: Hold on. You wanted to take somebody with you. You didn't want to come here alone. You wanted to watch what somebody looks like in the face of death. And here you are. This is what somebody who's about to die looks like. He talks. Shit.

Julie: He talks shit.

August: Yeah. That too. Maybe.

Julie: "In the face of death." Where do you get that kind of crap?

Are you gonna start weeping, or what?

August: No.

Julie: You're bawling.

August: No.

Julie: He's bawling, guys.

August: Which guys?

Julie: It's, like, an expression "He's bawling, guys."

August: Don't know it.

Julie: There you are. You learn something new every day.

August: What's it supposed to mean, that expression?

Julie. "I am bowled over by your bawling."

August: I'm not bawling.

Julie: I mean, your expression …

August: My expression?

Julie: "He's bawling, guys."

August: What are you talking about? I'm just looking around, dammit. I'm not bawling. I am just looking at the damn river. At the water. And at the ice.

Julie: You're bawling.

August: So what? It's not a crime, is it?

Julie: No.

August: No.

Julie: But you claimed you weren't bawling.

August: Because … because … shit. I claim whatever I want here. I don't have to justify myself to anybody here. I can say whatever I want here. Since I'm supposed to make my permanent exit here, I might as well act the way I want. I can cut loose any way I want. I can cut loose any way I want and find relief any way I want and say what I've never said before. Shit.

Julie: You already said that.

August: I'm gonna die of laughter, I swear.

Julie: Wait a minute. You said: "supposed to make my exit here."

August: Yes. And?

Julie: That sounds weird.

August: Yeah?

Julie: Yeah. As if you don't want to do it anymore.

August: What?

JULIE: Make your exit.

AUGUST: I don't want anything anymore.

JULIE: Wait a minute here. Making your exit, you've got to want that.

AUGUST: Yeah. Fuck it. I don't even want to know what I want. Guess I want it.

JULIE: I just got, like, a feeling.

AUGUST: I don't want feeling either.

JULIE: We made a deal.

AUGUST: Yes, I know.

JULIE: I just want to make sure. We made a deal.

AUGUST: Yeah.

JULIE: What's the deal we made?

AUGUST: There's no going back.

JULIE: And if one of us wants to drop out?

AUGUST: Yes, I know ...

JULIE: There you are.

AUGUST: And I still say whatever I want here. And I do whatever I want.

AUGUST quickly does whatever he wants.

JULIE: What are you doing?

AUGUST: I'm doing whatever I want.

JULIE slowly ventures toward the precipice.

JULIE: Come over here.

AUGUST: What for?

JULIE: Come over here.

AUGUST: What for?

JULIE: To look at this.

AUGUST: I don't want to look at anything now.

JULIE: Are you scared?

AUGUST: No.

JULIE: Then come over here.

AUGUST: I'm not coming over. It's slippery. There, where you are, it's slippery there.

JULIE: It's a dare.

AUGUST: A dare is the last thing I need now.

JULIE: I can't look down if nobody is holding me, dammit.
It's a long way down and I have no idea what might happen when I look down.

AUGUST: I thought you'd been here before. With your parents.

JULIE: I was a kid then.

AUGUST: And you didn't look down then?

JULIE: Sure. But my father held me.

AUGUST: He's not here now.

JULIE: No, he's not here now.
What? you coming?

AUGUST slowly ventures forward and is crawling on all fours towards JULIE. They crawl towards the edge.

AUGUST: No bullshit though, okay?

JULIE: You don't have to look down. Hold my feet.

AUGUST: Kant! His name was Kant.

JULIE: Who?

AUGUST: The philosopher.

JULIE: Which philosopher?

AUGUST: The one with the eyes and ears. Who said that they're not worth anything.

JULIE: You're changing the subject.

SCENE CHANGE. We see a cliff towering in front of us. Way up the white sky. We see JULIE'S head appearing over the edge of the cliff.

AUGUST: *(Off.)* What's happening? What do you see?

Say something. What's going on?

What's it look like?

JULIE: What?

AUGUST: *(Off.)* Whatever you're seeing.

JULIE: See for yourself.

AUGUST: *(Off.)* What?

Can't you say something?

JULIE: Don't know.

AUGUST: *(Off.)* No? What do you see?

JULIE: I don't know what you would like to hear. I see the butthole of New Zealand. What do you think I'm seeing? I see nothing. A goddamn bottomless abyss is what I'm seeing.

AUGUST: *(Off.)* And all the way at the bottom, what is there?

JULIE: It's dark down there. There could be something. Don't know. Maybe, like, hell or something.

AUGUST: *(Off.)* You mean, you can't see the bottom.

JULIE: No. Something's sticking out. Further down something's sticking out. We'll have to jump past that. We'll have to jump far out.

AUGUST: *(Off.)* Something's sticking out?

JULIE: Yeah.

AUGUST: *(Off.)* How much is it sticking out?

JULIE: Quite a bit. We'll have to jump past that.

AUGUST: *(Off.)* And if we crash into it, that wouldn't do the trick?

JULIE: Don't know. No. Some part of you might just get torn off and you'd continue falling. And your arm would be dangling there and wave at you for a little while.

AUGUST: *(Off.)* And you can't see the bottom?

JULIE: See for yourself.

AUGUST: *(Off.)* I'm gonna freak. *(August's head appears.)*

AUGUST: I can't look down.

JULIE: Then don't look.

AUGUST: Everything is starting to spin.

JULIE: Then look away.

AUGUST: Shit.

JULIE: What?

AUGUST: Why are we doing this?

JULIE: You've got to do something.

AUGUST: Yeah.
Do you think people have done this here before us?

JULIE: You can bet your life on that.

AUGUST: Why do you think?

JULIE: You don't imagine we're, like, the first ones to come up with this idea?

AUGUST: Nope.

JULIE: You can be dead sure that it's been around before. Like this or a little different, but basically the same.

AUGUST: I mean this way. Like, the two of us together, and all that.

JULIE: Together, alone, like the lemmings. It's all been done. But who cares about that now. I'm doing this for me. I'm not doing this for anybody else. I'm not doing a show or something.

AUGUST: No.

Julie: And I've never done this before. I have never killed myself before.

August: No.

Julie: That counts for something. It's completely unique. It elevates the whole thing above anything that's been done before. I've never done this before. And now it's time.

August: What? Now?

Julie: Yeah.

August: Wait a minute, now?

Julie: Yeah.

August: But …

Julie: What?

August: But I …

Julie: What?

August: You … I … we've got all our stuff. And the food and the tent and all that.

Julie: Right, so?

August: Right, and I thought we would sleep on it one more time.

Julie: We would sleep on it?

August: Yeah.

Julie: You mean you wanted to reconsider one more time?

August: No, no … no. Not that.

Julie: So there.

August: But, hold on a minute. Doing it now, that's so … I wanted to write something before and …

Julie: Come on.

August: Hold on.

Julie: Come on, let's stand up. *(Julie stands up.)* Come on, let's go!

AUGUST: No. Hold on. I can't stand up. I'm about to fall off here.

JULIE: That's the idea. Come on.

AUGUST: Wait. Wait. That … let go.

JULIE: Come on, let's go. I want to get this over with now. I want to get down there, now!

AUGUST: Hold on. I just want to …

JULIE: What?

AUGUST: I was going to …

JULIE: Sleep on it, right?

AUGUST: No. Yes.

JULIE: You can sleep all you want when you're dead. Come on, let's jump!

AUGUST: No!

JULIE: Let's go!

AUGUST: Let go of me!

JULIE grabs AUGUST's hand. They struggle. They are practically wrestling with each other. During the struggle they almost go over the edge several times.

AUGUST: Stop it!

JULIE: Coward!

AUGUST: Stop it! You let go of me, now.

JULIE: No.

AUGUST: Let go!

JULIE: We made a deal.

AUGUST: Let go, goddammit! We're gonna fall.

JULIE: Right.

AUGUST: That wasn't the plan.

JULIE: That was the plan.

AUGUST: Let go of me!

JULIE: If you won't jump, I'm gonna make you.

AUGUST: Let go!

JULIE: No.

AUGUST: If I fall off, they'll hang you for murder.

JULIE: I'll be jumping after you, you moron.

AUGUST: I don't want to.

JULIE: What?

AUGUST: I don't want to!

JULIE: You're coming with me ...

AUGUST: If you're not gonna stop, I'm ...

JULIE: What? What?

AUGUST: I'm gonna kill you, goddammit!

JULIE: Great! *(Julie trips and falls. She can barely hold on to an overhang with one hand. She's dangling over the precipice.)* I can't pull myself up. Help me.

AUGUST: *(Off.)* You are ... you are totally sick! I could have fallen off here!

JULIE: Yeah, so what. It was a blast wasn't it? Come on, help me.

AUGUST: *(Off.)* Hold on a minute. I've got a song for you here!

JULIE: Help me. Dammit. I ... I am sorry. I was really stupid just now.

AUGUST: *(Off.)* Hold on, almost there!

JULIE: I was just kidding. I would never have thrown you down there. Honest. Help me, dammit. What if I fall, dammit. What will you do then? I can't hold on anymore. Help! Fuck it.

AUGUST returns with a boom box, trying to turn it on.

AUGUST: Listen. Do you know this one? It's my brother's.

JULIE: Help me up you freak.

AUGUST: Hush! Wait. How does this thing work?

JULIE: If you don't pull me up I'm gonna fall.

AUGUST: So?

JULIE: So ... it will be on your conscience. You don't want that.

AUGUST: This thing's not working.

JULIE: Help!

AUGUST: How long was the ride actually, in the cab?

JULIE: Help me!

AUGUST: You think anybody can hear us?

JULIE: No.

AUGUST: No. Nobody can hear us. For thirty miles.

JULIE: Help me.

AUGUST: You can scream here as much as you like and nobody will hear you.

JULIE: That's right.

AUGUST: Let's hear it.

JULIE: What?

AUGUST: Go ahead, scream.

JULIE: Help me.

AUGUST: Louder.

JULIE: Why don't you scream, you freak?

AUGUST: I don't have any reason to just now.

JULIE: Neither do I.

AUGUST: No?

JULIE: No.

AUGUST: I would be a little scared if I were you.

JULIE: Why.

AUGUST: Because you don't know me.

JULIE: And so?

AUGUST: So you don't know who I am. I could be completely nuts. Wait, the song goes something like this: tumtumtum, tumtum, tumtumtum, tumtum …

JULIE: Boo. Bad, bad man.

AUGUST: Just tell me what I would get out of not letting you fall. What would I get out of that?

JULIE: Don't know. Pull me up. I can't hold on anymore.

AUGUST: What would I get out of it?

JULIE: Help me back up … fuck!

AUGUST: What do I get out of that?

JULIE: Anything you want.

AUGUST: Anything I want?

JULIE: Yes.

AUGUST: And if I don't want anything?

JULIE: If you don't want anything, you won't get anything. Come on, pull!

AUGUST pulls her up. They sit down, exhausted, at the edge of the cliff.

AUGUST: You were going to kill me. It's true, isn't it?

JULIE: You're totally nuts, you are.

AUGUST: You wanted to watch me fall.

They both stare down into the abyss. JULIE slowly takes AUGUST'S hand.

JULIE: I wanted …

AUGUST: Go fuck yourself …

JULIE: You fuck yourself.

AUGUST: Fuck you, really.

JULIE: You don't say.

AUGUST: You were going to fucking kill me just now.

JULIE: Totally fucking crazy.

AUGUST: At the very least you were going to kill me.

JULIE: I'll die laughing.

AUGUST: I'm gonna get hives. Because of the shock.

JULIE: Hives? You're thinking about hives right now?

AUGUST: Yeah.

JULIE: That is un-fucking-believable.

AUGUST: I can't help it. I always think about weird stuff.

JULIE: He's thinking about hives.

AUGUST: Who are you talking to?

JULIE gets up.

JULIE: We should set up the tent. It's getting dark. Soon. Maybe another half hour and it will be dark again. It's always dark here, in winter.

SCENE CHANGE. Same as before, but darkness. We're looking at a tent, dimly lit. AUGUST stands outside, looking up at the sky.

AUGUST: There was something ... up in the sky ... just now.

JULIE: *(Off.)* What?

AUGUST: Some kind of a light. Up in the sky.

JULIE comes out of the tent.

JULIE: Where?

AUGUST: Everywhere. It was all bright. Just for a split second.

JULIE: A light?

AUGUST: Yeah.

JULIE: Everywhere?

AUGUST: Yeah.

JULIE: Some kind of illumination?

AUGUST: Yeah. I don't know. I was just standing here, and I look up to see if there are stars. And then I see it. All of a sudden.

JULIE: And?

AUGUST: And what? It was weird.

JULIE: What did it say to you, that light?

AUGUST: You are such a moron.

JULIE: For real?

AUGUST: Yeah. It was awesome.

JULIE: Well, okay. I'm cold.

JULIE goes back into the tent. A gigantic wave of light flickers across the sky.

AUGUST: There! There! There it is again! It's absolutely awesome! You see it? Look!

JULIE comes out.

JULIE: The aurora borealis! That's the aurora borealis. The camera!

JULIE goes back into tent. She reemerges from the tent with the video camera and films the whole thing.

JULIE: Hold on! I've got it! I've got it! The aurora borealis ...

AUGUST: Have you ever seen it before? This thing?

JULIE: No. Never.

AUGUST: But didn't you grow up around here?

JULIE: Around here you get to see the aurora borealis every fifty years or so. That means basically never.

August: That's rare.

Julie: It's not the right spot for an aurora borealis. It's too far south. I don't know of anybody who's seen one before.

The light is fading.

August: It's gone.

Julie moves camera to August.

Julie: Say something.

August: How big is an aurora borealis?

Stop that. I mean, how big is it? It looks very big. But if it's as big as it looks, the light, then people should be able to see it everywhere. Why does nobody see aurora borealises? You don't know of anyone who's seen one, and neither do I. I mean, half of the world can see the moon, simultaneously. And if the aurora borealis is as big as it seems, then half of the world should see that too. Maybe not that much. But still quite a few people. Don't you think?

Julie turns off the camera.

Julie: You're sweet.

August: Let's see. Let's see if we got it ... Maybe it's impossible to catch this light on film. *(August rewinds.)* Maybe aurora borealises are really tiny. Some kind of a hallucination that you can't mention to anyone. Maybe all they do is flicker in front of our faces. Kinda like a home movie. For private use ... *(August pushes "play." As both of them watch the small monitor, behind them in the sky the same spectacle as before is taking place.)* There it is!

Julie: It doesn't seem very small.

August: Still, it's not the same, on video.

Julie: It looks like some kind of disturbance. Like something extraterrestrial.

August: It is just about the most beautiful thing I have seen in a very long time. Now imagine if we were some kind of cave people.

Julie: We would be totally shittin' our pants that some gods wanted to have our hides.

AUGUST: Yeah. Did they have pants, the cave people?

JULIE: Don't know. I'm sure they had hides.

AUGUST: I don't know. And you think they had gods?

JULIE: Sure. Aurora borealis, for example. Once every fifty years a god like that would flicker by and wave a little at them. And they would live on that for the next fifty years.

AUGUST: Sitting in their caves.

JULIE: Yeah.

The image behind AUGUST and JULIE pans from the light to AUGUST. Again we see AUGUST say the words, "How big is an aurora borealis?"

JULIE: How big is an aurora borealis. Genius.

AUGUST: I look like a total jerk. Completely fake.

Camera off. Night sky.

JULIE: I've been really awful to you.

AUGUST: What?

JULIE: I am sorry. I was awful to you, today. You must not believe a word I say, especially if I'm saying it when I'm about to kill myself. No one tells the truth then.

AUGUST: No?

JULIE: No. I like you. *(JULIE kisses AUGUST tenderly on the temple.)*

AUGUST: Why did you do that?

JULIE: I just felt like it.

AUGUST: You have such soft lips.

JULIE: You know, you can trust me.

AUGUST: I like you too.

JULIE takes the camera away from AUGUST and starts taping him. We see a close-up of AUGUST projected.

JULIE: Say it again.

August: What?

Julie: What you just said, say it again.

August: That's not possible.

Julie: That's not what you said before.

August: I can't say that again.

Julie: Never again?

August: Give me that. *(August takes the camera and tapes Julie.)*

Julie: Listen: we don't have much time. There are about four sandwiches left and ten cans of beer. And the music and cigarettes won't last us till spring either. And soon it's gonna be morning. And tomorrow morning is the end. That should be clear to us, right now. So—nothing really matters. You can act like a complete jerk if you like, it doesn't matter, you don't need to hold back anymore, okay? Nobody expects that here. You can let it all hang out. You can jerk off in front of this panoramic view, who cares? You can say every sentence there is on this earth. You can do whatever you want. You can repeat words or not. You can do a headstand. And that's why, if I ask you to do something for me, something really harmless, then please fucking do it, or I'm gonna freak. Or if you have an idea to do something else, then do that. Because it's fun to do something. It's much more fun than if you don't do it. Thinking is out. You can think when you have time. And we don't have any time to lose. Agreed?

August: Agreed.

Julie: What I mean is, we will have an eternity of time, later, to think.

August: Yeah?

Julie: Yes. If the part inside of us that thinks is the spirit, and if the spirit is eternal, as they say, then logically we will have an eternity to think. But only very little time to do anything, by comparison. There you are, and if you ask me for something, I shall do it.

I like you. You see?

August: Yeah. I like you too.

Julie: Hold on, give me that. *(Julie takes the camera and tapes August.)* What was it you just said?

August: Don't know.

Julie: Did we make a deal just a second ago or what?

August: Yeah.

Julie: And?

August: What?

Julie: And didn't you just say something, a second ago? Come on! Say it.

August: I don't feel like saying something on command.

Julie: Okay. Then say something else. Something new. Quickly. This is a rehearsal. Come on, stay loose. Thinking is out. Say something! Emotions, let's go! Trust your instincts. If you don't say something emotional in the next three seconds, I'll jump. One, two, three.

August: Heil Hitler!

Julie: Are you stupid, or what?

August: What?

Julie: That was really totally dumb just now.

August: It just came out. You were getting me all stressed out.

Julie: It was really way off. Totally embarrassing.

August: Nobody here to hear it. You said do anything.

Julie: But not something like that.

August: I saved your life after all.

Julie: Can't you come up with something more intelligent?

August: Why did you bring a camera with you?

Julie: No reason. Because I wanted … for them to … so something remains … first she's here, and now she's on here.

AUGUST: I want to make love to you.

JULIE: Why are you saying that?

AUGUST: Because you told me to say whatever I want.

JULIE: You got a rubber?

AUGUST: No.

JULIE: He doesn't have a rubber.

AUGUST: What for?

JULIE: Mom, he doesn't have a rubber and he wants to make love to me, is that okay? Nonono. No, I'm not gonna get pregnant, I'm gonna jump soon, down there. Don't worry. Disease? No, that'll go with me, won't survive the fall.

What?

AUGUST: Nothing.

JULIE: Is there, like, a problem?

AUGUST: Like?

JULIE: With me joking around?

AUGUST: No.

JULIE: Well, then I'm gonna go into the tent to freshen up.

AUGUST: Yeah.

JULIE: "Yeah …"

AUGUST: Yeah.

They disappear, taking the camera with them, into the dimly lit tent and zip it up behind them. We hear their voices, amplified.

JULIE: *(Off.)* You're shivering.

AUGUST: *(Off.)* I'm cold.

JULIE: *(Off.)* The way you're shivering, it's not gonna work. Turn that off there. Yeah. Give it to me. Turn it off. Is it off?

On video we see August and Julie in the tent. The image is flickering. Julie seems to take the camera to put it away. The picture is gone but then comes back. We see something colorful, may be a close-up of a piece of clothing.

Julie: We should breathe. Are you breathing?

August: *(Off.)* Do you have a sweetheart?

Julie: *(Off.)* A sweetheart?

August: *(Off.)* A boyfriend.

Julie: *(Off.)* You're sweet. Ask something else.

August: What gives … do you have one?

The picture jerks. Suddenly they're both in the frame.

Julie: Why don't you ask me how I like it?

August: How do you like it?

Julie: While doing a handstand on a horse.

August: And how does he like it?

Julie: Listen, if you'd rather do it with him, you're knocking on the wrong door.

August: With who?

Julie: What do I know? You're the one keeps asking about some guy.

August: I was just curious.

Julie: You're not, like, jealous?

August: No.

Julie: Because that's where I draw the line. That would be the most fucked up thing of all. The last thing I need is to sit at the edge of a cliff in a tent and listen to you make a scene because you're jealous. Your breathing's too shallow, it's never gonna warm up in here like this. What's the matter?

August: What do you mean, what's the matter?

Julie: You're still shivering.

August: It's cold.

Julie: Come here.

August moves closer to Julie.

You're shivering.

August: You are too.

Julie: Hold me tight.
You think Armageddon will happen at night?

August: Nope. At dawn.

Julie: So you do know the movie?

August: Which one?

Julie: *Rebel Without a Cause.*

August: No.

Julie: There's a scene, right before the end, where Plato, that's his name, he's much younger than the other two, more like their child, you know? They are a little like his parents, the two lovers, and he's asking the guy, the one played by James Dean, he asks him if Armageddon is gonna happen at night.

August: And so?

Julie: And James Dean says: "Nope. At dawn."

August: He's a genius, that guy.

Julie: It was in the script like that.

August: That's what I'm saying.

Julie: What guy?

August: The guy who wrote the script.

Julie: But maybe he ripped it off somewhere else, the way you just ripped him off.

August: I didn't rip it off.

Julie: You've seen the movie.

AUGUST: Yeah.

JULIE: And you know exactly who Natalie Wood is?

AUGUST: Yeah.

JULIE: And you just pretended that you didn't know?

AUGUST: Right.

JULIE: And I believed you.

AUGUST: Maybe you just pretended too.

JULIE: Possible.

AUGUST: Possible.

(They kiss briefly.) Yeah. But look. That we're getting it on and getting naked and like that, I bet you never imagined that would happen …

AUGUST: Imagined, yes.

JULIE: Okay. But we don't have to go through with it, right?

AUGUST: Nope. We don't have to. We could just imagine it a little more graphically.

JULIE: Yeah. We could do that.

AUGUST: Well, I would try to get into your blouse just about now.

JULIE: And I would put my hand there. Right there on the inside of your thigh.

AUGUST: So you would, like, go for it right away.

JULIE: Yeah.

AUGUST: That would irritate me a bit.

JULIE: Irritate you?

AUGUST: Yeah, or how do you say that?

JULIE: No idea. I never say anything like that.

AUGUST: Excite me.

JULIE: Yeah? If I put my hand there?

AUGUST: Yeah, sure. I would probably use the hand I'm not leaning on to touch your hair, and your neck.

JULIE: Then I probably would, like, move my hand back and forth like this.

AUGUST: And then I would go for your bra moving my hand kind of inconspicuously towards it.

JULIE: How?

AUGUST: Well, kind of along the side. My wrist would probably brush your breast coming down.

JULIE: Yeah, probably. I would probably stop stroking your thigh at that point and my hand would touch your face in order to caress you

AUGUST: I would probably feel encouraged by that. I would probably reach around your hip, with my hand, and touch your back.

JULIE: I would kiss your neck then.

AUGUST: And I wouldn't speak the whole time. But I would be shivering.

JULIE: Yeah. Me too.

AUGUST: I would be totally excited, because we are about to do it …

JULIE: I would take in your smell. But then I would have to look at you again. And I would think that you look damn good to me.

AUGUST: No, wait, that's what I think. That's what I would be thinking.

AUGUST comes out of the tent, while on screen we continue to see the two in the tent. AUGUST talks to himself and the audience.

AUGUST: I would be thinking, what's she doing with me here in this tent, this hot chick? She's so beautiful and, like, really cool all around. And I'm just me. She must be weird, making out here with me. Maybe she's crazy. So I would be, like, close to losing all my respect for her. There's got to be some fucked up mistake here. Some catch. A mix-up. She thinks that I'm not me, but I am. I can't tell her that, or I won't get any action.

JULIE comes out of the tent, on screen the scene continues as if nothing's happening. She stands next to AUGUST. She also looks into the audience.

August: I must now very carefully act as if it's perfectly natural for a woman like her to be interested in me. In a tent. As if it happens all the time. And as I keep telling myself this, I touch your breast with my hand and kiss you, just like some dude in the movies, because I have to appear really cool in this situation, because I have no idea how to act naturally in this kind of situation.

Julie: Well, probably your hands touch my breasts, like that ...

August: Right.

Julie: Right.

August: Right. And so I would kiss you, long and artfully, and I would tell myself, what soft lips she has.

Julie: And I would hope this kiss would never end and that all I was, up till then, would crumble and fall apart, and that there would be more and more space for you inside of me. And I wouldn't want to let you in, not yet, because I would be so ashamed of the mess inside of me, lots of unresolved things, but the kiss would go on and on, and actually at times I wouldn't even know who I am, kind of, anymore, I would be so busy with my tongue that just for a moment I would believe that it's all good, that it's over and that we will survive, you know? Survive it all.

Something about the image on screen doesn't match the reality of being in a tent anymore. The images evoked by Julie slowly become real in front of our eyes. A kind of "dialogue" begins to develop between screen and stage, the two seem to merge into each other.

Julie: That dying is done and that we're in a place that's ours, at home, under the covers, and that it's possible to be at home and the dying is over, we can go outside and everything's normal there, and the dying is over, get it? Nothing's pushing towards death anymore, everything just is, and in my thoughts I would be going outside, and the kiss would last as long as it takes me to get to the street, and it would be night and I would take you with me and walk through the streets and we would stop a cab and get in and I would hold on to your thigh, because it feels so firm.

August: And there would be a lot going on at the same time.

Julie: Look, the lights. The city lights.

Lights flash by.

August: Yeah.

JULIE: We would love making love in a taxicab the most, in public, because that's where we met, once.

AUGUST: Right, but not this time. I would start undressing you. First, the jacket and the blouse.

JULIE: And I would help you to make it go faster. And I would pull on your shirt like crazy to get it off. And then we would be lying next to each other and I would of course say, "I'm cold."

AUGUST: And I would lie on top of you, like, almost a little on the side. And your skin would be really cold, and mine too, but together we would get warm, somehow. And I would kiss you even more. And with my hand, with my free hand—the other one would be squeezed underneath you, but I would act as if it didn't matter—I would stroke your upper thigh, the same way you stroked mine, because I would know, she likes that, she did that with me, and it was good.

JULIE: And I would open my legs very slowly, so you know it's okay if your hand goes up a little higher. Because we haven't known each other that long.

AUGUST: Yeah. And I would come up with my hand a little more. But it's not so easy to feel anything with jeans on, so I would continue to kiss you wildly up top until I manage to open up the pants down there.

JULIE: And I would turn away from you to take everything off. And I would take everything off. And you would hold me and we would warm each other. We would lie there like two little teaspoons and hold each other tight. And I would look at the side of the tent that would flap in the wind and we would be in the desert, like two Bedouins, and I would feel your chest against my back. Do you have hair?

AUGUST: What do you mean?

JULIE: On your chest?

AUGUST: Nope.

JULIE: Good.

AUGUST: I would hold on to you and move my hip back and forth and try to hold on myself, with all that excitement.

JULIE: And, like, eventually I would give into all that lust that's all over the place.

And I would come up on all fours and scream, “Take me, come on and take me, take me” …

August: For real?

Julie: Why not.

August: Right. And I would tell myself, she’s totally wild, this cat, and I would … well, I would do it.

Julie: Like, how?

August: I would … with you … I would, you know …

Julie: You would grab my hips.

August: Yeah. With one hand. With the other, I would caress up and down your spine.

Julie: And I would look for you with my ass and press it up against you, and I would feel how you penetrate me. Slowly at first, and then faster and deeper. And my breath would go faster with each thrust …

August: I would love you.

Julie: You mean fuck me. We would fuck our brains out.

August: No, I would love you.

Julie: You mean, like, fuck lamely.

August: No.

Julie: You mean, you’d be in love then.

August: Right.

Julie: With all the stuff that goes with it, and you would say sweet things to me?

August: Yeah.

Julie: What would you call me?

August: Froggie.

Julie: Froggie.

AUGUST: Yeah, I don't know. No, kitten. Probably.

JULIE: Kitten, right? You're into animals, aren't you?

AUGUST: Or, like, baby.

JULIE: Sure, or babies ...

AUGUST: What's going on?

JULIE: I'm happy.

AUGUST: Me too.

JULIE: Tomorrow we will die.

AUGUST: Yeah.

JULIE: I'm so happy.

AUGUST: Me too.

JULIE: Let's go.

JULIE takes AUGUST's hand. They disappear into the tent.

JULIE: *(Off.)* Put on some music! Put some music on, let's go! What was it you were gonna play for me earlier? What was it? Let's see. *(Julie plays CD.)*

AUGUST: No, skip that. Go to track 4. That's it. *("Death of an Angel" by the Kingsmen.)* The organ. Awesome. They were totally ... You hear that? This music made history. It's Trash. They called it Trash. They were punks, twenty years before there were punks. Real punks. I mean, the punks later imitated them. The whole no-future thing is completely fake. For real. I mean, maybe Trash is fake too. But that doesn't matter. Listen to it: it's a perfect song. A light came on in their heads. Totally. They saw an aurora borealis and when it was gone, they got a song: "My Baby's Gone and Left Me Here To Stay."

JULIE: *(Off.)* Interesting ...

SCENE CHANGE. Same as before. Dawn. AUGUST crawls out of the tent. He's got the camera and walks to the edge of the cliff. He stops. He films the panoramic view, then pans slowly into the abyss. Then he zooms in. He turns off the camera. JULIE comes out of the tent. She looks like she didn't sleep much and is dressed up as if she's going to a party. She is wearing an elegant dress and high heels.

JULIE: It's kind of a black day today.

AUGUST: This morning when I was half asleep I dreamed that I was on the edge of creation, standing on the edge of the abyss, there, where it all began, and watching the creation of chaos.

JULIE: Come on, let's get it over with.

AUGUST: You first.

AUGUST moves away from the edge and directs the camera towards JULIE.

JULIE: Wait. Are you already recording?

AUGUST: Yeah.

JULIE: No, wait. Erase that.

AUGUST rewinds.

AUGUST: Okay.

JULIE: Hello Mother, hello Father … Shit. That sucked, erase that.

AUGUST: Okay.

Camera rolling.

JULIE: Ready? Hello Mother, hello Father, hello Grandma, hello Rune. As you can see, I am at the spot, where … what?

AUGUST: Did you want the ready to be on it, too?

JULIE: Of course not.

AUGUST: One more time then. Wait.

JULIE: You only start after I say "okay," okay?—Okay … Hello Mother, hello Father, hello Grandma, hello Rune. Well, as you can see I am here at the spot we once visited together when I was small and you, Father, held my feet so I could look down into the abyss, because you were afraid I would fall …

AUGUST: What's happening?

JULIE: Turn it off.

AUGUST: What is it?

JULIE: Nothing. I … Wait, let's see, what does it look like?

AUGUST: The whole thing?

JULIE: No, just the end.

AUGUST rewinds. On screen we see JULIE say: " … you, Father, held my feet so I could look down into the abyss, because you were afraid I would fall … "

JULIE: It sucks, somehow.

AUGUST: I don't know, I liked that take.

JULIE: It's totally pathetic. Isn't it?

AUGUST: Don't know. It's a special situation here. Keep going, we can always tape another version.

JULIE: Okay. Can you go from there? After "I would fall."

AUGUST: Yeah, hold on … okay.

JULIE: I say okay.

AUGUST: Okay.

JULIE: Okay … I am here today to make up for what I didn't do before. I am going to jump off today. That means that I am actually already dead. *(She is trying not to laugh.)* As I am telling you this, I am dead. *(She's laughing.)* It's a totally crazy idea, let me tell you … *(She's laughing more and more.)* But you already know that. Because otherwise the video … well … shit, now I lost my train of thought.

AUGUST: I'm gonna stop, okay?

JULIE: No! What for?

AUGUST: I thought, with all that laughing …

JULIE: That might have made it good! Like, offered some comfort maybe. Those can be, like, good moments.

AUGUST: But it seemed a little crazy, didn't it?

JULIE: crazy?

AUGUST: A little.

JULIE: Doesn't matter. Go on from there.

AUGUST: So you have to laugh a little more here, for continuity.

JULIE: What continuity?

AUGUST: The continuity.

JULIE: But it's a cut!

AUGUST: Yeah, but after the cut it has to have continuity. It picks up where we stopped before.

JULIE: No. It picks up a little later on. That's why I'm not laughing anymore now. You cannot decide to stop. Okay? Only I can. Okay?

AUGUST: Okay.

JULIE: Okay …

AUGUST: Camera rolling.

JULIE: After that, there isn't anything else.

After that, there isn't anything else. After that, it's the end. After the beginning there's nothing else.

You hear me?

Turn that thing off.

AUGUST: What? That was awesome. The Silence. You should leave more pauses, they're really cool.

Camera off.

JULIE: There is no "camera rolling." After "okay" there isn't any "camera rolling." After "okay," there's only me.

AUGUST: Did I say something?

JULIE: Yes. You said, "camera rolling." But everybody can see that it's rolling, or they wouldn't hear you say, "camera rolling."

AUGUST: Don't be so picky.

JULIE: It's not everyday I'm killing myself here, dammit. I want it to look really smooth.

August: Okay.

Julie: Okay. *(Camera rolling.)* We interrupt this program for a commercial break: Shop till you drop, motherfuckers. Here we are again, with our live coverage of two young, innocent middle-class people made in Europe who are dropping out of life by their own volition … Okay. Let's go … okay.

August: What?

Julie: I said "okay." So the camera should be rolling now.

August: It's been rolling for a while already.

Julie: It's been rolling for a while already. Well … I don't want it to look as if I don't know what I'm doing here. I know very well. I'm here with somebody who can be a witness to that. The one behind the camera, that's August, and he is my best friend. I love him. Very much. Show yourself. *(August briefly points the camera towards his own face and grins.)* Right, Rune, this is August. I'm sure you're thinking "what a loser." But it's a great success to be a loser. Think about it. It's a great success to be one. And August is a Super-loser. Don't laugh. And I love him for it. I don't want anything to happen to him. That's why we're gonna jump together. We're gonna hold hands, and we won't let go until we reach the bottom …

August: Hold on …

Camera off.

Julie: What?

August: I don't know. Wouldn't it be better if we stayed out of each other's thing?

Julie: Why?

August: Well, I don't know. This Rune, I don't know him, and I don't know if I want to leave anything behind for him. Like, I'm a loser and all that stuff. I don't know.

Julie: But that's just between me and him. I'm not saying that you're a loser in general. That's only between Rune and me. Let's just do separate tapes.

August: Yeah, but that doesn't make any difference. I mean, I have nothing to do with you killing yourself, as far as the reasons why.

Julie: I wanna finish saying my thing here.

August: Fine. But then you'll do a version without me, okay?

Julie: Whatever. Well. Okay. Where was I?

August: We won't let go until we reach the bottom.

Julie: Yeah. Right. What are you talking about, "a version without me"? There is no version without you. Come on, let's take it from there. Well, Okay… *(Camera rolling.)* Right. That's always been my dream, I'll have you know. I always wanted to die with my loved ones. At the same time. So that I won't have to go through somebody dying. All I've ever been able to imagine is to die together with all of you. During a picnic. All together. "Family hit by meteorite. Crater is the size of a football field." I could never bear the thought that one of us might die before the others. Right. Well, I'm gonna go first. I am sorry. You see, it's like this. When you, Dad, held me then, by my feet, that was a good feeling. I always got a good feeling from you guys whenever I needed it. You were such unbelievably good parents. Because you actually always held me by my feet, you, my friends and colleagues … I was able to gaze into any abyss in the world and didn't have to be afraid. Because you were there. And, and for that I wanna thank you, because I've had a wonderful life. Thank you, all of you. I've seen everything, I was able to eat up the entire world. And I always was able to have everything there is. Everything I ever wanted, I was able to have. Nothing was unattainable. I've been everywhere, and everything else I've seen in the movies. I went to Tierra del Fuego, hung out with the natives and saw the sunrise, I ate Big Macs and shopped at Prada and vice versa. I was loved, desired, I know how to sail and play golf, I was an Ace in computer science, developed PC games, made money, I did everything fun there is to do, I have a tattoo, look here … I took all drugs on Earth without falling apart and screwed around with guys, had a one night stand with Brad Pitt that wasn't particularly fun but interesting from a sociological point of view. That was years ago when you let me go to New York by myself. Rune, the guy was on the same flight, I'm so sorry. You were the love of my life, Rune, and I still love you … Even though you've become a winner. Take care of yourself. Right. Everybody will have his moment. In short: I had the world on a silver platter, I had it all, and spit it back out as soon as it was in my mouth. Because one thing can never make up for the possibilities of the next. My life … that is my past, consists for the most part of a future that didn't turn out to be much. For the longest time I didn't understand one thing … I didn't understand that the only way to have everything is not to desire anything. There is only one way to have it all: to have no desires. And I believe … that I'm not hungry anymore now. I've had it all, and I want nothing else. I want nothing more than I ever wanted anything. I don't know if you understand. Anyway, none of you can give me nothing, that's something none of you can give to me—only I can. Oh right, there is one thing I want: a beautiful death. And I wanted to tell you all goodbye and hold you tight and comfort you and say that it's all gonna be alright … because I … you … because it … because I … because … turn it off, okay … *(Camera off.)*

It just came to me that I'm a total idiot.

AUGUST: Why?

JULIE: Here I am, just talking about myself …

AUGUST: Well … after all, it's the last time …

JULIE: And nothing but crap on top of that. That's no good. I can't do this. Put a new tape in.

AUGUST puts a new tape in.

AUGUST: Yes you can. It wasn't bad. At least I understand you much better now. That you want to kill yourself and all that stuff. I get it. For real.

JULIE: It was total bullshit. That I, like, had it all. That the whole world held my legs, so I can gaze into the abyss. All bull. Complete drivel, that's what it is. Propaganda.

AUGUST: Yeah. But, all in all.

JULIE: Go again.

August tapes Julie.

Hello guys. Here I am again … right. Not to blame you for anything. Only somebody who's still attached to life would do that. Just wanted to say bye. Yeah, and don't worry about it, because, if I had realized earlier on that I have the same weaknesses and flaws as you all, I would have killed myself right then and there. Right? From that perspective, it went on for quite a long time anyway. Okay. Well …

AUGUST: I turned it off.

JULIE: I'm finished.

AUGUST: Right. I didn't know. It seemed so short.

AUGUST hands the camera to JULIE.

August: Well, hold on, I don't know if I can do it as short as that.

Julie: I'm ready.

August: Let's go then. *(Camera rolling.)* Hello. You. Dear ones. Here I am again … I … well … I always wanted to be a part of something, of life, of a story, but at the same time … shit. Sorry. Right. Ever since I could think, I never wanted to cause anything, you see? I never felt an urge to be the cause of anything on this earth. Maybe there is a word I would have liked to say, but right now I can't see which one. Oh, yes. Coward. I am a coward. Probably. My only bravery till now consisted of not having killed myself. I always lived in fear of sudden disaster. That really poisoned my time. Right. That's why I'm gonna beat fate to it today and throw myself down there, into disaster, before it hits me. Right. So. don't worry about it, will you? It might be a good thing, this disaster. Yeah, and don't forget to feed the fish. Right. Bye.

Camera off.

Julie: You have a fish?

August: Yeah. I actually wanted to bring him. But then I thought, the airplane … and after all, it's a saltwater fish.

Julie: That's saltwater down there.

August: For real?

Julie: It's a fjord.

August: Right. Well then, fuck it. I hope they feed him. Let's see, I wanna see what it looks like. You have to imagine that you are your parents and you have to watch this.

August takes the camera and rewinds. We see and hear the playback. The two of them are glued to the little control monitor.

Julie: … I would have killed myself right then and there. Right? From that perspective, it went on for quite a long time anyway. Okay. Well …

August: Hello. You. Dear ones. Here I am again … I … well … I always wanted to be a part of something, of life, of a story, but …

August turns it off.

That's not it somehow. It sounds super fake, somehow. I can't do this. I mean, I don't want my life to end with a lie like that. It's impossible to leave that lying here. It's so fake.

JULIE: We will have to go over it again. I'm standing around like I'm in a trance.

AUGUST: I'm just talking … I don't know.

JULIE: Well. That, too. But I look like that as well.

AUGUST: That's normal.

JULIE: What do you mean?

AUGUST: Everyone looks like that when they get up.

JULIE: It's just too depressing. I look like I'm in a cult. I don't want that to happen, for them to think that I was, like, out of my mind. Listen, that coward thing was total crap.

AUGUST: Well …

JULIE: Why would you say something like that?

AUGUST: To comfort them. I thought, if a coward commits suicide, there is something comforting about that.

JULIE: You wouldn't wanna tell them the truth? Instead of something fake? I mean, this would be a good occasion! And besides, I don't wanna jump with a coward.

AUGUST: Right. Right. That was bullshit.

Camera rolling. JULIE acts super casual.

JULIE: Hey guys. I've had enough. You won't get it, so I won't keep blabbing. Ciao.

Camera off.

AUGUST: That was definitely something. Short and sweet.

JULIE: Again. *(Camera rolling.)* Hello Mother; Father, I'll get to you later …

No. That's not a good beginning. Hold on, hold on. Dear Mom, dear Pop. I'm here with August. August is my new friend. We love each other.

Fuck. Really. Fuck. I can't do it. Come on, you go.

JULIE takes the camera.

AUGUST: Right. Wait. Well. Okay. Hello. I am so sorry I'm doing this to you. But with this whole thing I didn't really think about you. You really didn't matter in this moment which is about to happen. That's the truth ...

What do I know if they don't matter when the moment comes. Wait, again ... okay?

Hello. You have no idea what it's like to be me. I tell you, it's fucked up. I can't even come up with a good farewell message here. It's so desperate, and that's why I'm gonna go now ... Bye.

Camera off.

JULIE: You're not serious about that.

AUGUST: At least it's true. I don't know. Wait a minute, I've got it.

JULIE: Okay.

AUGUST: Dear Mother, dear Father, dear Brother and dear rest of the world. All in all ... if you look at it rationally, it is impossible not to lose your mind. See ya ...

Camera off.

JULIE: I don't know ... maybe we should just put the camera there, both stand in front of it, say something brief and then go.

AUGUST: Yeah.

JULIE places the camera and presses the "record" button. They both stand in front of it, holding each other's hands.

JULIE: I love you all.

AUGUST: So do I.

They go, holding hands, towards the edge of the cliff. Just before they reach it:

JULIE: It's pathetic.

AUGUST: Kinda, yeah.

JULIE: Besides, there is all the stuff from before still on there.

AUGUST: Right. *(AUGUST turns the camera off again.)* How about a little music?

JULIE: Music?

AUGUST: I don't know, to set the mood, in the background?

JULIE: Wait, I've got something. This always helped me, when I was sad. *(JULIE gets the boom box from the tent.)* The thing is, I didn't actually have it all. That's the thing. I don't know. I can't believe a word I say, somehow. The aurora borealis last night. I had never seen an aurora borealis. Fuck. I mean, if we had jumped yesterday, we would have totally missed it, that fucking aurora. I haven't seen anything at all. There it is. Hold on. Number six. Ready?

AUGUST: Yeah.

JULIE: Okay, let it roll. *(Camera rolling. JULIE puts in a CD—"Egg Radio" by Bill Frisell. She's about to say something, looks into the camera for a long time, but finally just cries. The song continues to play. JULIE turns off the boom box.)* I am so sorry.

AUGUST: Wanna try again?

JULIE: No. I think I'm just not capable. It can't be so hard to say goodbye.

AUGUST: Let me try again. *(He hands the camera to JULIE.)* Okay? *(JULIE nods. AUGUST begins again, thoughtfully.)* ... If death is something horrible, how come that after some time we consider each of our friends lucky who has ceased to exist?

Life to me is a problem I have to solve every day anew. If I would follow my deepest instincts, I would scream for help from morning till night.

All my contradictions are derived from the fact that it is impossible to love life more than I love it and simultaneously and incessantly experience the feeling of being an outcast and abandoned.

I have lived ruled by myself for many years and am unhappy. But today, today I'm happy. Maybe true happiness lies in the realization that you don't need yourself anymore.

Camera off. JULIE is totally blown away.

JULIE: Amen. That was genius!

AUGUST: Shit ...

JULIE: You're a poet. Where do you get that from? *(AUGUST gets a book from the tent.)* It sounded so real. I was so moved.

AUGUST: Nope. I stole it.

JULIE: Doesn't matter, does it?

AUGUST: I don't know.

JULIE: We can leave that.

AUGUST: You mean, that was it?

JULIE: Yeah. No?

AUGUST: No. It was stolen, it doesn't count. I want to say something of my own.

JULIE: Okay. But you must act the way you just did, kinda thoughtful. That was great.

AUGUST: I have to act like something?

JULIE: It was totally believable, believe me.

AUGUST: You mean, I have to fake it?

JULIE: Looks like it.

AUGUST: To make it believable?

JULIE: That's what it looks like from over here.

AUGUST: It was fake. I was totally faking it.

JULIE: But it looked real.

AUGUST: But if it's … it was fake!

JULIE: So what? Obviously, fake doesn't always need to be fake. Fake can be completely real, sometimes.

AUGUST: Fake can be real?

JULIE: Yeah. Fake is only when it's nothing at all. That's fake.

AUGUST: That's what you say.

JULIE: That's what I say.

AUGUST: It's only fake, when it's nothing at all.

JULIE: Yeah.

AUGUST: But nothing is ever completely nothing.

JULIE: Right.

AUGUST: So nothing is fake.

JULIE: Right.

AUGUST: So that means that all this has to be taken seriously? From now on?

JULIE: Looks like it. *(Laughs.)*

AUGUST: You're kidding me.

JULIE: No. Not right now. Not this time. *(Laughs.)*

AUGUST: We can take all this seriously here?

JULIE: You're shivering.

AUGUST: Yeah. I'm scared.

JULIE: Of what?

AUGUST: The future.

JULIE: What future?

AUGUST: My future, I don't know. Up till now my future never scared me because I knew that I could always kill myself. You understand? But now …

JULIE: But now?

AUGUST: I'm suddenly not so sure anymore … that I can still kill myself. Get it?

JULIE: Let's go.

AUGUST: Okay. *(Camera rolling.)* Hey there folks. I'm here in Norway today. I told you I was going to go to Mats over the weekend. But that was a lie. You wouldn't have let me go. So I told you a big ol' lie. Julie here paid for the flight. Right. And it was worth it. I mean, we're just about to jump here … I mean that's why we're here. To go. But it was worth it anyway, because even this short time was really cool. I mean, I felt alive here, for the first time basically. Last night we saw the aurora borealis. We taped it. You can take a look. It was such a beautiful, gigantic light. It covered almost the entire sky. And I thought of you, and also why you can't see the light at home, even though it's so big. The thing is, on video it looks much smaller, and darker. Looks as if you're seeing it through a mist. You had to be there. I can only recommend it to you. Julie here had never seen one either. We stood there like lunatics. Yeah. You should see that one day. But it's very rare supposedly, says Julie. Right. Yes and Julie is a friend. Julie. I … she is … well I am … basically … yeah. Well I actually meant to … I meant to tell you why I'm gonna do what I'm about to do, but … to be honest, I don't know why anymore right now. No idea. So sorry. *(Camera off.)* Do you know?

JULIE: Nope.

AUGUST: Well, then.

JULIE: Yeah.

AUGUST: Hold on.

AUGUST packs up all the tapes in a bag and takes them to the edge of the cliff. JULIE stands next to him. They look at each other. AUGUST throws the bag over the edge. They watch it fall.

JULIE: It got caught.

AUGUST: It's very possible that we were just hit by a stroke of luck that we won't recover from anytime soon.

JULIE: I wanna get out of here.

AUGUST: Me too.

They both exit.

The Death of the Squirrel-Man

Małgorzata Sikorska-Miszczuk

Translated from Polish by Jadwiga Kosicka

"Oh my God, they killed Kenny! You Bastards!" —*South Park*

The Death of the Squirrel-Man premiered at the Teatr Usta Usta in Poznań, Poland, in December 2006, directed by Marcin Liber.

This translation has received the generous support of Instytut Teatralny im. Zbigniewa Raszewskiego, Warsaw.

CHARACTERS

Ulrike Meinhof: Member of the RAF (Red Army Faction), an intellectual

Gudrun Ensslin: Member of the RAF, a radical terrorist

Andreas Baader: Member of the RAF, later as Anti-Man

Policeman (later, pigeon-hearted; later, with a hole in his chest; finally, with a new heart): Fights against the RAF

Lucky: Gudrun Ensslin's son, abandoned by her when he was six months old

Squirrel-Man: Collective RAF victim, the subject of an experiment, dies once a day over and over again

And (*Off.*) Voice of the Host, Sound B, Sound C, Wing, Voice Over the Telephone

The history recounted in the play actually happened.

Ulrike Meinhof helped to free Andreas Baader, abandoned her children, went underground to fight for a New Germany.

She wrote the RAF manifesto, participated in or helped to organize bank robberies, threw bombs.

She was arrested; her skull was forcibly x-rayed.

In prison she went on a hunger strike along with the other imprisoned members of the RAF.

She committed suicide in her cell by hanging herself on Mother's Day.

Andreas Baader and Gudrun Ensslin also committed suicide in prison.

A fashion show of over-the-head paper bags with audience participation

Paper-bag head wear accounts for only one percent of paper-bag sales, but it is a market that is constantly expanding. In order to launch a new German line, a fashion show with audience participation has been organized. An attractive head in a paper bag can promote a new brand—that's why the manufacturer concluded that this unusual form of promotion will be remembered by a hitherto abused public. The German public loves to be abused—what about you?

VOICE OF THE HOST: *(Off.)* Numbers one, two, three, four, five, six, step forward!

The designated numbers step forward. Their heads are covered with gray paper bags with cutout openings for the eyes and the mouth. They come out on the runway. Right, left, right, left—movements geared to the runway.

VOICE OF THE HOST: *(Off.)* Ulrike Meinhof has agreed to become the face of our latest paper-bag collection! Ulrike Meinhof, hidden under a paper bag, unsubmissive, rebellious, true to her principles to the very end. Let's greet her with a hearty round of applause!

We applaud and applaud; after all she's a real star.

VOICE OF THE HOST. *(Off.)* We know her face from TV appearances, we've admired her in many fabulous car chases, attempted killings, hold-ups, murders, mass executions punctuated with black humor and wit.

The numbers come to a stop facing the public.

VOICE OF THE HOST: *(Off.)* Ladies and gentlemen, you can surely point out which bag our star is hidden under...?! Thanks to Ulrike, you dear lady, you dear sir, and our entire global village, soon we'll all put bags over our heads and view the world from a totally new perspective. Please point out Ulrike Meinhof!

Silence. Silence. Silence.

VOICE OF THE HOST: *(Off.)* It's not easy to point out Ulrike Meinhof since she has a bag over her head. Because of the bag we don't know who is under it. Anybody could be under the bag; we are all equals in an encounter with the bag. Bag-given liberty, equality, and fraternity. Show yourself to us, Ulrike Meinhof, we want to see the human face of the bag!

ULRIKE MEINHOF: *(Tears off the bag.)* I'm Ulrike Meinhof!

Andreas Baader: *(Tears off the bag.)* I'm Ulrike Meinhof!

Gudrun Ensslin: *(Tears off the bag.)* I'm Ulrike Meinhof!

Policeman: *(Tears off the bag.)* I'm Ulrike Meinhof!

Squirrel-Man: *(Tears off the bag.)* I'm Ulrike Meinhof!

Lucky: *(Tears off the bag.)* I'm Ulrike Meinhof!

All together to the Public; that is, to us:

Ulrike Meinhof: I spit on you, you pigs!

Andreas Baader: I spit on you, you pigs!

Gudrun Ensslin: I spit on you, you pigs!

Squirrel-Man: I spit on you, you pigs!

Lucky: I spit on you, you pigs!

Ulrike Meinhof: This show is a farce! It's only a performance!

Andreas Baader: This show is a farce! It's only a performance!

Gudrun Ensslin: This show is a farce! It's only a performance!

Policeman *(pigeon-hearted)*: This show is a farce! It's only a performance!

Squirrel-Man: This show is a farce! It's only a performance!

Lucky: This show is a farce! It's only a performance!

Ulrike Meinhof: I'm Ulrike Meinhof. I spit on you, pigs. This show is a farce. It's only a performance.

The stone

Squirrel-Man is lying on the ground in an uncomfortable position. He'd like to talk to Ulrike, but it's not easy. The various voices in her head that reverberated some seven years ago, or was it just yesterday, now resound even louder than the crude moaning heard coming from Squirrel-Man, lying under the wheels of her car.

Squirrel-Man: Excuse me, down here, down here!

Ulrike Meinhof: I couldn't hear what you said. Are you talking to me?

Squirrel-Man: I'm glad that you can hear me now.

Ulrike Meinhof: What are you doing down there?

Squirrel-Man: Honestly, that's what I'd like to know myself.

Ulrike Meinhof: Come out from under there at once.

Squirrel-Man: I just wanted to say that you ran over me when you were parking your car.

Ulrike Meinhof: I have my own opinion on the subject.

Squirrel-Man: Could you please drive off me? I'd feel relieved. By the way, you ought to practice parking.

Ulrike Meinhof: Nonsense.

Squirrel-Man: All the same, you should give it some serious thought. Otherwise you'll end up running over somebody else.

Ulrike Meinhof: Let me explain what really happened to you. You've been cheated, your freedom was stolen and instead you got a pitiful sham. It's a disgrace.

Squirrel-Man: I saw your car approaching, but I felt safe.

Ulrike Meinhof: You're living a lie; you're unaware of the real situation, just like all the rest.

Squirrel-Man: You speeded through the parking lot, over the sidewalk, and rammed into a store; on the way you ran over me.

Ulrike Meinhof: I won't let people I despise mark off zones or set limits "from here to there" for me! Freedom! Freedom not of this world! That's how I want to live.

Squirrel-Man: You're an unusual person, really quite different from me. I completely agree with you with respect to restrictions. There's not enough parking space. Our authorities have nothing to be proud of in this business.

Ulrike Meinhof: Don't say "authorities." Say "pigs."

Squirrel-Man: Animals.

Ulrike Meinhof: Getting better.

Squirrel-Man: Like me.

At this moment Squirrel-Man *dies from injuries sustained in being run over. He died as he usually does, but since he is the object of an ongoing experiment, and his death has already been included in the operating expenses, it made no impression on anyone. But* Ulrike, *on the other hand, had to explain her poor parking and did so. The case seemed to have come to a close, but on the contrary, it was just getting started. She had a basic feeling that everyone has the right to express one's views, and that means that she does too. The only discordant note that blemished an otherwise highly successful day was a stone that fell from the sky and damaged the hood of her car.*

An Anti-Man from an anti-world

A Poet went for a walk when a pot of poetry broke above his head, and a cluster of bubbles was formed. From one of the bubbles there sprang a small moon-maloon, a galaxy, little stars, and a cosmos, and from all of that Anti-Man *was born and popped up to the surface to make his self-presentation.*

Anti-Man: My name is Anti-Man. I don't have kidneys, lungs, heart, spleen, stomach, or any of the rest of that crap inside me. Therefore I have no need of a can, doctors, the achievements of civilization, health food, laundry detergent and the coupons on laundry detergent boxes, washing machines, washing machine factories, unions in washing machine factories, government commissions investigating the financial fraud by the unions in the washing machine factories, or any government that sends government commissions to washing machine factories.

In my opinion that's all shit, but it's your shit, not mine, because I don't shit.

Applause.

That's what his self-presentation sounded like, but there were also witnesses who insisted that it sounded different.

Sound B: My name is Anti-Man and I protest the postwar policies of the German state concerning employment in the washing machine factories. Those factories employ former Nazi party functionaries, members of the SS, and war criminals who now are washing their bloody rags there. To sum up, the bureaucratic machine of the German state has in its belly instead of decent entrails one big hunk of shit, which I repudiate.

Sound C: My name is Anti-Man and I spit on you pigs. Capitalism has stuffed your bellies with the riches of the Third World, which rots away miserably there, and your pig anuses excrete unrecognizably altered bananas from Bolivia, gold from Africa, and oil from the Persian Gulf. The bombing of Vietnam is still going on, which means that you've failed to learn anything from your last pig war; it serves you right that as punishment the German Democratic Republic came into being!

It is evident that SOUNDS B and C are quite different in content, so let's stick with SOUND A.

Freedom not of this world

ULRIKE was walking across terrestrial grass, passing street lamps on which perch pigeons classified in terrestrial atlases. She kept absorbing the sounds with all her senses. The sounds were German sounds, and the state was Germany, so she heard in sequence: the creaking door of the Deutsche Bank branch, the pig voices of German policemen, shooting during a German demonstration, weeping, the wail of sirens, and victorious military marches hummed softly. Her walk brings her finally to a cozy café. All this is happening during one German autumn, although it was in fact spring, and the now is taking place right now.

A Deutsche mark coin rolls on the café table; SQUIRREL-MAN catches it deftly.

SQUIRREL-MAN: I wanted to meet you to explain myself. You appeal to me a lot.

ULRIKE MEINHOF: You caught that German mark quite deftly.

SQUIRREL-MAN: Thanks. Well, last time I didn't have a chance to tell you much about myself, because I died, a fact which I'm afraid made me unattractive in your eyes. However, I'd like to tell you that I die once a day because I'm the object of an experiment.

ULRIKE MEINHOF: I beg your pardon, I have a splitting headache.

SQUIRREL-MAN: Can I be of any help to you?

ULRIKE MEINHOF: Your voice reaches me with great difficulty. I keep hearing German sounds that drown out everything else.

SQUIRREL-MAN: I'm German myself.

ULRIKE MEINHOF: What did you say?

SQUIRREL-MAN: German! You parked on top of me. I had hoped that somehow that would bring us closer. You appeal to me enormously, but as a victim of your parking, I don't stand a chance, do I?

ULRIKE MEINHOF: I'll tell you what I hear: the snapping shut of handcuffs, gagging, choking, shooting, bombing. A door creaks in despair, the voices of the police give the order to stop, the wail of sirens establishes the boundaries!

SQUIRREL-MAN: That's me! It is about me! That's my life!

Ulrike Meinhof: I see your lips moving, but I don't hear anything.

Squirrel-Man: I'm the one being handcuffed, gagged, choked, shot, blown sky-high, and scattered to the winds! It is my door that creaks in despair, the voices of the police order *me* to stop, the wail of sirens establishes the boundaries!

Ulrike Meinhof: You seem like an animal in your fierce, soundless movements. The freedom not of this world that I long for is the pure Absolute. I give it to all humanity, and all of us will become angels. It's no laughing matter; it demands victims.

Squirrel-Man: I'm ready. Too bad you can't hear me.

Squirrel-Man picks up the one-mark coin and drops it in the jukebox.

The strains of the famous hit song, "Too Bad You Can't Hear Me," fill the café. Squirrel-Man dances to the music and sings along with it. Ulrike can't hear him and thinks he's a dumbbell.

Color Red

Ulrike hears a knock at the door. She gets up and opens the door. A large package is lying on the doorstep. Ulrike brings the package in and looks it over. She finds a note attached to the package. She reads: "To my beloved U with best wishes from your loving God."

She opens the package. It contains a left wing with a label, on which is written: "Made from the matter of light."

Ulrike hesitates. Now she knows what to do. And she knows what to think. Now she doesn't know what to do. And she doesn't know what to think. Finally she decides to interrogate the left wing.

Ulrike Meinhof: Who sent you here?

The wing is silent.

Ulrike Meinhof: Don't tell me it was God. I don't believe in parcels from God.

The wing is silent.

Ulrike Meinhof: I don't believe, period. Could it be the Americans? The German government? The police?

The wing is silent.

Ulrike Meinhof: And why just one wing?

The wing is silent.

ULRIKE MEINHOF: Ha, ha, how unfathomable are God's judgments! Of course! Why precisely a left wing? Is that supposed to be some kind of political allusion?

The wing is silent.

ULRIKE MEINHOF: Do you think God can't make allusions? Enough of this nonsense. You're bugged, is that it?

The wing is silent.

ULRIKE MEINHOF: Don't deny it. That won't help you. Admit it, you won't suffer for it.

The wing is silent.

ULRIKE MEINHOF: So you're not afraid? Let's see.

ULRIKE picks up a knife and cuts the wing open. She lights a match and sets the wing on fire. She hangs it upside down. Wax drips out of the wing. It contains no bug.

Another knock on the door. Someone is knocking as if seeking shelter. ULRIKE wakes up. She hears the knock. She gets up and opens the door.

ULRIKE MEINHOF: I heard a knock on the door as if someone were seeking shelter.

ANTI-MAN: I don't need shelter. I appear on the doorstep and simply am. She's the one *(Points to GUDRUN ENSSLIN.)* who knocked as if she needed shelter.

ULRIKE MEINHOF: I must tell my children a fairy tale about who you are.

ANTI-MAN: Say we're Reds.

GUDRUN ENSSLIN: Say we go from house to house and tell fairy tales about the Color Red.

ULRIKE MEINHOF: I can't make up my mind. I don't know what to do. I don't know what to think.

GUDRUN ENSSLIN: Listen. Once upon a time there was the Color Red. Nobody liked it. Baneberry took it, and got squashed under foot; blood took it, and got hidden under the skin; red shoes took it, and got burned at the stake. The Color Red grew angry and began to bite. The bomb took it, because it wasn't afraid of it. The bomb exploded and started a fire in the big department store. The store burned red hot.

The Color Red called the Deutsche Presse Agentur and said in my voice, "This is the Color Red taking revenge," and went its own way.

Ulrike Meinhof: What happens next?

Gudrun Ensslin: If you let them in, Uncle Hans and Auntie Grete will tell the children what happens next.

Ulrike lets them in. As a result God changes his plans and did not send Ulrike the right wing, and with only one wing—and a burned one at that—it's impossible to fly.

The Policeman and Anti-Man

Maybe it's true that Anti-Man is an enemy of civilization, but sometimes he makes exceptions. Right now he's racing down the open highway at a speed that makes his hair stream back, and his soul soars to the heights of the moon-maloon. The BMW races along, and the BMW Company will thank him for it some day, mentally, since it wouldn't be proper to do so openly.

This racing lasts a bit longer than the twinkle of an eye, but the Anti-Man does not let himself be taken in by appearances. Germany is a police state, although the police of one Bundesland do not cooperate with the police of another Bundesland. Those are problems of establishing contact. Nonetheless, the appearance of the Policeman at this point is inevitable.

Policeman: It's my pleasure, Sir, to pull you over for excessive speeding in your comfortable and fast automobile.

Anti-Man: Do what you're supposed to, police pig, and as for the automobile, I agree with your assessment.

Policeman: Alright, let me tell you something. The events of the last war have caused a part of society to look at the German uniform with suspicion, but it isn't really such a large part.

Anti-Man: I do all I can to shake the conscience of this horrible German nation. Owing to my efforts, you will be called "police pig" more and more frequently, "you police pig."

Policeman: Possibly, possibly, but for the time being you are in the avant-garde of invective, but socially you're nothing but an outcast.

Anti-Man: Wretched cop, dogcatcher, limp prick.

Policeman: Now that's getting personal. Your papers, please.

ANTI-MAN: Here, you fucking loser.

POLICEMAN: *(Reads.)* Peter Chenowitz. *(Looks ANTI-MAN over.)* That's not true.

ANTI-MAN: What's not true, uniformed asshole?

POLICEMAN: Your name isn't Peter Chenowitz.

ANTI-MAN: And just what is it, you dimwitted hammerhead of the regime?

POLICEMAN: I was present at your self-presentation. You sprang from a bubble, from the moon-maloon, which means you're Anti-Man!

ANTI-MAN: Verdammt!

POLICEMAN: I arrest you for possession of forged documents.

The POLICEMAN locks ANTI-MAN in a cage and covers him with a dark cloth, like a canary.

The telephone rings.

POLICEMAN: Berlin Police Station. Please speak quietly, the birdie's asleep in his cage.

VOICE ON THE TELEPHONE: You pig snout, you imperialist uniformed bastard don't you dare touch even one hair of our great, dear Andreas Baader, whom you arrested illegally!

POLICEMAN: I'm very glad that I've arrested Herr Baader. I had no idea who it was. Could you come to Berlin to confirm his identity?

Unfortunately, at this point the connection is cut off, but we already know that the ANTI-MAN is ANDREAS BAADER, and ANDREAS BAADER is ANTI-MAN.

The Pigeon-hearted Policeman

The POLICEMAN is guarding the cage containing ANDREAS ANTI-MAN, and casts stern glances, now here, now there. At the bottom of his soul, however, the POLICEMAN is pigeon-hearted. Probably due to an error on the part of nature. Once nature becomes aware of the error, it will replace his pigeon heart with a new one. The POLICEMAN's menacing glare does not scare GUDRUN and ULRIKE.

POLICEMAN: Guten Morgen! What are you looking for, ladies?

ULRIKE MEINHOF: We brought seeds for the canary.

POLICEMAN: He's not a canary. Did you ladies think he's a canary?

Gudrun Ensslin: Yes.

Policeman: He's not a canary. He's Andreas Baader.

Ulrike Meinhof: You locked him up in a cage and covered him with a cloth like a canary.

Policeman: I'll admit it may look that way. Like a cage with a canary. But it's a bubble.

Ulrike Meinhof: A bubble!

Policeman: I made Herr Baader's cage in the shape of a bubble so he'd feel at home.

Gudrun Ensslin and Ulrike Meinhof: *(In unison.)* How do you know that Herr Baader came out of a bubble!?

Policeman: The German police know more than meets the eye. *(Pause.)* But since you ladies also seem to know that Herr Baader came out of a bubble, why did you bring him seeds, eh? After all, he doesn't eat, he has no guts.

Gudrun Ensslin: The seeds are for the canary, not for Herr Baader.

Policeman: Whew. Do I feel relieved. Please give me the seeds. *(Takes the seeds and nibbles some.)* I'm pigeon-hearted, and food for canaries is good for me—it's rich in minerals. That's very good for the heart. And then there's this dovish trustfulness of mine, somewhat out of place in a policeman. I'm trying to overcome it, and that's why I ask these questions that are embarrassing to all of us, whew. So you ladies don't know Herr Baader?

Ulrike Meinhof: No, how could we? We're conducting scholarly research, and bird feeding in police stations is our contribution to the study of the threatened ecosystem.

Gudrun Ensslin: *(Introducing herself.)* Doctor Grete W.

Policeman: I think scholarly research should be done on Herr Baader. He's unusual in every respect. He doesn't eat, as I have already mentioned, in the human sense of the word. You understand, ladies, wurst and that kind of thing—not a bit of it …

Gudrun Ensslin: He must eat something, or he'd croak.

Policeman: I can see right away that you are a doctor! *(Pause.)* I thought and thought about it, and it occurred to me that I'll try to feed him something out of the ordinary.

Ulrike Meinhof: You should have asked for help from science instead conducting experiments on your own.

Policeman: I did not experiment on my own. I consulted Herr Baader. He's asked for a good book.

Ulrike Meinhof: And what happened?

Policeman: He threw them all away, except for one. That one he devoured from start to finish. But it took me a lot of searching to find that one …

Gudrun Ensslin: I want to see Baader as soon as possible.

Policeman: Easy, easy. I figured out that since he's occupied with planting bombs himself, this book would meet with his approval. The title is—tata, tata—*Minimanual of the Urban Guerilla* by Carlos Marighella! Now I'm waiting for your praise.

Gudrun Ensslin: I don't give a shit about any of that, and I simply speak my mind: How could you lock up in a cage such an extraordinary person, who devours the latest works published?

Policeman: But he is Andreas Baader, isn't he?!

Gudrun Ensslin. You locked him up in a cage only because his name is Andreas Baader.

Policeman: I'm only following orders, that's all

Gudrun Ensslin: Moron.

Policeman: Please try to understand me, ladies: I'm not without a heart. I've a family and dear ones.

Gudrun Ensslin: Moron.

Policeman: He behaved badly, ladies. He blew up a large department store—you can't do things like that—and please don't draw any parallels to the Nuremberg trial here.

Ulrike Meinhof: Did you ever give a thought to what's happening in the world right now?

Policeman: I can't grasp the entire world with my reason. I have a relative in Poland, a six-year-old girl … I have a premonition, I tell you, ladies, that at this very moment she stepped with her bare feet on a shard of glass, and that she's crying her eyes out. That's an example of what is happening in the world right now.

Ulrike Meinhof: I'll tell what's happening in the world right now: Persian crude oil flows in a broad stream, along with Bolivian bananas and African gold. Exploitation of the Third World.

Policeman: You've counted how many worlds there are, because you're in the sciences, but I am not. I'm afraid that blood is flowing from the little girl's foot and that her mother is not at home.

Gudrun Ensslin: Moron. The German police are morons.

Policeman: You're wrong there, lady. We're looking for Gudrun Ensslin, who was an accomplice in planting the bomb in that store. Do you happen to know her?

Gudrun Ensslin: And why should I know her?

Policeman: Too bad. I'm simply asking, I ask here and there, all the time, that's my job. I ask people in the streets: "Have you seen such and such person? Her name is Gudrun Ensslin." And they say, "Unfortunately, no, but if we do see her, we'll let you know." Maybe she'll turn herself in, who knows?

Ulrike Meinhof: That's likely.

Gudrun Ensslin: Now can we finally see Baader?

Policeman: Of course. *(He removes the cover from the cage, opens the door, and lets Ensslin and Ulrike go in.)* You've got visitors, Herr Baader, they'll cheer you up.

Andreas Baader: *(To Enslin.)* Gudrun!

Policeman: The lady's name is Grete.

Andreas Baader: I'll call her Gudrun. Now please get out of here, I have to fuck her.

Gudrun Ensslin: For scientific purposes.

Ulrike Meinhof: And I'll watch.

Policeman: I'm going, I'm going. *(To himself.)* Youth, youth, oy, and all I've got are seeds, oy, could make you envious.

Tactfully, the Policeman *leaves the premises. Although he feels that one of the ladies who claims to be Doctor Grete W. is in fact* Gudrun Ensslin, Baader*'s girlfriend, and who, at this very moment, is discussing an escape plan with the well-known leftist journalist and screenwriter,* Ulrike Meinhof. *But no one would believe him if he were to report this to the authorities. The authorities cannot believe in premonitions. In any case, the* Policeman *decided to put in a call to Poland to find out how the little girl is doing. But the call cannot go through because in those days there were no cell phones, only rotary ones with six-digit numbers: 22–93–22. Rain quickly washes away the blood from the girl's cut foot. The janitor cleans up the broken glass from the beer bottle.*

The Poles drank a lot because they were oppressed by Marxism.

Circus

The Chancellor of Germany said that the Germans are as likable and hard-working as squirrels. He would like to see the squirrel on the German coat of arms, but for the time being it is a black eagle with wings outspread on the shield, like "tsiplata-tabak" (roasted chicken), a popular dish in Soviet railroad stations.

The chancellor is pleased. "Everything bad is already behind us," he says, but not all Germans agree with him. Gudrun Ensslin, *for example, is also pleased, but does not agree.* Ensslin *considers that the time has come to start a decent circus.*

Gudrun Ensslin: *(Cracks her whip.)* Here comes the famous Squirrel-Man!

Squirrel-Man *runs in.*

Gudrun Ensslin: Squirrel-Man—if you haven't seen him, take a look; if you haven't heard him, give a listen! Squirrel-Man hoards provisions for winter-time, nurtures his young, shelters them tenderly, looks to the future apprehensively, checks the current prices, pays his debts on time, worries about losing his hair, hops around, writes verses, is useful, easy to get to bed, on a cot, on a grill, propagates rapidly!

Squirrel-Man *listens to* Ensslin.

Gudrun Ensslin: And now Squirrel-Man will kick the Policeman in the ass!

Gudrun *cracks her whip. The* Policeman *runs in.*

Policeman: *(Good-naturedly.)* I've decided to take part in this German circus. People deserve some fun and entertainment after this horrible war. A kick in the ass is a somewhat crude form of entertainment, but the art of circus isn't particularly intellectually demanding, and I accept that.

Gudrun Ensslin: The intellectuals will take part in the show too, I promise you! *(Cracks her whip again. Ulrike runs in.)*

Gudrun Ensslin: Now the intellectuals join the show! They spew out the scholarly Kick the Policeman in the Ass Manifesto!

Squirrel-Man looks at Ulrike.

Squirrel-Man: What good luck—to see you again! I thought of you during long sleepless nights; with my heart pounding I composed endless scenarios about our meeting, in the course of which I always died of love. Can you hear me?

Ulrike again doesn't listen to him; she is absorbed in her own thoughts.

Policeman: *(To Ulrike.)* Dear Frau U. Although I'm standing in the arena of events in the spotlight in a somewhat uncomfortable position—well—of necessity bent over, backside raised, so it won't sound comical I'll only say: no, dear Madame, go on reading Count Tolstoy, or do research on the secret life of dolphins.

Gudrun Ensslin: A jabbering ass! Who ever saw a jabbering ass?

Squirrel-Man: I'm used to dying once a day. In my dreams I die even more often, but of my own free will. I won't kick the Policeman in the ass. If I do, you'll be forced by this lady here to write a manifesto.

Gudrun Ensslin: Stupid critter full of squirrel guts! That's exactly what she's waiting for.

Policeman: All that's a joke, a fairground amusement, Herr comrade. Go ahead, kick me in the ass, let the public have a healthy laugh. Frau U. is a part of the show, there's nothing to get upset about. It makes me feel uncomfortable too, keep that in mind.

Ulrike Meinhof: The words keep blurting out of my mouth as if they'd grown wings, but I can't get started.

Squirrel-Man: I won't kick.

Gudrun Ensslin: Well, all right then. Now I'll beat the living daylights out of you, or else you kill yourself.

Policeman: Easy does it, my friends, it's all just a part of this lousy show.

Squirrel-Man: I'll hang myself with my tie, although that's a tricky business.

He hangs himself in the air with his tie, although that's a tricky business. ULRIKE, *watching him, is carried away by inspiration. At last the words fly out of her mouth like birds. How far they'll fly depends on the quality of their wings.*

ULRIKE MEINHOF: At the sight of this person's death, my semi-radical words have become one-hundred percent radicalized. The ideological foundations for ass-kicking are one thing, and those for death are another. This person gave his life defending imaginary values. My answer is: Enough! I demand the immediate withdrawal of the troops from Indochina!

POLICEMAN: Stop pretending, my friend. You can't hang yourself in the air by your own tie.

GUDRUN ENSSLIN: *(To* ULRIKE.*)* Avoid intellectual shortcuts, we need to fill twenty-two pages of fine print.

ULRIKE MEINHOF: In life's goodness I'm no believer.

POLICEMAN: Here's what I'll add: in life's no-goodness I'm a believer, since you seldom get laid by a beaver. *(Pause.)* A circus should be a real circus!

GUDRUN ENSSLIN: End of show.

The POLICEMAN *immediately resumes his search for* GUDRUN ENSSLIN *since he's a person who goes and goes until he finally gets up on his toes and does his duty. Meanwhile,* ULRIKE *admiringly regards her winged words, which are already landing on a blank sheet of paper.*

Tree and wind

ULRIKE *would like to go underground.* ULRIKE *does not know if she would like to go underground.*

A female member of the Red Brigades declared: "I was convinced that I was endangering my life, but that the revolution would eventually come—and it wouldn't be in twenty years, but much sooner. (...) Frontline soldiers in the struggle [like me] had to sever all ties with their former way of life, have no contact with their families or their communities, and go underground."

If we're citing quotations, making wise faces, earning a doctorate, compiling a decent bibliography for the play, then, for the sake of balance, why shouldn't we also say something stupid, recite blank verse for example: "What shall we do with him? Let him dance, let him dance! What shall we do with him? Let's kill him, but let him dance!"

ULRIKE MEINHOF: Woman is earth, damp, darkness. To be down there, underground, draw strength from darkness, from the dark, damp, terrifying interior, is to draw directly from the source of strength. Life and death: all-powerful.

Gudrun Ensslin: Anybody peeked into your small, dark, terrifying interior lately? Been doing any fucking?

Ulrike Meinhof: At night I can manage to die of love, but during the day I scoff at it. No one in my life now, and never will be.

Gudrun Ensslin: You're still young.

Ulrike Meinhof: I'm old and wise. I want to go underground. I'm afraid of going underground.

Gudrun Ensslin: Little coward. Hypocritical bitch.

Ulrike Meinhof: A tree buffeted by doubts.

Gudrun Ensslin: You're the tree, I'm the wind.

Ulrike is a tree. Gudrun is the wind.

Gudrun Ensslin: *(Wrestling with Ulrike.)* I'll knock you over. You'll disappear from the face of the earth.

Ulrike Meinhof: You won't be able to.

Gudrun Ensslin: I'll knock you over.

Ulrike Meinhof: Two small identical apples, my fruit.

Gudrun Ensslin: Shake them off, then you'll go underground.

Ulrike Meinhof: I'm rooted underground.

Gudrun Ensslin: Shake them off, then you'll go underground.

Ulrike Meinhof: Kingdom of shadows, of ghosts, of non-existences, of false identities, of forged passports, of stolen registration plates, of rented apartments, of arms dealers, of double agents, of spies from the First, Second, and Third World.

Gudrun Ensslin: Underground is not for bitches.

Ulrike Meinhof: Roots are underground. I bid farewell to the tree.

Gudrun Ensslin: The apples roll. The tree is no more.

ULRIKE is no longer a tree.

ULRIKE MEINHOF: Anyone who stands in my way, but does not yet know it, wakes up with a scream, without knowing why fear takes away one's breath. What shall I do with him? Let him dance, let him dance. What shall I do with him? I'll kill him, but let him dance!

When was the last time you woke up with a scream?

When was the last time you woke up with a scream?

Window

Let us take a look at the window of the cage through which the little bird BAADER flew away. There is nothing unusual about it. And yet the special agents of all the police investigative services in the world are staring at it as if they were spellbound. Even Emperor Bokassa, who took a break from cutting off the ears of his subjects, stops and stares at it. No wonder—he senses competition. That is why the Emperor Bokassa decides to devour a few of his subjects and to teach a chimpanzee how to smoke cigarettes. Emperor Bokassa jealously guards his position of leadership

At the moment we are in the reading room of the Institute for Social Studies in Berlin. SQUIRREL-MAN and ULRIKE MEINHOF are among the readers.

SQUIRREL-MAN: *(To himself.)* Every day I wake up thinking that this time I'll say that something special that will make this woman love me. *(To ULRIKE.)* Did you know that Karl Marx wrote *Das Kapital* in this reading room? *(Silence. To himself.)* I made that up; Marx wrote it in the reading room of the British Museum. *(To ULRIKE.)* I thought it might move you, but if not, I'll try to amuse you with Lenin. Did you know that Lenin sat in this reading room and wrote under the pseudonym Jacob Richter? It's a joke, of course, but do you hear me?

ULRIKE MEINHOF: *(To herself.)* Every day I wake up thinking other people do something real, while I only deceive myself with make-believe actions. This time I have decided to do something that surprises even me. I deny myself the right to lead an ordinary life in a country that is marked by a monstrous crime everyone wants to forget as fast as possible.

SQUIRREL-MAN: What crime are you talking about?

Enter the POLICEMAN and BAADER. BAADER in handcuffs.

POLICEMAN: What crime are you talking about?

Squirrel-Man: I'm deeply in love with this lady without her loving me in return, and, to make her pay attention to me, I'm ready to take up any subject that's of interest to her, no matter how strange. Unfortunately, I am too individual for her. She cares only for humanity in general.

Policeman: Crime as a subject interests me professionally. I can contribute to your discussion from my own point of view.

Andreas Baader: I intend to commit a series of crimes, you pig of a policeman, but I do not consider my future crimes to be crimes.

Policeman: I've grown fond of your provocative way of conducting a conversation. In the depths of your heart you are a good man, an extremely good man. Yes, I know that belief in the goodness of man has many a time been put to the test and failed. As a policeman, I've decided to fulfill my professional duties by trusting people. *(Takes off Baader's handcuffs.)*

Ulrike Meinhof: *(To the Policeman.)* Trust him, he doesn't lie; and he will certainly commit many crimes, in your understanding of the word—and I'll help him. I actually stand on the border between two worlds, do you understand? One of these worlds is here, inside this reading room, and the other is there, outside the window.

Policeman: I already told you that you see the borders between worlds, between first, second, and third worlds—although for others they are invisible. What I perceive outside this window is the springtime greenness of Berlin.

Ulrike Meinhof: Springtime greenness, laughing children, the colors of autumn—the triteness of all that slices my ear like a razor.

Andreas Baader: *(To the Policeman.)* Now I can tell you openly that I possess superhuman abilities. I can catch a bomb falling on a rice-paddy and hurl it at Frankfurt or Munich. The inhabitants of those cities can, thanks to me, experience the horrors of a war that is not their own and inhale the smell of burned flesh.

Ulrike Meinhof: Bravo!

Squirrel-Man: *(To Ulrike.)* Are you in love with him? I feel myself so unattractive compared to that extraordinary Herr Baader … Besides, I'm afraid he's talking about my flesh.

Policeman: Herr Baader poses no threat to us. He came here to probe himself sociologically with the help of Frau Meinhof.

ULRIKE MEINHOF: Gentlemen. I'm starting a new life. I give you my word. Two witnesses please.

POLICEMAN: I'm really here to keep an eye on Herr Baader, but I trust him. *(Goes over to ULRIKE and extends his hand to her.)*

SQUIRREL-MAN: My friend, who loves German literature more than anything, told me that no one ever talked to him like you. I'm here to keep an eye on Herr Baader, but—although I don't trust him—I'll be a witness to your oath *(Goes over to ULRIKE.)*

ULRIKE MEINHOF: I solemnly swear to do everything possible so as not to waste my life.

Enter GUDRUN ENSSLIN.

GUDRUN ENSSLIN: I've been standing at the door listening for a few minutes, because I was curious as to what you'd swear. But it wasn't worth waiting for. Cunt.

ANDREAS BAADER: Enough of boredom! With my superhuman strength I open this window! *(Goes to the window and opens it.)*

POLICEMAN: You're not allowed to leave the reading room; you have to probe your own depths, not run away!

SQUIRREL-MAN: *(To ULRIKE.)* Stay here, please!

SQUIRREL MAN goes over to the window and blocks the exit.

GUDRUN ENSSLIN: I won't shoot you, Squirrel-Man; it's for your sake that we are starting the revolution in Germany.

She shoots SQUIRREL-MAN. Fatally hit in the liver, SQUIRREL-MAN falls to the ground.

SQUIRREL-MAN: Halt! Fatally hit in the liver, I just had a dying vision connected with this window!

Listen to the story of a dying man.

ANDREAS BAADER: But make it short.

GUDRUN ENSSLIN: Let's hurry, Baby, I missed you so much!

ANDREAS BAADER: Let's hear his vision; and you, Meinhof, accustom yourself to the sight of someone fatally hit in the liver and other organs.

Policeman: That's a big, big mistake, Herr Baader, you're unleashing a spiral of violence, oh, my, what's coming next, this is no longer a circus.

Squirrel-Man: Can I finally say something?

All, somewhat contrite, nod "yes."

Squirrel-Man: The title of my vision is "The Story of a Guy Who Had an Airplane Fly Through the Window."

Andreas Baader and Gudrun Ensslin: Oh, no! Even the title is too long! We're leaving.

They start to leave.

Squirrel-Man: A plane flew in through the first window. A plane flew in through the second window. A plane flew in through the third window … *(He dies.)*

We'll never know what he had in mind. Perhaps a story about how a plane flew in through the window? If so, Emperor Bokassa and his chimpanzee pale in comparison.

Desert and pumpkin

Ulrike Meinhof and Gudrun Ensslin, like two lizards, leave a trail in the sand. They are in the desert—only sand and sky. The Promised Land. One grain of that sand represents good, another evil, and so on ad infinitum. Ulrike and Gudrun carefully separate out the right grains of sand and load them into the howitzer, mortar, hand-held bomb launcher.

Bang, bang. The grains fly.

You can learn anything; you just have to be properly motivated.

Gudrun Ensslin: *(Fires a round at the pumpkin—misses it.)* That pumpkin is no good.

Ulrike Meinhof: *(Looking at the unscathed pumpkin.)* What an ironic twist of fate! You have, before your eyes, clearly delineated against the blue sky, the classic American symbol of inanity, of spookiness, of death. Provided, of course, that you first disembowel it like a pig with automatic firepower, pluck out its eyes, force its snout to scream.

Gudrun Ensslin: Sure as shit. That pumpkin is somehow shady.

Ulrike Meinhof: A shapely, chubby, juicy pumpkin. It's waiting for you to slaughter it and stick a burning candle inside it. It'll light the way to hell for some American pig in Heidelberg.

GUDRUN ENSSLIN: Words, words. Even when you fart, you find a catchy name for it.

ULRIKE MEINHOF: That's the only thing I do well, my dear.

GUDRUN ENSSLIN: *(Fires another round; the pumpkin is shattered into little pieces. With satisfaction.)* That shitty Heidelberg will wake up from its sleep when American entrails fly into its gardens.

ULRIKE MEINHOF: Don't get me wrong, but can I bow down to you?

GUDRUN ENSSLIN: Go ahead, bow down, I don't give it a thought. I keep on loading and shooting. *(Fires again.)*

ULRIKE MEINHOF: *(Bows.)* You're the personification of firmness, of pure energy, of strength. I bow down to you, I wish I could erect a temple in your honor, et cetera.

GUDRUN ENSSLIN: You're talking shit, just get to the point.

ULRIKE MEINHOF: An overheated Kalashnikov, fired up from shooting, loads me up with energy and clarity of thought. I see, I finally see what else I can give of myself besides words.

GUDRUN ENSSLIN: Out with it.

ULRIKE MEINHOF: I have twin girls, two useless daughters. I'll take them away from the volcano at Mount Etna where they have a safe but inane shelter, and I'll shut them up here in the camp in the Promised Land.

GUDRUN ENSSLIN: Children mean trouble even in a camp.

ULRIKE MEINHOF: But my children can be useful. They'll be my eyes and my fingers. They'll pull the trigger and die for the Vietnamese, Angolan, Cuban, Guatemalan, and Palestinian cause.

GUDRUN ENSSLIN: They're big enough. Thinking, by heck, you're good at that all right. You've got a head like that pumpkin.

But this ingenious, maternal plan was thwarted by a number of people of good will who failed to recognize its merits. The girls flew from the inane volcano at Mount Etna in the opposite direction, that is, to Germany, where the sole Kalashnikov they encountered was depicted on the logo RAF, which was later replaced by a Heckler und Koch (a submachine assault rifle).

The book of names: Felix means lucky

Lucky is talking to Gudrun Ensslin on a wanted poster. "Wanted ENSSLIN." The poster was put up by the Policeman.

Lucky: Mummy, Mummy, I'm burning.

Gudrun Ensslin: I know, because I decided to burn you up. Uncle Hans set you on fire, that's why you're burning.

Lucky: I'm glad you know all about it, but I'm suffering terribly. I'm burning up.

Gudrun Ensslin: I'm very sorry we didn't succeed in burning you up entirely and that you're still burning.

Lucky: What am I supposed to do? Am I responsible that I'm still burning and suffering terribly?

Gudrun Ensslin: I feel bad about it myself. If you'd burned up entirely, we could've scattered your ashes and ended the whole thing.

Lucky: Mummy, I'd really like you to do something … for me. But it's so hard for me to ask for anything that all I'd like to say is, "Mummy, Mummy, Mummy."

Gudrun Ensslin: I want to do something for you, too.

Lucky: What is it, Mummy, Mummy, Mummy?

Gudrun Ensslin: I've got some poison for you.

Lucky: To drink, something from Mummy to drink? I'm afraid to drink it. It's hard to do, Mummy.

Gudrun Ensslin: It's easy to do. It's a present. The Color Red went for a walk and gave out presents. Drink it to a better world.

Lucky: Really, Mummy, Mummy? When I call you "Mummy," I believe you.

Gudrun Ensslin: Then call me "Mummy" all the time and give me your hand..

Lucky: That's what I have to do? Call you "Mummy" and give you my hand like this?

Gudrun Ensslin: You do that very well. You say what is necessary, and your hand is outstretched. I'm your Mummy. You have to grab the glass. Hold on to it tight so as not to spill. Keep thinking, "Mummy."

Lucky stretches out his hand in a firmly clenched fist.

Gudrun Ensslin: Hold the glass tight, your hand is burned and weak. Drink.

Lucky: It's hard.

Gudrun Ensslin: It's best.

Lucky: I don't want to.

Gudrun Ensslin: Repeat the words.

Lucky: Mummy, Mummy ... Help me.

Gudrun Ensslin: It'll be much easier now.

Lucky: Yes, it's easier.

Policeman: *(Butting in.)* Don't give him poison. That's illegal.

Gudrun Ensslin: In life's no-goodness I'm a believer.

Policeman: Since you seldom get laid by a beaver, I know. Please comply and don't give him poison.

Thanks to this intervention Lucky continues to burn. He falls asleep and dreams a dream: his burned hands fly over the desert. The wind carries them into a garden. The hands fall to the ground, a pumpkin grows out of them. His Mother picks the pumpkin and sets it in the sand. "This pumpkin is no good," she says. What could that mean?

The pumpkin is a magical vegetable

Ulrike Meinhof: I heard the strange story of what happened to that man, although I don't know who he is. Why did he talk to Gudrun's photo on the wanted poster? The pigeon-hearted Policeman came up to him and forbade him from talking to the wanted poster. Why didn't the Policeman forbid the wanted poster from talking to the man? That's not a fair law! If German law prohibits wanted posters from talking to strangers, then the Policeman could arrest a poster like that and put it in jail.

Since I came back to Germany, I've noticed there are pumpkins everywhere. Even in banks: Guten Tag, Herr Pumpkin, how was your vacation, Frau Pumpkin ... No, that was a joke, pumpkins don't go on vacation. What's most important is that I've changed my life. I no longer deceive myself, I no longer get raped, nobody rapes me. That's supreme happiness, the absolute tops. Anyone who was ever raped knows what I'm talking about. Now I exist in a new reality. I'm a different person. I'm *(Laughs.)* Robin Hood.

I say things, like in the movies. For example, I say … *(Laughs again.)* … seriously, for example, I say things like … like … *(Trying to smother her laughter.)* … say it for me, Gudrun …

The bank robbery begins. Baader *turns on a boom box. Loud music.*

Ulrike Meinhof: … Say it, Gudrun …

Gudrun Ensslin: *(Shrieks; holding a submachine gun.)* This is a hold-up …

Ulrike Meinhof: *(Laughs.)* Yes, this is a hold-up …

Andreas Baader: *(Shrieks.)* This is a hold-up!

Gudrun Ensslin: *(Shrieks.)* Hands up! Face to the wall!

Ulrike Meinhof: *(Laughs.)* Yes, hands up … right now … or I'll blow your pumpkin heads off!

Laughter.

Andreas Baader: *(Shrieks.)* Hands up!

Gudrun Ensslin: *(Shrieks.)* Face to the wall! Keep quiet!

Baader *jumps on the counter and takes aim with his gun.*

Ulrike Meinhof: Gudrun says that for all these words we'll get a total of two-hundred and eighty-five thousand Deutsche marks! *(Laughter.)* I have a gun too. Gudrun says we must have guns, because they want to kill us.

Enter the Policeman *on all fours.*

Policeman: Lower your voices, please. I've been shot in the back, and my face was cut by flying glass.

Ulrike Meinhof: Why are you on all fours?

Policeman: Because I'm bleeding—you know how debilitating that is? There's a car parked in front of the bank, from which somebody shot at me.

Andreas Baader: That's our car.

POLICEMAN: Herr Baader, I told you, you can't disregard the "no parking" sign. I have to write you a ticket.

ANDREAS BAADER: I don't give a shit about your "no parking" sign.

GUDRUN ENSSLIN: Neither do I.

POLICEMAN: You're not doctor Grete. You're Gudrun Ensslin on the wanted poster.

ANDREAS BAADER: You're a pigeon-hearted moron.

POLICEMAN: I trusted you. I was a trusting policeman.

ANDREAS BAADER: And my eyes are blue.

BAADER jumps off the counter, lifts the POLICEMAN up on his knees, and shoots him through the heart. The POLICEMAN falls to the ground.

GUDRUN ENSSLIN: *(Peering into the hole in the POLICEMAN's body; to BAADER.)* You got him right through his pigeon-heart, Baby.

ANDREAS BAADER: Let them replace it with a piggy-heart since he's a pig.

ULRIKE MEINHOF: *(Peering into the hole in the POLICEMAN's body.)* What a terrible hole.

GUDRUN ENSSLIN: Come on, Ulrike, we didn't come here to peer into that hole.

ULRIKE MEINHOF: *(To herself.)* I'm running a fever. I'm running a fever and I'm raving. Somebody has turned my pumpkin into a carriage. I'm racing, I'm racing and I'm realizing my dreams. I must get back by twelve, then I'll turn back again into that other Ulrike, *(In whisper.)* the one that got raped. I have to hurry.

Ulrike subjects herself to self-analysis, but also listens to public opinion

ULRIKE MEINHOF: Yesterday I was ill; I don't remember much, but I am aware that I can easily be classified as a Sacred Female Fanatic character—and just what does that mean, gentlemen? It means that extreme variations and emotional instability affect me, perhaps even suppress and repress me. On the one hand, I fluctuate between mystical states and total doubt; on the other, my fanaticism sometimes changes into its opposite, that is to say, lack of faith. To sum up: yesterday doubt and lack of faith, today energy and optimism—you surely know what I'm talking about, gentlemen? Maybe you too have got all the makings of terrorists? *(Cups her hands into a megaphone, through which she speaks.)*

War is war! Members of society, form ranks!

Society forms ranks: The Policeman with the hole in his chest, Andreas, Gudrun, Squirrel-Man and Lucky.

Ulrike Meinhof: Count off!

Policeman: Eenie.

Andreas Baader: Meenie.

Gudrun Ensslin: Minie.

Squirrel-Man: Mo.

Lucky: Catch.

Policeman: A Tiger.

Andreas Baader: By the.

Gudrun Ensslin: Toe.

Squirrel-Man: If he.

Lucky: Hollers.

Policeman: Let.

Andreas Baader: Him.

Gudrun Ensslin: Go.

Squirrel-Man: You're.

Lucky: It!

Ulrike Meinhof: The winner is the gentleman who talked with Gudrun Ensslin's picture on the wanted poster. The well-known and respected Allensbach Institute for Public Opinion Research has an important question for you: What is your feeling for the Red Army Faction terrorists?

Lucky: Empathy.

Ulrike Meinhof: I'm delighted to hear it! Tell us something about yourself, please.

Lucky: I'm every fifth and every tenth German.

ULRIKE MEINHOF: The next important question: Would you let a member of the RAF in need of shelter stay overnight in your apartment?

LUCKY: I would.

GUDRUN ENSSLIN: My flesh and blood!

ULRIKE MEINHOF: *(To GUDRUN.)* You haven't spilled any yet.

GUDRUN ENSSLIN: My flesh and blood—my son! *(To LUCKY.)* I'm proud of you, my son.

ULRIKE MEINHOF: *(To LUCKY.)* Is she your Mummy?

LUCKY: Yes, she's my Mummy.

ULRIKE MEINHOF: *(To herself.)* Life provides solutions to riddles when we least expect them. *(To LUCKY.)* Now you are grown up, but I heard that Gudrun abandoned you when you were six months old. Aren't you angry at her for deserting you?

LUCKY: No, I'm not angry. I'm proud.

GUDRUN ENSSLIN: *(Cutting in.)* After all, who has a Mummy like me? Whose Mummy fights as I do? Without me, he wouldn't know that politicians tell lies, that Vietnam is being bombed, and if somebody says "no," he'll be shot!

LUCKY: Yes, Mummy.

ULRIKE MEINHOF: Next question: Could you name the well-known German politician, whose title begins with "F," responsible for crimes against humanity?

LUCKY: The Few-roar?

ULRIKE MEINHOF: N-n-no.

LUCKY: The Fur-rear? The Furry-ear? No? … Exactly what did he do? What crimes did he commit?

ULRIKE MEINHOF: This is a crime. I told you at the time, when I crossed over the invisible border between the world of peace and the world of terror, when I jumped out the window, and when I changed my life. I said: "I deny myself the right to live an ordinary life in a country marked by crimes every one wants to forget as quickly as possible."

ANDREAS BAADER: *(To ULRIKE.)* Don't be too smart for your own good.

Ulrike Meinhof: *(To Andreas.)* You promised to tell us all a fairy tale about The Color Red. Where's the fairy tale?

Policeman: I don't trust you anymore, Herr Baader! You said you had no entrails and that you don't shit ... and yesterday you said, "I shit on your no-parking sign. I shit on it!"

Squirrel-Man: And I'd like to step out of the ranks of society. I bought a new car and I want to show it to a friend.

Andreas Baader: Get the fuck out of here! Only members of the RAF get to stay!

The RAF members gather in a tight circle.

The Policeman feels bad with a hole in his chest. Lucky wants to boast that he once saw his Mummy Gudrun acting in a porno movie, but he's embarrassed and decides to keep the information to himself. Squirrel-Man goes to the parking lot to get his car, and the RAF plans the total fairy tale about The Color Red.

Seeds of fear

Squirrel-Man: I told her I wanted to show off my new car, but I was lying. It was just one more attempt to make a statement that would make her fall in love with me. I made her understand—between the lines—that I could leave her, that she meant nothing to me. That I was in a hurry to get back to my car. That she had miscalculated. That I didn't love her anymore. Pretty clever, eh? But a convincing delivery cost me a lot of effort: "I bought a new car and I want to show it to a friend." Now my whole jaw aches and my throat is hoarse from saying those words. You can hear that, can't you? She doesn't love me because she loves the Vietnamese, the Angolans, the Guatemalans, the Enteropians, and not me. I'm pitiful, aren't I? I'll go and tell her: "I take back the words 'I bought a new car and I want to show it to a friend'—I take back those words, they're burning my throat."

Policeman *(with a hole in his chest)*: I can't sleep. Those RAF terrorists formed a circle and plotted. One out of five and one out of ten Germans likes them and is willing to give them shelter, although they killed me straight through the heart. Perhaps that Baader, the Anti-Man from moon-maloon, was right after all to call me a pig? Perhaps people on the moon see better from high up that I'm a pig—and who would shed a tear for a pig?

Squirrel-Man: They have sown a seeds of fear in us, haven't they, Herr Policeman?

Policeman *(with a hole in his chest)*: They have sown a seeds of fear, yes, Herr Squirrel-Man.

Squirrel-Man: They have sown, they have sown a seed of fear.

Policeman *(with a hole in his chest)*: They have sown, they have sown a seed of fear.

Squirrel-Man: And where in *you* did they sow it?

Policeman *(with a hole in his chest)*: And where in *you* did they sow it?

Squirrel-Man: Let's look for it.

Policeman *(with a hole in his chest)*: Let's look for it.

They search themselves, looking for the seeds of fear everywhere: in their pockets, in their wallets, under their belts, in their underwear. They find what they were looking for.

Squirrel-Man: I've got it here.

Policeman *(with a hole in his chest)*: And I've got it here.

They show each other the seeds of fear they have found.

Policeman *(with a hole in his chest)*: *(Carefully examines seeds.)* Oh, I'm afraid they're not seeds.

Squirrel-Man: Not seeds? Then, what are they then?

Policeman *(with a hole in his chest)*: Bombs.

Squirrel-Man: Bombs are seeds too.

Policeman *(with a hole in his chest)*: Oh, no. I know all about seeds. These are bombs.

Squirrel-Man: Bombs—"the seeds of fear." Just a metaphor.

Policeman *(with a hole in his chest)*: It's no metaphor. Let's get out of here.

Squirrel-Man: Do you think Frau Meinhof sowed this bomb in me?

Policeman *(with a hole in his chest)*: I wouldn't rule it out, it's altogether possible, Herr Squirrel-Man.

Squirrel-Man: Then why should I flee?

Policeman *(with a hole in his chest)*: The bomb will explode, you'll be killed.

SQUIRREL-MAN: Frau Meinhof already ran over me once, when she was parking, but it was unintentional.

POLICEMAN *(with a hole in his chest)*: My intuition tells me she wants to kill you.

SQUIRREL-MAN: Then you'd better flee. I have something to tell her.

The POLICEMAN listens to his intuition.

SQUIRREL-MAN clears his throat once. Then clears it again. The bomb explodes. Something goes down and lodges in his throat.

ULRIKE MEINHOF: *(To the SQUIRREL-MAN.)* How are my seeds of fear doing?

SQUIRREL-MAN: *(Rattling.)* I bought … a new …

ULRIKE MEINHOF: Why are you rattling like that?

SQUIRREL-MAN: *(Rattling.)* … car …

POLICEMAN *(with a hole in his chest)*: He's rattling, because a splinter of glass from the window cut his throat. From that bomb of yours.

ULRIKE MEINHOF: *(Picks up another piece of glass.)* I recognize this piece of glass! It's from the window I jumped out of so I could go fight.

SQUIRREL-MAN: *(Rattling.)* … and I want to …

POLICEMAN *(with a hole in his chest)*: It's glass from the window through which the plane flew. You opened that window, and then a plane flew through it. He said so. *(To SQUIRREL-MAN.)* Did you say so?

SQUIRREL-MAN: *(Rattling.)* … to show … to show it … to a friend …

ULRIKE MEINHOF: I don't know what he's trying to say.

POLICEMAN *(with a hole in his chest)*: He's taking back the statement that he wants to show a friend his car. He lied, because he loves you.

ULRIKE MEINHOF: I don't want to hear about it.

POLICEMAN *(with a hole in his chest)*: I have a question about the glass that cut his throat. Didn't you advise your friends to fly their plane through some window or other? Was that your idea?

ULRIKE MEINHOF: *(Reflects.)* Maybe ... I'm always thinking; I think up things even if I don't want to.

SQUIRREL-MAN: *(Rattling.)* I love you. *(He dies.)*

ULRIKE MEINHOF: *(To herself.)* I'm not going to worry about him; the resurrection is tomorrow.

We look for Europe, we build the New Germany

ANDREAS BAADER: *(Pokes in trash cans containing unidentified body parts.)* What could this be? Liver? Heart? Hands?

GUDRUN ENSSLIN: Let's just bury all that, Baby, it's all the same.

ANDREAS BAADER: No, it makes a difference. You plant some old gut in the ground and shit grows out of it.

ULRIKE MEINHOF: *(To ANDREAS.)* Admit openly that you don't know what it is. That you have to ask me for help. That intellectuals are really needed.

ANDREAS BAADER: *(Uncertainly poking around in the hands and legs—not his own of course.)* I'll remember.

ULRIKE MEINHOF: Good luck ... You don't even have a high-school diploma.

GUDRUN ENSSLIN: How much longer is she going to insult you, Baby?

ANDREAS BAADER: *(To ULRIKE.)* While you're jabbering, these trash cans are beginning to stink.

ULRIKE MEINHOF: *(On cue.)* ... Intellectuals are needed.

ANDREAS BAADER: They're fucking needed all right.

ULRIKE MEINHOF: Okay. *(Begins.)* Cadmus looked everywhere for many years, but found no trace of his sister, Europa.

ANDREAS BAADER: Cut it short.

ULRIKE MEINHOF: Boor.

GUDRUN ENSSLIN: Shut your noise, twat.

ULRIKE MEINHOF: Cadmus challenged the dragon to single combat and dealt it a mortal blow. The goddess bid him pull out the dragon's fangs and sow them in the earth.

Andreas Baader: The dragon's teeth, its fucking teeth!

Ulrike Meinhof: Cadmus did as he was told, and from the earth there sprang up armed warriors who immediately fell upon each other with hate, wounding and killing one another in fratricidal battle. The earth greedily drank their blood. Five of them survived and built the city of Thebes on that ground poisoned by the spilled blood.

Andreas Baader: Get at the teeth, girls! The earth is waiting!

With unexpected skill they pull out the teeth, sow them in the ground so that a new city-state, the New Germany, can arise. They sow the teeth, sticking them in the freshly dug ground. They look and wait. The Policeman *emerges from the ground.*

Policeman: Two-hundred thousand Deutsche marks identity cards and passports official seals from the town hall two-hundred eighty-five thousand marks thirteen wounded one fatality one bomb in the police station in Augsburg provincial bureau of criminal investigation in Munich material losses wife of a federal judge seventeen wounded two bombs three killed seven wounded U.S. Army supreme headquarters in Heidelberg Petra Schelm commando Thomas Weissbecker commando movement 2 June commando movement 15 July commando.

Andreas Baader: What are you yapping about, pig face?

Policeman: Greetings, Herr Baader, there's a time to sow and a time to reap, dear ladies. We'll celebrate it together.

A Thanksgiving House was built on a potato field in the Stammheim district of Stuttgart at a cost of twelve-million marks. It was the best-guarded Thanksgiving House in Europe, for which Cadmus once searched in vain.

The Policeman x-rays Ulrike

Ulrike Meinhof: No, no, it wasn't at all like that. The Policeman didn't grow out of the contaminated ground. They caught each of us separately. Baader was picked up in Frankfurt; they showed it on television. They got Gudrun Ensslin in Hamburg as she was buying clothes. And I'm going to be caught in a moment.

A bell rings.

Ulrike Meinhof: "Who's there?" I say, not suspecting anything.

POLICEMAN: Open up!

ULRIKE MEINHOF: So I have to open the door. *(She opens the door. To the POLICEMAN.)* Oh, it's you, Herr Policeman. Where's the hole in your chest, did you get a new heart implanted?

POLICEMAN: It grew back all by itself, dear lady, there's so much blood everywhere, scraps of meat in the air, the air as heavy as in a pig slaughterhouse. The RAF company's best fertilizer for heart growth.

ULRIKE MEINHOF: That's wonderful, you must feel better now. And what's your business with me?

POLICEMAN: I'll tell you right away and show you. By the way, I have greetings for you from Squirrel Man. He went to show his new car to a friend. Your bomb went off and he was blown to pieces; his head went one way, and his legs another ... His head was still looking at the car, his legs were hanging in a tree. Funny, isn't it?

ULRIKE MEINHOF: There are no innocent civilians.

POLICEMAN: I'll convey that to his head.

ULRIKE MEINHOF: Now *they* are really afraid of us. You are too, aren't you?

POLICEMAN: I have a new heart. Thanks to you, I'm a new man.

ULRIKE MEINHOF: But did we achieve our goal? Are you really afraid?

POLICEMAN: Now I'm going to tell you and now I'm going to show you. It will be a performance. *(Bows.)* You say: "Goslings, goslings, what are you afraid of?"

ULRIKE MEINHOF: That's silly, stop it.

The POLICEMAN kicks her in the face with zest and zeal.

POLICEMAN: Goslings, goslings, what are you afraid of?

ULRIKE MEINHOF: *(On her knees.)* At that point I realized I'd really been caught. I started to cry. He was such a nice Policeman. He got all his nourishment from birdseed.

The POLICEMAN kicks her in the face with zest and zeal.

POLICEMAN: Goslings, goslings, what are you afraid of?

ULRIKE MEINHOF: *(Lying on the ground.)* The big bad wolf.

The Policeman kicks her in the face with zest and zeal.

Policeman: Wrong answer.

Ulrike Meinhof: I am afraid of you.

Policeman: Clever girl. Clever girls give the best blow jobs. *(Kicks her in the face with zest and zeal.)* On your knees. Don't move.

Ulrike Meinhof: You're not allowed to do that.

Policeman: I'm going to x-ray you. Has anyone x-rayed you before?

Ulrike Meinhof: You're not allowed to do that.

Policeman: I'll shine the light clean through you.

Ulrike Meinhof: You're not allowed to do that. You're not allowed to do that. You're not allowed to do that.

Policeman: Good. Good. Good.

Ulrike Meinhof: My head is no longer mine, my mouth is no longer mine, my body is no longer mine.

Policeman: I don't feel sorry for you, you sick brain, you sick brain, you sick, sick brain, I've made an X-ray of you, the right way, I've made an X-ray, whether you wanted me to or not, you asked for it, you brought it on yourself, and now I'm meting out your punishment, I'll lock you in a box, I'll starve you, I'll force-feed you, I'll starve you ... Funny, isn't it?

The X-ray showed the presence of a metal pin that was inserted in Ulrike Meinhof's head during brain surgery that she had undergone some years ago. It was the best proof that Ulrike Meinhof was Ulrike Meinhof.

The silent revenge of the potatoes

Numbers 1, 2, 3 are sitting with paper bags over their heads. They've been put behind bars. So now they're locked up on the inside, although they'd probably prefer to be strolling about on the outside, looking at terrestrial grass, street lamps on which perch pigeons classified in terrestrial atlases. They'd probably prefer to listen, to hear with their own ears, the sounds of the Heimat: the creaking of the door at the Deutsche Bank branch, gunshots during a demonstration, a one-mark coin rolling across the table in a cozy café.

The Policeman *is well aware of all that, but he doesn't allow them to get up, walk around, or listen. He has different plans for them.*

There can be heard in the background the singing of the cannibals from Kealakekua Bay who ate Captain Cook.

Policeman: Welcome to Stammheim, ladies and gentlemen. Our prison cost twelve-million marks. It is perfectly equipped to provide you with everything needed for the life sentence to which you have been condemned. I must also inform you that Stammheim prison is located in the middle of a potato field. Should you want someone to help you, ask the potatoes for assistance. Funny, isn't it?

Number 1: I spit on you, pig!

Number 2: I spit on you, pig!

Number 3: I spit on you, pig!

Policeman: I'm a pig, I'm a pig! *(The* Policeman *stirs some grub in a metal bowl, goes up to* Number *1. Pushes a spoonful of food at him.)* Yum, yum.

Number *1 turns his head away.*

Policeman: *(Tries again.)* Yum, yum.

Number *1 turns his head away. The* Policeman *holds* Number *1's chin and forces him to swallow the food. It turns out that* Number *1, like the other* Numbers, *is tied to the chair with top-quality leather straps.*

Policeman: Taste good?

Number *1 spits the food out.*

Policeman: Seems you didn't like it. *(Goes up to* Number *2 and gives him a spoonful of food.* Number *2 passively swallows it.)*

Policeman: Was it good?

Number 2: I can't taste anything, I can't taste anything, I can't taste anything …

Policeman: Then how can we tell if the Stammheim kitchen deserves four stars or not … *(Goes up to* Number *3. Hands the food to him.)* How is it?

Number 3: *(Swallows the food.)* Excellent, is that what you want to hear, pig snout? Delicious!

Policeman: Bravo! Bravo! Bravo! Guess who won our gourmet test? *(Removes the paper bag from Number 3's head.)* Herr Baader, man in the moon, liked our Stammheim dinner, today's special dish, excellent, excellent! And what was it? Attention: tatatata! ... chopped Captain Clyde Bonner of the U.S. Army supreme headquarters in Heidelberg!

That's right, Herr Baader, you've just eaten Mister Bonner, the one who bombed Vietnam, and as punishment, as pun–ish–ment, you ate him, bravo, and you liked it, you've won my contest, and as a reward you'll get the rest of Captain Bonner!

Andreas Baader: I don't believe you, you pig!

Policeman: Oh, are you implying that I could have been lying?! After all, you blew him up with your bomb! Yes! You didn't like him! To punish Bonner you blew him up, that's what you did! *(Pulls out Bonner's leg that has not yet been chopped.)*

And what did I cook up? *(Swinging the leg around.)* I saved Bonner's leg to be roasted, and from the rest: I made grilled ribs from the torso, I used the heart and the lungs for *paté*, I fricasseed the kidneys with basil, *sautéed* the liver with onions, roasted the neck with green peppercorns, pan-broiled the brains, boiled the tongue in cream of course; the eyes, the veins, and fat went into breakfast sausages, and I don't remember what else; oh, yes, there's the tripe, Bonner's tripe will be prepared too, with spices ...

Andreas Baader: Hold it, hold it, hold it. I declare a hunger strike.

Policeman: Gobble him down! I said, gobble Bonner down! Gobble him down! He's your political enemy!

The Policeman is completely carried away. For one thing, he worked hard to make something tasty out of Bonner's remains—for another, he doesn't like to waste food. He takes the bowl with Bonner's stew and sticks Baader's head into it. We can understand his frustration. If Emperor Bokassa ate his political enemies, then why shouldn't Baader be willing to eat his?

Meanwhile Gudrun Ensslin and Ulrike Meinhof have been furiously shaking their heads covered with paper bags, crying for help. The potatoes hear their cries but do not react. The potatoes still have their own accounts to settle with humankind, and now they take their revenge, silently and with satisfaction.

Lucky at last

GUDRUN ENSSLIN is alone in her cell. Nothing unusual about that, Stammheim prison is full of cells. She would so much like not to be alone. It is night.

LUCKY: Cuddle close to me.

GUDRUN ENSSLIN: It is so dark, I can't see a thing, what a night.

LUCKY: Cuddle close to me.

GUDRUN ENSSLIN: I long for you, Baby. I dream that I'm talking to you.

LUCKY: I long for you, too.

GUDRUN ENSSLIN: Do you love me?

LUCKY: And how. You can't imagine how much.

GUDRUN ENSSLIN: Love me, Baby.

LUCKY: I love you.

GUDRUN ENSSLIN: That's wonderful.

LUCKY: Can you feel me?

GUDRUN ENSSLIN: Oh, yes.

LUCKY: Can you feel me inside you?

GUDRUN ENSSLIN: Oh, yes, Baby, yes.

LUCKY: Can you feel me deep inside you?

GUDRUN ENSSLIN: Yes, deep inside me, Baby.

LUCKY: Do you feel my dick inside you?

GUDRUN ENSSLIN: Don't talk like that, Baby.

LUCKY: It was small, and now it's big. Can you feel it?

GUDRUN ENSSLIN: Stop.

LUCKY: It was so small, so small the last time you saw it. Can you feel it? It was only six months old then. Do you feel it, Mummy? Do you feel it?

Gudrun Ensslin: Life is no goodness.

Lucky: I'm inside you, Mummy, do you feel it? I always wanted to be inside you, I wanted to return there, get inside you, get back into your belly, can you understand that, Mummy? I'm there, Mummy, I'm coming there, Mummy, love me, Mummy.

The final death of the Squirrel-Man

Squirrel-Man and Ulrike are together in a cell and knot a rope.

Ulrike Meinhof: *(Knotting a rope from her prison towel torn into strips.)* Work is much easier done together. *(Pause.)* Why don't you say anything?

Squirrel-Man: *(Joins her in knotting the rope.)* I no longer believe that I'll ever say those words that would make you to fall in love with me. *(Pause.)* I'm pathetic, right?

Ulrike Meinhof: *(Warmly.)* A bit.

Squirrel-Man: We can be quiet and twine the rope. That's pleasant, too. *(Pause.)* Do you remember running over me that first time?

Ulrike Meinhof: *(Smiling.)* Yes. I didn't hear you at all then.

Squirrel-Man: *(Smiling.)* That's true. And I was terribly jealous. Because you heard others, but not me.

Ulrike Meinhof: But later on I did talk to you a little.

Squirrel-Man: That's a fact, you did.

Ulrike Meinhof: All that was so long ago. Ages ago.

Squirrel-Man: Do you also remember the time that Gudrun Ensslin shot me?

Ulrike Meinhof: Of course.

Squirrel-Man: We've been through so much together. But even so, you still didn't fall in love with me.

Ulrike Meinhof: Your wishful thinking alone wasn't enough.

Squirrel-Man: You're right, you're right.

Ulrike Meinhof: Will you help me hang myself?

Squirrel-Man: I'll help. But why do you want to do that?

ULRIKE MEINHOF: What does it matter why?

SQUIRREL-MAN: Everybody's curious. And as for me personally, I love you so much.

ULRIKE MEINHOF: That's your problem. *(Pause.)* Let's say because I've wasted my life. Will you help me hang myself? If you won't, please get out of here. Oh, what's the difference, you can watch me.

SQUIRREL-MAN: *(Ardently.)* I'll hang myself in your place! Please let me!

ULRIKE MEINHOF: What for? I don't want to go on living.

SQUIRREL-MAN: Here's my plan: I'll hang myself in your place. You'll take the rope and keep on knotting it. It has to be a hundred stories long. When you've finished knotting it, God will send you wings. He sent you a single wing once before! Then you'll fly out this window and fly around and give this rope to the people whose window the plane flew through. A super-plan!

ULRIKE MEINHOF: I'll have wings like an angel? How do you know?

SQUIRREL-MAN. I know, that's all. All you have to do is finish knotting this rope! Please!

ULRIKE MEINHOF: Are you really willing to hang yourself in my place?

SQUIRREL-MAN: For you. For love.

ULRIKE MEINHOF: And what will you hang yourself with?

SQUIRREL-MAN: My tie. I have a knack for that. What do you say? Please! One last time?!

ULRIKE MEINHOF: And I'll become an angel of God. That's wonderful.

SQUIRREL-MAN: All you have to do is believe me. I will die for you for love.

ULRIKE MEINHOF: All right. Die!

SQUIRREL-MAN hangs himself.

ULRIKE watches.

SQUIRREL-MAN's body swings back and forth.

ULRIKE stops knotting the rope. She starts to swing just like him.

They swing together. Finally they are doing something together. That's an improvement.

The big bang

ULRIKE MEINHOF, ANDREAS BAADER, and GUDRUN ENSSLIN are wearing paper bags with their mug shots on them.

ULRIKE MEINHOF: I'm Ulrike Meinhof!

ANDREAS BAADER: I'm Andreas Baader!

GUDRUN ENSSLIN: I'm Gudrun Ensslin!

ULRIKE MEINHOF: I spit on you, pigs!

ANDREAS BAADER: I spit on you, pigs!

GUDRUN ENSSLIN: I spit on you, pigs!

ULRIKE MEINHOF: We will live forever, even though we die!

ANDREAS BAADER: We will live forever, even though we die!!

GUDRUN ENSSLIN: We will live forever, even though we die!

They remove the paper bags from their heads and burst them with a big bang.

Bang. Bang. Bang.

Silence.

Now their fresh corpses bare their teeth at everybody.

The POLICEMAN enters carrying Bonner's leg.

POLICEMAN: *(Through a microphone.)* Ladies and gentlemen, I have an announcement to make: All's well that ends well!

With the microphone, approaches different people in the audience.

POLICEMAN: Isn't that right? The evil people died. Good. Isn't that right? Good. Isn't that right? *(He looks at the corpses with their bared teeth.)* Well, all right ... if that's the way it is ... I'll eat Bonner's leg myself.

Funeral music, suitable for a dance and for a meat cutlet, or, more precisely, for a roasted leg.

Hotel Europa

Goran Stefanovski

Original text in English

Hotel Europa premiered at Vienna Festwochen, May 2000, and was staged by nine directors.

Author's Note

Hotel Europa was a complex project that took over a year to prepare and perform. I originally wrote the concept and the first draft of the script, which was followed by a meeting with all the directors in which the material was discussed. Afterwards I wrote further drafts of the script.

The production was staged by nine directors and performed by twenty-five actors from several, mainly Balkan and Baltic, countries. Every director worked with their own team and their own style. Some scenes were written as drama, some as dance librettos, and some as installations. Some scenes mutated from their original version to suit the style of the director and the actors.

"Europeretta" was directed by Viesturs Karišs and the visual artist/designer Ieva Jurjane (Latvia). "Do Not Disturb," was directed, mainly as a dance piece, by choreographer Matjaž Farić (Slovenia). "One-Night Stand" was directed by Oskaras Koršunovas (Lithuania). "Room Service" was directed by Dritero Kasapi (Macedonia). "Hotel Angels" was directed by Piotr Cieplak (Poland). "Maiden Voyage" was directed by Ivan Popovski (Russia). "The Empty Rooms" were installations staged by the Art Action Group Škart from Yugoslavia. "Grand Hotel Casino Europa" was the central scene, directed by Nedyalko Delchev (Bulgaria). The Roving Characters (Locals) were directed and performed by local artists from the co-producing parties and countries.

Hotel Europa was performed in five European cities in the summer of 2000, in specially adapted huge spaces of "derelict buildings." In Vienna it was co-produced by Wiener Festwochen, and performed at the Kabelwerk, an old cable factory. In Bonn-Bad Godesberg it was co-produced by the Bonner Biennale and performed in an empty ex-department store in the center of town, Das Ehmalige Hertie Warenhaus. In Avignon it was co-produced by Festival d'Avignon, and performed in the Usine

Volponi, a warehouse twenty minutes by bus from the walled old town. In Stockholm it was produced by Intercult, and performed at Medborgarhuset, a huge public building featuring a swimming pool in the center of the southern part of town. In Bologna it was co-produced by the City of Culture of Bologna, and performed in a building that used to be an aquarium.

The project was produced by Chris Torch of Intercult in Stockholm. He is an American and a naturalized Swede, originally an actor in The Living Theatre, a real artistic and human live-wire force. Sören Brunés created the overall complex production design. The project resembled a military operation, and required military precision. An audience of three hundred would enter the building for an opening scene. Then it would be split into six groups of fifty and taken to separate rooms for individual scenes. There were six scenes going on simultaneously, each lasting roughly fifteen minutes. After each scene a Roving Character would lead the audience from one room to another, where another scene would start. Groups of audiences would sometimes brush shoulders with each other in corridors during these journeys.

It was extremely important for these transitions to go smoothly, which was not easy at the best of times. In the middle of the performance all of the audience would gather in a big "banquet" hall for the longer central scene. After this, there would be further journeys of the audience for the remaining scenes. All of the audience were together only in the central scene in the middle of the performance, and also at the very end. This means that people saw the production in a different order of scenes, and consequently with a different narrative flow.

All these years later I'm still reeling with excitement when I think of the sheer sweeping breadth of the project of *Hotel Europa.*

Goran Stefanovski
February 2009

CHARACTERS

HUSBAND

WIFE

MOTHER-IN-LAW

ODYSSEUS

CIRCE

YOUNG MAN

PROSTITUTE

PRINCE IGOR

IVANA

KRT

MAMA

VISITOR

PROFESSOR

ANGEL

DRIFTER

BRIDE

BRIDEGROOM

ROVING CHARACTERS (LOCALS): THE BELLHOP, THE SOCIAL WORKER, THE MAÎTRE D'HÔTEL, THE RECEPTIONIST, THE DAUGHTER, AND THE CARETAKER

From the outside the place looks bleak and unfriendly. A neon light on it says "Hotel Europa." The audience enters. It's the seedy world of the railway inn, the one-night stand, the makeshift bed-and-breakfast on the outskirts of town.

The audience moves through the space. It is welcomed by the locals—Roving Characters—who remember the "hotel" when it was an industrial plant, before it became a temporary accommodation for immigrants and travelers. The locals lead groups of the audience from one door to another, and talk to them. They are THE BELLHOP, THE SOCIAL WORKER, THE MAÎTRE D'HÔTEL, THE RECEPTIONIST, THE DAUGHTER, and THE CARETAKER.

THE BELLHOP speaks to his audience group. At the same time, each of the Locals speaks to their group in different spaces.

THE BELLHOP: *(Very old man, finicky in his manners, well-dressed, naturally elegant.)* I apologize for this mess. Such idiotic overbooking. Mind you, it's not that it hasn't happened before. They get it painfully wrong at Reception sometimes. We'll try to straighten things out. But there is only so much a man can do. I shouldn't take things so personally. But I take pride in my work. I am the only one here with any qualifications. I come from a family with a long tradition in fine hotels. My grandfather worked at the Imperial. He waited in the most beautiful dining rooms in the country. Opulent Louis XVIth decor. And a terrace with an *al fresco* restaurant. Ah, the elegance of the bygone era. Look at one of the menus of those days. *Haute cuisine* with no compromise. A menu for a particular *divertissement* on Sunday, the 18th of January, 1908:

Mousseline de Saumon en Feuilletage

Fillet de jeune Renne de la Calotte Boreale au Genievre

Parfait de Fausses-mures des Tourbieres

Domaine Sainte-Anne 1903

Aloxe-Cortons 1903

Chateau Bel Air 1901

What else can I say? Do I have to say anything? Oh, well.

He introduces the next room.

There is a loud and proud Latvian family living here. The husband drinks a lot. His mother grows vegetables inside. The wife takes care of two twin babies. There's the smell of alcohol coming from the room all the time, but we have no idea why.

Europeretta

CHARACTERS

HUSBAND

WIFE

MOTHER-IN-LAW

A stuffy room. On the windowsill there are pots of indoor plants and a whole vegetable garden: home-grown tomatoes and potatoes. Steamy atmosphere. There are baby clothes hanging on a clothesline stretched across the room. There is a twin baby cot. A stove with pans and pots boiling. The MOTHER-IN LAW *is sitting and knitting.*

MOTHER-IN-LAW: *(Recitative.)* We are children of Latvia. We came to the West one summer, many moons ago, to earn some money, to make our ends meet. We worked on the fields, we helped with the harvest. Time passed on. And then we stayed. They put us in this hotel. And then they forgot about us. This is my daughter-in-law.

WIFE: *(Curlers in her hair, singing an aria.)* I'm taking care of our baby twins. With one hand I'm cooking pasta. With the other I'm flicking through a beauty magazine. *(She scratches a page of the magazine with a fragrance advertisement and sniffs at it.)*

MOTHER-IN-LAW: *(Recitative.)* We don't cry and we don't complain. Our souls are made of steel. We are self-contained. We grow our own fruit, we grow our own veg. This is soil from the old country. We brought it specially from home, in plastic bags.

WIFE: *(Sings.)*

> Nothing smells here, Mother.

MOTHER-IN-LAW: *(Sings.)*

> Nothing smells here, Daughter, but nothing stinks either.

MOTHER-IN-LAW/WIFE: *(Duet.)*

> Nothing smells here,
> But nothing stinks here either!

They finish the duet.

WIFE: Oh where, oh where is my derelict husband?

At that moment the HUSBAND enters, drunk. He pushes a shopping cart with a traffic cone and a huge traffic sign in it.

HUSBAND: *(Sings a drinking song. This is just a suggestion. He would most likely be singing a Latvian tune.)*

> So we'll drink-a-drink-a-drink
> to Lily the Pink-a-pink-a-pink
> the savior of the human race
> she invented medicinal compound
> most efficacious in every way!

WIFE: Where have you been?

HUSBAND: Fighting for Latvia!

WIFE: Again?

HUSBAND: These bastards asked me where I was from. Latvia, I said! Where the fuck is that, they said? I'll show you where it is, I said! *(He shows his heart.)* Here! I said. This is where "the fuck" it is I said! And fuck you too! Next thing I know I'm fighting these six big motherfuckers.

WIFE: That's what happened last time.

HUSBAND: Exactly.

WIFE: Every time you come home drunk, you've been fighting for Latvia.

HUSBAND: Our enemies are many.

WIFE: Must you fight them all?

HUSBAND: I never start a fight. But when provoked, I never run from a fight either.

The WIFE throws the traffic cone at the HUSBAND. He defends himself with the traffic sign. The WIFE takes out a knife, singing.

WIFE: *(Aria.)*

> I will kill you, if that's the last thing I ever do.

MOTHER-IN-LAW: *(Sings.)*

> You're not going to kill my son!

WIFE: *(Sings.)*

> Oh yes, I will. I have no husband. My children have no father.

HUSBAND: Please mother, let her kill me. *(He shows his bare chest to his wife.)* Strike here! I have no fear! My enemies, I can fight! But you, my closest and dearest, in front of you I stand naked.

MOTHER-IN-LAW, HUSBAND, WIFE: *(Aria.)*

> I will kill him.
> Oh no, you won't!
> Please Mother, let her kill me.
> Oh, what has the cruel West done to us?
> Thus left and forsaken!

The sound of the twin babies screaming can be heard from the cot. The Mother-in-law *brings everyone to their senses by a master stroke: she opens her mouth and breathes—fire! They both look at her and feel crushed. The* Wife *starts crying. The* Husband *embraces her and consoles her by patting her on her back. The* Mother-in-law *opens up a curtain, behind which there is a bathtub. In it there is a little alcohol distillery. It is a copper contraption with long pipes.*

Mother-in-Law: We make brandy from wine, applejack from hard cider, rum from molasses, whisky from grain mash and vodka from wheat mash. Fifty-percent strong or one-hundred proof. It's smooth, unaged, odorless, and colorless.

The three of them start working in the vodka distillery. The old woman makes the spirits and the Husband *and* Wife *put it in bottles. On the bottles they put labels with the symbol of Latvian freedom and independence. They sing a work song.*

Mother-in-Law, Wife, Husband:

> Distill, bottle, label and sell,
> distill, bottle, label and sell,
> distill, bottle, label and sell,
> distill, bottle, label and sell
> as well!

They work in rhythm. Harmony is restored, for the time being. There are happy baby noises coming from the cot.

Mother-in-law: The babies goo-goo. A good sign! I can see the future on the horizon. It is pink!

She points to the future on the horizon. They all look at it.

Husband: *(Trying, but he cannot see.)* Where?

The Wife *hits the back of the* Husband*'s head. The* Wife *points up again. The* Husband *can now clearly see it or at least pretend he can. They all look at the future.*

The audience leaves the first room and moves on. They are met by The Social Worker*, an energetic, intelligent, young woman. She talks to them as she takes them to the next room.*

The Social Worker: My name is Eurydice. *Nomen est omen.* I was destined to be married to Europe since birth. I am a social worker. I'm only a supply worker here. Otherwise, I'm a student of sociology. I love my work. Although I can see lots of injustice. I can see greed and exploitation. I can't start to tell you what goes on in here.

Undercover, you know. I believe in Europe as a common home for all. A Europe in which the lamps of hope will be lit again, in our lifetime. I'd love to go to Brussels and see the European politicians in the flesh. And tell them a few horror stories.

In the nightmare of the dark
All the dogs of Europe bark,
and the living nations wait
Each sequestered in its hate.

We musn't let hell happen again. We've seen it all before. We have no excuses. What shall we tell our children if we let it happen again? That we didn't know? Well, we do know. *Je regrette l'Europe aux anciens parapets!* (I pine for Europe of the ancient parapets!), as the poet said: We must bring back the age of chivalry! We must put an end to the sophisters, economists, and calculators. *Oui, c'est l'Europe, depuis l'Atlantique jusqu'a l'Oural, c'est l'Europe, c'est toute l'Europe, qui decidera le destin du monde.* (Yes, it is Europe, from the Atlantic to the Urals, it is Europe, it is the whole of Europe, that will decide the fate of the world.) Do you understand what I'm talking about?

She introduces the next room.

There is a weird woman in this room who looks like a witch. She says her name is Circe. Somebody called Odysseus came to see her a few weeks ago. They haven't left the room at all since. I wouldn't be surprised if it was drugs.

Do Not Disturb

CHARACTERS

ODYSSEUS

CIRCE

ODYSSEUS and CIRCE have been locked in the hotel room for ages, taking drugs and tripping. It's been ten years since the collapse of the Berlin Wall, the last European Troy. ODYSSEUS was prominent in his fight against Troy, and is now on his way back home. CIRCE has decided to bring ODYSSEUS to this sleazy place because she perversely enjoys run-down hotels and shabby places. She likes to disguise herself and her lovers in old clothes, and mix and drink with the poor people.

ODYSSEUS carries with him the bag out of which the winds come. In it he has a stone. It is a leftover of the Berlin Wall. He is feverish, as if in a coma.

ODYSSEUS: My spirit has failed me. Shall I jump overboard and drown, or stay among the living and quietly endure? I am detested by the blessed gods. My heart is eaten with grief.

CIRCE feeds him a mixture of cheese, barley-meal and yellow honey flavored with Pramnian wine. She mixes her brews that keep them drunk and high for days.

ODYSSEUS: *(Speaking to himself.)* Comrades in suffering, friends, listen to me. We are utterly lost. We do not know where East or West is, where the light-giving Sun rises or where he sits.

CIRCE sings in her beautiful voice as she goes to and fro at her great and everlasting loom, on which she is weaving one of those delicate, graceful, and dazzling fabrics that goddesses make. She shouts at him.

CIRCE: Off to the pigsty, and lie down with your friends. Who are you and where do you come from? Where is your native town? Who are your parents? You must have a heart in your breast that is proof against all enchantment.

She rubs him with ointments. ODYSSEUS is a very powerful man, and his image of power preceded him wherever he went. He wants to go back to his wife and old life. But somehow he can't find his way back home. He is physically and mentally falling apart. One part of his body seems to move independently from the other.

Suddenly the sirens of a ship can be heard. A huge ship has arrived at their window. ODYSSEUS is overwhelmed with memories of home. He is yearning to go and yet he is burning to stay. He doesn't know what to do.

ODYSSEUS: Circe, keep the promise that you once made me, to send me home. I am eager now to be gone.

CIRCE: Heaven-born Laertes, resourceful Odysseus, do not stay on unwillingly. But first you must make another journey and find your way to the Halls of Hades.

ODYSSEUS starts weeping.

ODYSSEUS: Beautiful Circe, child of the Sun and Perse, the Daughter of Ocean. Goddess, do not be angry with me. My wife Penelope is not as tall or as beautiful as yourself. She is only a woman, whereas you are an immortal. But I want to get home, and can think of nothing else.

CIRCE: But my dear Odysseus. I am Penelope.

ODYSSEUS: You cannot be.

CIRCE: Look at me. I have no wish to set myself up, nor to depreciate you; but I am not struck by your appearance, for I very well remember what kind of a man you were when you set sail from Ithaca.

ODYSSEUS: You can't even recognize me any more. I will sleep alone, for you have a heart as hard as iron.

CIRCE: Oh, you're weak, Odysseus. You are weak and confused. And I like that. I like that so much.

Drug-induced visions. CIRCE bares her breast. She brings out a snake! She dances for ODYSSEUS. He falls into a sweet trance. The memory of home becomes dim and hazy again. The ship sets sail without him. CIRCE has inner power. She is like a spider in her web. She is strongly infatuated with him. She plays all kinds of tricks. She makes the room look big and small at the same time. She cuts his body in half with light.

ODYSSEUS: What is this red smoke? Comrade Elpenor, is that you? Have you not been laid beneath the earth? How did you come down here into this gloom and darkness?

CIRCE: *(Speaking in the voice of Elpenor)* Sir, it was all bad luck and my unspeakable drunkenness. I fell from the great red staircase and broke my neck, so my soul went down to the house of Hades. And now I beseech you. Do not go thence leaving me unawakened and unburied behind you!

ODYSSEUS: Your ghost is bleeding.

ODYSSEUS decides to leave. He makes the final effort to cut himself loose from the powers of CIRCE. It is a deadly struggle. He dances with CIRCE. He manages to extract himself from her poisonous embrace.

He leaves. CIRCE composes herself. She is going to wait for the next powerful man to come along her way. But whoever it will be, he will never be the equal of ODYSSEUS.

The audience leaves the room and moves on. They are met by THE MAÎTRE D'HÔTEL, an enterprising, freshly-coiffed lady. She talks to them as she takes them to the next room.

THE MAÎTRE D'HÔTEL: There used to be a factory across there. These were barracks for the workers. I bought them when the factory closed down. I turned them into a housing estate for immigrants. For the government, you know. They pay me directly, through the local council. But there is so much red tape and paperwork. I don't know how they expect us to make a profit. I'm doing the state a service by taking these wretched cases off their back, and what do I get? I'm actually paying out of my pocket to give these people shelter. Do you know what the running costs of a place like this are? Maybe I should close this place down and open a hotel for dogs and cats. The profits are much higher and at least you work with animals. It's a challenging job. I have to fight the housing association, the local councils, the social security officer, the citizens advice bureau, blah, blah, blah. I have to solve their problems every day. They all come from God's forsaken places, they all take all kinds of things for granted, they all speak their own God's forsaken languages. Repairs, grants, health issues. I'll go insane. Either that or I'll die of a heart attack one sunny morning soon.

He introduces the next room.

There is a prostitute who operates in this room. She has a client in there at the moment. A boy. He comes to see her every second week. She makes him think he is superhuman. She makes him feel like a national hero.

One-Night Stand (Koršunovas)

CHARACTERS

YOUNG MAN

PROSTITUTE

The woman PROSTITUTE is lying on the sofa, covered up with a funeral shroud. She is pretending to be asleep. The YOUNG MAN stands, like a knight in shining armor, holding a sword. He has an improvised breastplate (perhaps made of plastic). The PROSTITUTE turns on a tape recorder and lies down.

VOICE *(On tape.)*: . . . they were caught up in the thorns and died . . .

The PROSTITUTE rewinds the tape. She turns it on again. There is a musical intermezzo on a section of the recording. The PROSTITUTE lies down on the bed again and puts the shroud over herself. The YOUNG MAN stands motionless, watching all this.

VOICE *(On tape.)*: And the Prince heard rumors about that country of the beautiful sleeping Rosamond. Many princes came and tried to force their way through the hedge. But they were caught up in the thorns and died there. There a beautiful enchanted Princess Rosamond had slept for a hundred years, and with her the King and Queen, and the whole court and the whole country and the whole Nation. But our Prince did not fear to try—to wind through and see the sleeping beauty. For now the hundred years were at an end, and the day had come when Rosamond should be awakened.

With his sword the YOUNG MAN takes the shroud off the woman.

YOUNG MAN: *(Whispers.)* Rosamond.

The PROSTITUTE opens her eye. She is twice his age—she could be his mother. The YOUNG MAN kisses her lips.

PRINCE'S VOICE *(On tape.)*: Rosamond! Rosamond! Wake up! I've come to give yourself to yourself.

The PROSTITUTE pretends to wake up. She rubs her eyes. She stirs and sits up in bed.

ROSAMOND'S VOICE *(On tape.)*: I took a spindle into my hand. But as I touched it, the evil prophecy was fulfilled. I pricked my finger with it. I collapsed on the bed in a deep sleep. This sleep fell upon the whole Nation. The King and Queen fell asleep, and with them the whole court. The horses in their stalls, the dogs in the yard, the pigeons on the roof, the flies on the wall, the very fire that flickered on the hearth became still. Everything stopped. The meat on the spit ceased roasting. The cooks went to sleep too. And the wind ceased, and not a leaf moved in the trees. Then round about that place there grew a hedge of thorns thicker every year. At last the whole country was hidden from view. Nothing could be seen but the weathervane on the castle roof.

The YOUNG MAN bathes the PROSTITUTE's eyes with water full of rose petals. She takes her high-heel shoe off and puts cheap fizzy drink in it. She gives it to the YOUNG MAN.

VOICE *(On tape.)*: Then the wedding of the Prince and Rosamond was held with all splendor, and they lived happily ever after until their lives' end.

They drink. She takes the shroud off. She is wearing a heavy national costume. But underneath, she has black stockings and suspenders. She is heavily made-up. She puts her hand on his crotch.

PROSTITUTE: Oh, my savior. Your holy sword.

Prostitute pats his crotch.

PROSTITUTE: Your nationalist Excalibur, Arondigh, Ascalon, Balmung, Naglering, Durrendal, Glorious, Flamberge, Gram, Azoth, Zuflagar.

She kisses him.

PROSTITUTE: The war you fought was sacred. Let me kiss your heroic wounds.

She takes off his shirt and kisses his shoulders. The YOUNG MAN takes off his trousers. He stands naked in his socks.

YOUNG MAN: "They shall beat their ploughshares into swords, and their pruning-hooks into spears: nation shall lift up sword against nation, and they shall learn war again!"

She takes a Polaroid picture of him. The YOUNG MAN puts his head in her lap. Pause.

PROSTITUTE: For me the old state was a prison. I had no food, no water, no shelter.

YOUNG MAN: No air to breathe.

PROSTITUTE: No air to breathe. But now I have freedom. I have food, water, and shelter.

YOUNG MAN: And air to breathe.

PROSTITUTE: And air to breathe. Your Nation wants to thank you. I was a slave, but now I'm free. I was blind, but now I can see.

Pause. He sings a lullaby that his mother must have sung to him when he was a child. Pause.

YOUNG MAN: Mother.

Pause. PROSTITUTE starts giggling. The YOUNG MAN looks at her.

YOUNG MAN: What's the matter?

PROSTITUTE: Sorry. I'm not laughing at you. I just remembered something.

YOUNG MAN: What did you remember?

PROSTITUTE: My mother.

She gets serious. The YOUNG MAN embraces her.

YOUNG MAN: When I get married I want my sword to be plunged into the main beam of the house. When I die, I want to be buried with my sword. Or go with it out to sea in a boat funeral.

The woman takes off her wig. The session is finished. The *YOUNG MAN pays up.*

YOUNG MAN: Next time I want to be a soldier of the United Nations on a peace mission.

PROSTITUTE: We've done that.

YOUNG MAN: We'll do it again.

The PROSTITUTE lights up a cigarette. The YOUNG MAN leaves.

The audience leaves the room and moves on. They pass by a series of empty rooms. These are special art installations. Each of these rooms is a separate self-contained world, left behind by ex-guests of the hotel.

One of them has a pizza left in the trouser press. Another has a telescope. The third one is a room upside down, the next one a room sideways up. One is full of hotel language signs and maps of fire escape routes.

All have various leftovers (dry bread, moldy fruit, blood stains, soiled condoms). One room has a book of dreams of the hotel guests chained to the wall, which the audience can read. One has a TV screen with a video loop of guests' activities in their rooms. Another TV screen shows soup kitchens for refugees, another one a "real" lawyer giving advice on obtaining visas and residence in the country. One room has actual political materials concerning refugees and immigrants from the various parties of the country in question.

The audience gathers in the canteen/restaurant of the hotel, which is also known as the "banquet hall." There are tables there, with expensive candleholders and tablecloths, which look out of place in the larger context of the run-down building.

The audience takes refreshments. They are shown to their seats around the tables.

Grand Hotel Casino Europa

CHARACTERS

PRINCE IGOR, Eastern European entrepreneur

IVANA, his girlfriend

KRT, IGOR'S bodyguard

MAMA, accountant and spiritual adviser

There is music coming from a small band of musicians. They all wear black suits and are a part of PRINCE IGOR's entourage.

KRT, a huge bodyguard, stands at the side wearing black sunglasses and chewing gum, scanning the audience as they enter. He leads a German shepherd dog on a leash, with a muzzle on its mouth.

MAMA is an Eastern-European manic witch who pretends she's an executive woman. She animates the audience. They are treated as crème-de-la-crème of the town. They've been personally invited for this occasion by IGOR. MAMA looks at their RSVP invitations; she says hello to them and shows them their places at their tables.

IVANA is heavily made-up and wearing a "dumb blonde" wig. She improvises a song. It is a combination of plaintive, bluesy, cabaret-like music, with elements of the kitschy type of turbo-folk characteristic of the Balkan countries in transition. She improvises around a few strange phrases.

IVANA: *(Singing.)*

> Madonna … an eye for optical theory … the Coca-Cola garden is becoming a robe room … Don't start now … Eurostar prawn watching … The long trail to justice … Shut up … I want to eat the wall … You can't eat the wall … I know I can't. I just want to …

When the break finishes and the audience has taken their seats at the tables, the scene begins. The lights dim. There are two Islands of light at the opposite ends of the hall. The characters walk in and out of these Islands.

Island 1

MAMA and KRT. She brings a golden lighter that works like a revolver. KRT immediately uses it to light up a cigarette. MAMA starts a belly dance. KRT joins her. The dance gets quicker and quicker. KRT goes down on his knees and closes his eyes. KRT breaks a bottle on the floor.

MAMA: Oh, Krt!

KRT: Oh, Mama.

MAMA: You were so wonderful last night.

KRT: I know.

MAMA: You give me so much pleasure.

KRT: There's nothing I can do about it.

MAMA: Is that what they taught you in the happy days when you worked for the state security?

KRT: I knew it all before I joined them.

MAMA: Is that why they took you?

KRT: I was overqualified.

Island 2

Igor and Ivana. Igor is dressing.

Igor: What's the matter with you?

Ivana: I'm fine.

Igor: Are you drunk?

Ivana: Yes.

Igor: Get yourself together. Europe is looking at us tonight.

Ivana: Fuck Europe.

Igor. Don't you ever, ever again say something like that about Europe. Europe is my love. My life.

Ivana: What are you to Europe, and what is Europe to you?

Igor: Europe taught me everything I know.

Ivana: You're a criminal.

Igor: Exactly. I learned from the best. Italian *mafiosi*, German car thieves, Swedish human rights money launderers, French drug barons.

Ivana: You're such a cliché

Igor: I'm what?

Ivana: Never mind.

Igor: Watch your language, young lady. Whatever I am, you are living with it.

Island 3

Igor and Mama. He is eating a dish of broth. He is slurping. She is singing a folksong to him that she intersects with the dialogue.

Mama: Is it nice?

Igor: Mmm.

Mama: Did I put enough salt?

IGOR: Mmm.

MAMA: They've all come all the way from town. With their shiny cars and shiny shoes and minks. You've made it. They've come to kiss your hand. They've come to see you on your terms.

IGOR: Fuck them.

MAMA: You will have to do that, dear.

IGOR: Mmm.

MAMA: Eat first. Is it nice?

IGOR: Mmm.

MAMA: Did I put enough pepper?

IGOR: Mmm.

MAMA: Are you thinking of the company image you want to project?

She keeps singing the song.

Island 4

KRT and IVANA.

KRT: Will you let me get into your pants, Ivana?

IVANA: Your honesty is disarming, Krt, but I wouldn't dream of that.

KRT: I will wait. Maybe my time will come when you're in a retirement home.

IVANA: I will die young.

KRT: Maybe I should simply rape you then.

IVANA: Then you'll find your cock and balls finely chopped and cooked in a stew.

KRT: I love talking to you.

IVANA: The pleasure is all mine.

Island 5

Ivana and Mama.

Ivana: I can't stand them.

Mama: Don't put your heart in it, darling.

Ivana: They're beasts.

Mama: They know how to take care of a lady.

Ivana: How can you live with this?

Mama: A woman must serve her man.

Ivana: Do you really mean that?

Mama: No. But I really live that.

Island 6

Igor and Krt.

Krt: Come Europe!

Igor: Come whore!

Krt: And sit on my manhood!

Igor: On mine, on mine!

Krt/Igor: Your refugee mongrels are waiting for you!

They give each other high five.

Krt: Praise be to the mongrel. Abused, abandoned, three-legged, beaten, chased, hungry, thirsty, but never vanquished! Agile, virile, ever ready for action.

Igor: Here, here! We are the new type of dog, a mongrel uber-race. Patented under the name of Dusha. Top species! We'll put all other pedigree dogs out of business. Customers will queue for our services! They'll pay to mate with us.

Krt: I once served a Lady. The ugliest motherfucker I've seen in my life. Every time I serviced her I had to close my eyes and think of something else.

Igor: Sheep.

Krt: Fuck you.

The lights change. Now the larger space of the hall becomes the performance area. Mama *takes the microphone.*

Mama: Good evening ladies and gentlemen, and thank you so much for coming to join us for our unique little celebration. The launch of our extraordinary capital venture! This is a direct, active marketing platform. This is an IPO, i.e., an Initial Public Offering. We are canvassing investors to subscribe and we are able to offer you a certain amount of shares prior to floating our company on the stock market! Let me introduce to you our host! Our very special man! Igor! Or Prince Igor, as most of you know him. Let me introduce to you—the future!

Mama *claps her hands and urges the audience to clap their hands too. The doors open. The band plays a special entrance roll. Enter* Igor, *wearing expensive clothes.*

The band plays the music of "Happy Birthday." Mama *sings in the style of Marilyn Monroe.*

Mama:

> Happy future to you
> Happy future to you
> Happy future, Prince Igor
> Happy future to you!

Igor *sits down. There is a film projection as illustration of what follows. The film images are opposite of what the text suggests.*

Mama: Igor was born in the little picturesque village of Dobri Dol.

IMAGE: A run-down village

Mama: He had a happy childhood, taking care of the village sheep and playing a reed pipe he made himself.

IMAGE: Igor strangling a chicken

Mama: Even at a very early age he knew he was someone special. He had recurring visions of Europe.

IMAGE: Igor pissing on a model of the Eiffel Tower made of matchsticks

Mama: This symbolized his fearless nature and huge ambition. He couldn't wait to grow up and go out into the big world. On the day he left the village there was an eclipse of the sun.

IMAGE: Old men and women crossing themselves, relieved that he's leaving

MAMA: It was a small step for Igor, but a big step for Europe. As a refugee, he first stayed at this place, where we are now gathered. This was his first home. This is where he started from. For Igor this is a sentimental journey. He was lonely.

IMAGE: IGOR happy and drunk

He found modest work as a dog jogger. He was taking a rich lady's bulldogs for walks. The lady had long waiting lists of international customers who wanted to mate their dogs with her champions. Igor was overseeing the mating business.

IMAGE: IGOR collecting dog shit

The dogs didn't like him. Igor had to leave

IMAGE: IGOR strangling a bulldog with bare hands

Igor forged his plans for the future! The rest is history. Today he is an established businessman in the West and a leading light and example to many a young man in the East.

IGOR approaches something covered with a white sheet. He uncovers it. It is a cage with a sad, mongrel dog inside.

IGOR: I am a philanthropist. I have seen too much human misery and I want to see an end to it. I have suffered and I don't want to see others suffer the way I did. I want to see others have what I never had. I want to build a real Hotel Europa. I want to build a Grand Hotel Europa. A place where refugees will feel at home. A cozy nest where they will keep their pride and dignity. It will be a charitable institution. It will have a resource room, a library, an institute. A swimming pool. A sauna. A Jacuzzi bath. A museum. We will run an internal lottery. We will become an integral part of the ever-expanding human rights industry. We will be ever so politically correct. A diplomatic tourist attraction, an Embassy of Good Will. A school for love, tolerance, and democracy. A greenhouse of multiculturalism. We will be darlings of the various European funds, UN departments, NGOs, agencies and goodhearted individuals. We will siphon government monies for food, lodgings, and legal costs, and redistribute it justly and evenly. We will organize refugee poetry readings, exhibitions of refugee children drawings, a festival of refugee plays. Of course, we will also run a casino. The refugees will be given decent jobs as waiters and cleaners. The more ambitious ones could become croupiers. The most talented ones will be guards. They'll have regular fitness training and target practice. We will create a pool of youth and energy and muscle. An elite force. Full of brotherhood and unity. We will act as a recruitment agency. Somebody wants a dog jogger—they call us. Somebody wants a job done—they call us. We listen, we contract, we deliver. Money will be generated and poured back into the community. I can see prosperity. I can see roulette wheels, roulette tables. I can see black jack, *chemin de fer*, baccarat. Make your wagers, ladies and gentlemen! Get your bonds and shares, here and now! The wheel is spinning. When it stops don't you want to see the ball rest in our compartment? Don't you want to see your number and your color?

Igor is carried away by the enthusiasm of his speech. He's looking around at the audience.

IVANA: Madonna, an eye for optical theory, the Coca-Cola garden is becoming a robe room.

IGOR: Don't start now.

IVANA: Eurostar prawn watching. The long trail to justice.

IGOR: Shut up.

IVANA: I want to eat the wall.

IGOR: You can't eat the wall.

IVANA: I know I can't. I just want to.

IGOR: Shut up.

IGOR: I would also want to take this opportunity to announce my marriage.

IVANA looks at him.

IGOR: As of now you are my wife.

IVANA: And what if I say no?

IGOR: You can't say no.

IVANA: Why not?

IGOR: 'Cause you're my woman.

IVANA: How am I yours?

IGOR: I found you in the gutter and decided to drag you out of the mud and give you a new life.

IVANA: And if I disobey, you're going to throw me back where you found me?

IGOR: Yes.

IVANA takes her wig off. She turns out to be a wild young woman.

IVANA: I'm not buying this story. I'm not buying the mafia, the alcohol excesses, the prostitution, the stray dogs, and abandoned children in run-down railway stations! It's a big soap opera.

IGOR: Oh shut up silly cow!

IVANA: I'm not buying it. This is not my stage! This is not my play!

IGOR: What is your play? You don't have a play anymore.

IVANA: I have my country. I have my house. I know how the sun shines there, when it is on my front door and when it is on my back door. I have my saints. I have my daughter. I have my home.

IGOR: Oh. I've seen the light. I'll give all my money to charity and go back to the old country to try my luck at chicken farming.

IVANA: The old country wouldn't have you.

IGOR slaps IVANA's face.

IVANA: The Earth is ashamed of you.

IGOR hits her again. Suddenly IVANA produces a gun and shoots at IGOR six times. IGOR just stands there and looks at her. Pause. IVANA drops the gun and looks at it. IGOR goes to her and slaps her again. Blood starts running from IVANA's mouth. She falls on her knees.

MAMA: Sorry for this inconvenience.

MAMA turns to the musicians. They start playing again. The audience is shown to leave the hall.

The audience leaves the reception and moves on. They are divided into groups again. One of the groups is met by THE RECEPTIONIST. Fat, officious, sweating all the time, he wears a jogging outfit and trainer shoes. He's drunk.

THE RECEPTIONIST: When I was young I could swallow little frogs and then throw them up again. I did this for money on a few European squares, including St. Mark's in Venice. People would stand and stare. Most of them giggled. Some ladies fainted. I'm a self-made man. I've had enough of Europe. What has Europe ever given me? What have I got from Europe? Culture? Monuments? Can I eat them? Am I right? Can I drink them? I've seen them, thank you very much, but I'm not a tourist. I live here. They're a bloody nuisance, if you ask me. Am I right? I'm going to emigrate to Africa. I have a friend down there. We went to school together. Now he has a coffee plantation. I fly to Nairobi, I take my jeep, I go to my plantation. Early evening: I sip my gin and tonic, three young naked black beauties shake banana leaves to keep me cool. Very gentle people. They actually enjoy giving you pleasure. The thing is those civil wars. Have they got any at this point, do you know? I have to check that out. But then, so what? Civil wars come and civil wars go, but land stays forever. Am I right or am I right?

He introduces the next room.

There's a professor of some kind in this room. He's a bit paranoid. He's afraid someone is after him to kill him. I must admit that the young man who went into his room a while ago, does look like that someone.

Room Service

CHARACTERS

VISITOR

PROFESSOR

The PROFESSOR sits in an armchair. He drinks. He is dozing away. There is a book open on his lap. There are knocks on the door. He opens his eyes. He is unsure whether he should open the door. He gets up. He opens the door. The VISITOR, a young man, is standing at the door. He is holding a tray. On it there is a large silver dish with a silver cover.

VISITOR: Room service.

The PROFESSOR looks at the VISITOR. He makes way for him. The VISITOR comes in. The PROFESSOR closes the door behind him. The VISITOR doesn't know what to do with the tray. The PROFESSOR makes space on the little table for the VISITOR to put it down. The VISITOR puts down the tray. The PROFESSOR sits down and looks at him.

PROFESSOR: Welcome.

The VISITOR is confused. He can't look the PROFESSOR in the eye. Long silence. Finally they look at each other. The VISITOR is nervous.

PROFESSOR: Yes?

VISITOR: What?

PROFESSOR: You've come to see me. *(Pause.)* Would you like to sit down?

The VISITOR sits down. Pause.

VISITOR: You've been here a long time.

PROFESSOR: I like to keep myself to myself.

VISITOR: Nobody knows anything about you. Some say you were a sailor—the only survivor of a shipwreck. Some say there was a *femme fatale,* who left me poisoned and half-dead.

Pause.

PROFESSOR: You must have been looking for me for a long time.

VISITOR: I have.

PROFESSOR: Can I offer you a drink?

The PROFESSOR gives him a drink from the drinks trolley that he has next to him. The VISITOR drinks.

PROFESSOR: How's life?

VISITOR: Piece of shit.

PROFESSOR: You're young. You must keep your head up. Hungry?

VISITOR: No, thank you.

PROFESSOR: Where did you sleep last night?

VISITOR: I didn't.

PROFESSOR: You're shaking.

Pause. The PROFESSOR gets up. He takes out a razor. He puts shaving foam on his face. He looks at his face in a broken mirror on the wall around which are loose photographs. He starts shaving. The VISITOR looks at him. Pause. The PROFESSOR points at the book on the table. It's a big encyclopedia.

VISITOR: Page 237.

The VISITOR looks at the book. He opens it up on that page. He looks at it.

PROFESSOR: Read.

VISITOR: *(Reads.)* Blood revenge?

PROFESSOR: That's it.

The VISITOR reads.

PROFESSOR: Read aloud.

VISITOR: Also called "blood feud." A continuing state of conflict between two groups within a society (typically kinship groups) characterized by violence, usually killings and counter-killings. It exists in many non-literate communities in which there is an absence of law or a breakdown of legal procedures, and in which attempts to redress a grievance in a way that is acceptable to both parties have failed. *(Pause.)* Heavy stuff.

PROFESSOR: Yes it is. *(Pause.)* And, no it isn't.

The PROFESSOR is shaving.

VISITOR: Did you write this?

PROFESSOR: I'm the authority on the subject.

VISITOR: You?

PROFESSOR: I've been helping academics in Western Europe with their PhDs. Every dog has its day.

VISITOR: *(Looks at the text in the book.)* I kill you and you kill me.

PROFESSOR: I kill you and you kill me and I kill you.

VISITOR: You kill me and I kill you and you kill me and I kill you.

The PROFESSOR has now put on a new black suit, but he's barefoot. He takes the photos from the mirror. He throws them on the table in front of the VISITOR.

PROFESSOR: Ilir and me. Best friends. Children on a sledge. Those were snows. I haven't seen snows like that since. Nature is shriveling up.

The Visitor *looks at the photo.*

Professor: Our first bike. He taught me how to ride. He held the saddle for me. One day I turn around, Ilir is a hundred meters behind me. I was on my own. I could ride a bike. Dusty country road.

The Visitor *looks at the photo.*

Professor: Us eating watermelon. Look at this monster. Twenty kilos. We only ate the heart. Left the rest to the pigs.

The Visitor *looks at the photo.*

Professor: Later. We had girlfriends. They pressed the blackheads on our foreheads. What bliss!

The Visitor *looks at the photo.*

Professor: Even later. Young man playing marbles.

The Professor *and the* Visitor *start exchanging gibberish words used in the marble game. They start laughing. They throw words at each other. Their laughter grows. Pause. The* Professor *gets dark again.*

Professor: Ilir kills my brother. So I go after him. I follow him around Europe. It takes me months to track him down. I finally catch up with him in a hotel room. Not unlike this one. I kill him in cold blood.

The Professor *puts a rose in his lapel.*

Professor: I'm ready now.

The Visitor *takes the cover off the dish on the tray. There is a gun there. The* Visitor *and the* Professor *look at each other. Long pause.*

Visitor: I can't do it.

Professor: Of course you can. I thought I couldn't do it. I did it.

Visitor: I can't.

Professor: Blood is thicker than water.

Visitor: I thought I'd come to do it. But I haven't. I've come to … forgive you.

Professor: Don't be ridiculous. Might is right. An eye for an eye. Let's get it over with. I cannot forgive myself.

The Professor takes the gun and gives it to the Visitor.

Professor: Don't be a wimp. Don't be an "intellectual." Ilir wants you to revenge him. He was your brother. I shot him in the head.

The Visitor jumps up. He grabs the Professor by the throat. He wants to strangle him.

Professor: Six bullets with a Zastava. Ex-Yugoslav regulation item.

The Visitor lets out a long shriek into the Professor's face, as if he was fighting some murderous inner demons.

Professor: Yes! That's more like it! Now you're talking!

The Visitor lets go of the Professor and throws him back into his armchair. The Visitor is angry and excited and breathing heavily. The Professor grabs the gun. He shoots into his mouth. He jolts back into the armchair. But the gun is empty. The Professor has his eyes closed. Then he slowly opens them. He is surprised he is still alive. He has made the leap of faith and has metaphorically killed himself. There is a sense of exorcism in the air. Both revenge and forgiveness have happened. Murder has met mercy.

The Visitor tears up the pages of the Professor's text from the book. He tears them to pieces. He leaves them on the silver tray. He takes out six bullets from his pocket. He leaves them on the tray with the pieces of paper. He leaves and closes the door behind him.

The audience leaves the room and move on. They are met by The Daughter, who is nearsighted and wears thick glasses like jam jars, is awkward, autistic, and has long, girlish plaits.

The Daughter: I like Ulysses. He's really nice. He's a bit of a quiet type though. But very nice. Very nice. The man in the family is always drunk. One evening he asked me if I wanted a ride in his shopping cart. It was mad. Midnight and I'm having a ride in a shopping cart. But I enjoyed it. I can't complain. I like the young man who entered the Professor's room. Very tall, and dark and handsome. I stood in the middle of the hallway. He was coming towards me. And I thought, I'm not going to move. Maybe he's coming for me. I have also seen an angel. He was inside this room. He was on the ceiling. You don't have to believe me, but I'm telling you the truth, only the truth and nothing but the truth. Two newlyweds came into this one last night. You can always tell a bed if it's been used for that thing in the night. The sheets are messed up beyond belief. Nothing else could produce the same effect on the sheets. That's what I'd like to happen to me. I'd like to run away somewhere far, far away. In white. And mess up the sheets of a few hotels. My sign is Pisces. My horoscope says that I'm highly impressionable. And that my nature is receptive and that I lack firmness. Can you notice that in me? I mean when you're looking at me like this, can you tell I'm Pisces?

She introduces the next room.

A tired young woman checked into this room last night. She looked like someone on the brink of killing herself. The rumors are that this room has a resident angel. Maybe he'll help her. Maybe she'll help him.

Hotel Angels

CHARACTERS

ANGEL

DRIFTER

A woman DRIFTER enters the hotel room carrying a suitcase. She looks fragile, tired, and depressed. She wears a long raincoat. She sits on the suitcase. She gazes ahead of herself. Suddenly a voice is heard coming from the cupboard. The cupboard door opens. There is the "cupboard skeleton" of the ANGEL, a YOUNG MAN in his twenties. He is only visible from his waist up. He is wearing a uniform, a combination of police, army, and customs officer.

He addresses the DRIFTER in officious gibberish. He produces a nonsensical, high-pitched whine.

ANGEL: Passport!

The DRIFTER gives him her documents. The ANGEL closes the door of the cupboard like a counter window. Pause. The ANGEL opens up the window again.

ANGEL: Is this your photograph? Is this your hair? Your nose? Are these your eyes? Is this your signature? Your visa is invalid. Your passport is out of date. Who are you? Where are you going? What do you want? Anything to declare? Open suitcase!

The DRIFTER unpacks everything: a toothbrush, underwear, a teddy bear, a photo album. It all ends up in a mess on the floor. The DRIFTER woman tries to pack them back in again, but they end up in a bulge in the suitcase which she is unable to zip up. She sits on it and hangs her head. She starts crying desperately.

DRIFTER: *(She speaks quickly and silently to herself, as a mantra.)*

How many miles to Babylon?
Three score miles and ten.
Can I get there by candlelight?

Yes, and back again.
If your heels be nimble and light,
You may get there by candlelight.

ANGEL listens to this. He likes the DRIFTER woman.

ANGEL: Yes?

DRIFTER: I want to go home.

ANGEL: Let's go.

DRIFTER: Where?

ANGEL: I'll take you home.

The ANGEL has an idea of how to exorcise her sadness. The ANGEL first takes the DRIFTER woman to see again everything she knew in her life. He takes her on a mental trip in which they seem to fly over towns and countryside. They can see people and houses. They wave at them.

The ANGEL teaches the woman how to speak. He has his hand over her forehead as if he were helping her vomit. She spurts out words.

ANGEL:
A! A!

DRIFTER:
angel,
engel,
engle,
enngell,
angil,
eangel,
angle,
aungele,
angell,
angelle,
angele,
englas,
engles,
angles,

ANGEL: Thou hast maad me a litil lesse than aungels.

DRIFTER: I saw thee mounte into heuen on hye.

ANGEL: We are bright still, though the brightest fell.

DRIFTER: We of depnesse and bottomelesse pit.

The DRIFTER takes out a Swiss Army knife. She threatens the ANGEL with it. He runs away from her, walking across the ceiling. There is a strong sexual pull between them. They dance. They sweat and cry. Now she catches him.

DRIFTER: B! B!

ANGEL:

border,
bordure,
bordur,
bordeure,
bourder,
bordore,
bowerdur,
bordeure,
border,

DRIFTER: A lyne, that cometh down to the nethereste bordure.

ANGEL: The border northwarde, is from the see coast and goeth vp vnto Beth Hagla.

DRIFTER: I shal enlarge thy borders.

ANGEL: I sall gif peace to all your bordouris.

DRIFTER: A beggerly Beast brought out of barbarous borders.

ANGEL: Who walks on the borders of eternity.

Slowly and painfully he manages to touch the deep center of her alarm. She transforms into a lighter being. But now he looks tired and depressed. As if a strange transfer of energies has happened. Now she picks him up.

DRIFTER: What is the matter with you?

ANGEL: I want to go home.

DRIFTER: Let's go.

ANGEL: Where?

DRIFTER: I'll take you home.

Together they fly out of the window. Has the ANGEL *become human or the woman become an* ANGEL*? Have they flown up or down?*

The audience leaves the room and moves on. They are met by THE CARETAKER*, young, cocky, very short hair, well-built. He talks to them as he takes them to the next room.*

THE CARETAKER: Deadbeat fuck-ups. Gimps. Gonners. Jerks. Bums. Flim-flams fallen off the back of a truck. One of these days they'll wake up dead. How many unemployed in this country? Millions! And the government gives accommodation and cash to whoever comes under a truck. We work our guts off to make a living, they want everything for free overnight. Bloody mongrels. They multiply like rabbits. They stink. Never learn our language. The only word they know is "benefit." Excuse me, can I have a flat? Here's a flat. Excuse me, can I have food vouchers? Here are food vouchers! Excuse me, can I have health insurance! Here is health insurance. Excuse me, can I have a color TV, not 17-inch, 19-inch! Excuse me, can you scratch my balls? And they snigger like rats with golden teeth. *(Shows his tattoos on his shoulders and arms. They are neo-Nazi symbols.)* It's time for a crusade. If you know what I mean. The gloves are off! The day of reckoning! There will be rivers of blood. And when that day comes—I want to be ready. The great unwashed duds. Shit-kickers. Baboons. Low-lifes. Ball-busters. Freeloaders. Leeches. Faces like toilet seats. Don't know whether to suck or blow. They'd fuck a snake if somebody would hold its head!

He introduces the next room.

Two Russian newlyweds arrived in this room a few hours ago. I think they're in a hurry to do whatever newlyweds do.

Maiden Voyage

CHARACTERS

BRIDE

BRIDEGROOM

Two young immigrants have just arrived at the hotel as hitchhikers, wedding dress and all, straight from the wedding in the "home country." The BRIDEGROOM looks around. He loves everything he sees.

BRIDEGROOM: Look at this! Oh, yes! Look at this!

BRIDEGROOM kisses the bed.

BRIDE: What are you doing?

BRIDEGROOM: Kissing the bed.

BRIDE: Why?

BRIDEGROOM: It's a real Western European bed.

BRIDE: So?

BRIDEGROOM: The West is best!

He kisses the curtains.

BRIDEGROOM: Western curtains.

He kisses the floor.

BRIDEGROOM: Western floor.

He breathes deeply.

BRIDEGROOM: Western air.

He nearly cries tears of joy.

BRIDEGROOM: This is it!

BRIDE: Don't overdo it.

BRIDEGROOM: We've made it!

BRIDE: Don't jinx it.

The BRIDEGROOM starts undressing. He smells his armpits. He's getting ready for the nuptial ritual. The BRIDE is sitting on the bed nervously.

BRIDEGROOM: Shall we?

BRIDE: What?

BRIDEGROOM: Get down to it?

BRIDE: Get down to what?

BRIDEGROOM: Make a Western baby!

BRIDE: A Western baby?

BRIDEGROOM: A new man. Who will not suffer the Eastern fate of his parents.

BRIDE: What if it's not a man?

BRIDEGROOM: Of course it will be a man.

BRIDE: What if it's a girl?

BRIDEGROOM: A man first, then a girl.

The BRIDE sulks. Silence. The BRIDEGROOM touches her from behind. She turns on the TV. She starts zapping through the programs. Myriad commercial quiz shows and soap operas. The BRIDEGROOM sits next to her. They watch TV. Pause. The BRIDEGROOM gets uncomfortable with the competition.

BRIDEGROOM: Okay. Sorry. First a girl, then a boy.

BRIDE: I hoped this would be a spiritual and memorable moment.

BRIDEGROOM: It will be.

BRIDE: We hitchhiked for three days from home. Straight from the wedding.

BRIDEGROOM: Exactly. So turn that off! *(Pause.)* Turn that off!

BRIDE: Don't shout!

BRIDEGROOM: I'm not shouting.

BRIDE: You can't hear yourself.

The BRIDEGROOM starts kissing the BRIDE's neck. Pre-recorded audience laughter comes from the TV.

BRIDEGROOM: Please.

The B*RIDE presses the "mute" button on the remote control. Silence. She keeps on watching the program.*

The B*RIDEGROOM takes out the little icon of their local saint and puts it on the bedside table. He crosses himself. He says a prayer. The* B*RIDE is still watching television. The* B*RIDEGROOM turns off the light. The room is now lit only by the flickering light of the television. The* B*RIDEGROOM kisses the* B*RIDE's neck. She keeps watching the TV program.*

The B*RIDEGROOM has problems with his concentration. He gets up. He turns on the radio. He's trying to find some soft romantic music. He goes through various stations. There are all kinds of music, but nothing soft. Suddenly he tunes into a nice soft tune. He goes back to kissing the* B*RIDE's neck. The soft music stops and there is a change of program. A political broadcast starts. He changes the station. He finds another soft music program. The* B*RIDE is watching the TV. The* B*RIDEGROOM jumps up. He starts thrashing the sheets.*

BRIDE: What is it?

BRIDEGROOM: A cockroach.

BRIDE: A cockroach?

BRIDEGROOM: A bloody cockroach!

BRIDE: Isn't it a lovely Western cockroach!

BRIDEGROOM: That's funny!

The B*RIDEGROOM finishes thrashing the bed and turns off the TV set. They get back on the bed. There is now only the light of the neon light coming through the windows.*

The B*RIDEGROOM now gets into form. But suddenly there are faces coming through the walls. The* B*RIDE can see them.*

BRIDE: Jesus!

BRIDEGROOM: What?

BRIDE: Wait!

BRIDEGROOM: What?

BRIDE: My grandfather!

BRIDEGROOM: Who?

BRIDE: I saw my grandfather.

BRIDEGROOM: Where?

BRIDE: His head came through the wall.

BRIDEGROOM: Don't be silly.

BRIDE: I swear.

The BRIDEGROOM looks at the wall. Pause. Nothing happens. The BRIDEGROOM turns his back to the wall. There is a face coming out of the wall.

BRIDE: There!

The face disappears. The BRIDEGROOM turns back.

BRIDEGROOM: Where?

There is nothing there.

BRIDE: What does it mean?

BRIDEGROOM: Nothing.

BRIDE: It's a bad sign. My forefathers are angry with me.

The BRIDE gets up. She lights a candle to the local saint. She crosses herself. She opens a bag. She takes out a jar of honey and nuts. She takes a spoonful. She gives one to the BRIDEGROOM. The spoon falls on the floor. The BRIDE reaches for it.

Suddenly she sees something under the bed. She pulls out an attaché case. They have trouble opening the coded lock. They open it. It's full of money. They count the money. Then, underneath the money they find something wrapped up in a dirty cloth. They unwrap it. It's a bloody heart.

BRIDE: What's this?

BRIDEGROOM: It's a heart.

BRIDE: A heart?

BRIDEGROOM: Isn't it a heart?

BRIDE: What heart?

BRIDEGROOM: I don't know.

BRIDE: Whose heart?

BRIDEGROOM: Why do you ask me?

BRIDE: Who can I ask?

They are scared. The BRIDE touches the heart. Blood spurts out on her white underwear. She screams.

BRIDE: Blood.

BRIDEGROOM: Don't shout!

BRIDE: It's blood.

BRIDEGROOM: I can bloody well see it's blood!

The BRIDEGROOM puts the heart and the money back under the bed. But his hands are bloody. Blood is dripping on the sheets.

BRIDE: Blood!

He gets up and washes his hands. He goes back to bed. The telephone rings. They look at each other. The BRIDEGROOM is about to pick up the receiver.

BRIDE: Don't!

BRIDEGROOM: What?

BRIDE: Don't answer it.

BRIDEGROOM: Why not?

BRIDE: Something tells me.

The BRIDEGROOM takes the telephone and rips it out of the plug. Silence.

BRIDE: Let's go home.

BRIDEGROOM: Now?

BRIDE: Now.

BRIDEGROOM: Let's.

They look at each other. They start kissing and making love furiously as if there were no tomorrow. Their lives will never be the same.

The audience leaves the room. They are met by the first person who welcomed them at the beginning of the evening. He/she tells them of the dramatic changes that have happened in the course of the evening—that due to an unexpected twist they're all invited to a dance on the open-air terrace of the hotel. All of the audience gathers at a terrace outside. There is a long table there, around which all of the actors from all the rooms are gathered. They still have their costumes on, but they have taken their make-up off. IVANA *gets up and starts singing.*

IVANA:

> Freude schoner Goter funken,
> Tochter aus Elysium
> wir betreten feuer trunken
> Himmlische, dein Heiligthum
> Deine Zauber bin den wieder
> was die Mode streng getheilt
> all Menchen werden Bruder
> wo dein sanfter Flugel weilt.

They all raise their glasses. There is wind coming from somewhere, blowing in their hair.

Hotel Europa looms in the night under the sweet and sour moonlight.

Tales of Ordinary Madness

Petr Zelenka

Translated from Czech by Stepan S. Simek

Tales of Ordinary Madness premiered at Dejvické Divadlo in Prague, Czech Republic, November 2001. It was directed by the author.

CHARACTERS

Peter: Employee of a shipping company, a desperate seeker of normalcy. In his mid-thirties.

Midge: Peter's friend, an experimental masturbator, and a romantic. In his mid-thirties.

Jeanette: Peter's former girlfriend, a reluctant nymphomaniac engaged to Alex, but perhaps still in love with Peter. In her late-twenties, early thirties.

The Mother: Peter's mother, an obsessive blood donor, concerned about the state of the world. In her late-fifties, early sixties.

The Father: Peter's father, a former newsreel commentator who wants to change his voice. Also wants to find out if a lightbulb would fit in his mouth. In his fifties or sixties.

George: Former dissident, composer of elevator music, obsessive litigator, and a veteran of countless complicated relationships. In his late-forties, early fifties.

Alice: George's girlfriend, who achieves orgasm only if someone watches her having sex with George. In her twenties.

Alex: Jeanette's fiancée, a little dull, repeats everything other people say. In his late-twenties or early thirties.

Sylvia: A young sculptor. Later on, Father's girlfriend, and later his manager. Slightly hysterical, but full of life. In her twenties.

Anna: Midge's cleaning lady, and briefly his girlfriend. Also a dancer and an admirer of the ballet. In her twenties.

The Boss: Peter's boss, a theoretical pedophile—he likes little boys, but he doesn't throw himself on them. In his thirties or forties.

Eve: A plastic mannequin from a department store. Later brought to life by Midge's devotion and love for her. In her twenties.

A Female Dancer

A Man in the Audience

A Chechen Soldier

Party Guests

Mailmen

Setting

The play takes place in Prague in the early years of the twenty-first century. The action takes place in the apartments of the various protagonists, a visiting room of a psychiatric clinic, an elevator, and in SYLVIA's sculpture studio.

Note on Staging

The staging of the play relies on continuous stage action. The different spaces, such as the apartments of the different protagonists, etc., don't need to be specifically defined—the text and the actions of the characters should take care of such definition. Major scene changes would only break the continuity of the plot, and would be detrimental to the production. That is not to say that some major scenic elements might not be required at certain times. Those however, should be introduced as seamlessly as possible.

"Most people live in agony, and they are so miserable that they prefer risking further agony to facing their actual situation in life." —*Charles Bukowski*

There is only one way to get out of that mess. To tape yourself into a box and mail yourself away as a package.

PETER, age thirty-six, is waking up with a terrible hangover. He slowly gets up. He picks up his pants from the floor. They are full of leaves. He searches through the pockets, and finds a wad of woman's hair. He sniffs the hair and smiles. He picks up the phone, dials a number. His friend MIDGE, who is about the same age, picks up. He too has just woken up.

PETER: Hi, it's Peter.

MIDGE: Why so early?

PETER: It's about the hair.

MIDGE: What hair?

PETER: Jeanette's hair. I forgot what I should do with it.

MIDGE: Wait a minute! Did you really cut off her hair? Have you got it?

PETER: It was pretty easy, actually. I pulled it out of her hairbrush. You know how women's hairbrushes are always full of their hair. It's disgusting, but this time it came in handy.

MIDGE: I thought you really cut it off.

PETER: Come on, I'm not crazy.

MIDGE: You have to boil it in milk, then dry it, burn it with apple leaves, and scatter the ashes in the place where you first met.

PETER: O . . . K . . .

MIDGE: What's the problem? You don't trust this method or what?

PETER: I do. It's just . . . what do I do next?

MIDGE: You want her to come back to you, don't you?

PETER: Sure, but not like that.

MIDGE: It's a proven method.

PETER: But I want her to come back because of me, not because I cut off her hair.

MIDGE: You have to do it within twenty-four hours. So hurry up.

PETER: Right . . .

MIDGE hangs up. PETER gets a carton of milk. He pours the milk into a pan, puts in the wad of hair, and studies the strange mixture with some curiosity. Phone rings. It is JEANETTE, an attractive, energetic woman of around thirty. We see her on the phone on another part of the stage. ALEX, her current boyfriend paces around her, agitated.

JEANETTE: Peter?

PETER: Oh . . . Jeanette! I was just putting you in . . .

JEANETTE: Peter! I just can't believe that you could have done something so horrible!

PETER: What. . .?

JEANETTE: The kids saw you.

PETER: What kids?

JEANETTE: Auntie's kids!

PETER: Right . . . Auntie's kids. What aunt?

JEANETTE: Alex's aunt. They were in bed upstairs, and they saw you walking into her room with scissors and cutting her hair.

PETER is speechless. He frantically pulls more and more wads of hair from his pockets. He tosses them away, as if JEANETTE could see him.

PETER: I'd never do anything like that.

JEANETTE: Shut up!

PETER: Why did they let me do it? Why didn't the stupid brats start yelling? Normally they scream all the time. Why didn't they just wake somebody up to stop me?!

JEANETTE: I don't know why they didn't yell, but that's beside the point.

PETER: Why didn't Alex stop me?

JEANETTE: You know Alex, he ... Look Peter, Auntie is on the verge of a nervous breakdown. She's afraid to even go out.

PETER: I haven't gone out for quite some time either.

JEANETTE: But this is something very different. Alex's aunt wants to sue you. You are in big trouble, my friend. We expect you to come by tomorrow and sort it out.

JEANETTE hangs up. So does PETER. He starts dressing. Offstage we hear two voices—a man and a woman trading insults ...

GEORGE: Your mother is so stupid she eats marinated cat farts!

ALICE. And your brother is so dirty, he can't tell his ass from a hole in the dirt!

GEORGE: Leave my family out of this, you ...

PETER bangs on the wall, and the voices die out. Enter MIDGE. In front of him he is pushing a lavatory sink mounted on a wheeled metal frame. He starts to wash and polish the sink.

PETER: I told you it was too difficult! In the darkness I mixed her up with Alex's aunt.

MIDGE: How on earth could you mistake her for his aunt?!

PETER: I was drunk. Couldn't make myself do it sober.

MIDGE: Great! You're a genius!

PETER: It was your idea.

MIDGE: My advice to you was to stop dating altogether.

PETER: I don't want to end up like you.

Midge: I didn't end up like anything. Unlike you, I'm figuring things out.

Peter: Yeah! You don't even leave your place anymore.

Midge: That's because I don't want to run into some woman somewhere.

Peter: That's exactly what I'm talking about! You're hopeless. So don't tell me what to do. When did you last go out?

Midge: Not since Lizzie left. I do think about women, I even fantasize about them when I make myself happy, but I haven't talked to any. I'm scared to come close to them. They have some sort of a scent around them, or something. When you come too close, you may fall in love. And as soon you fall in love, they leave you.

Peter: What about food?

Midge: I have a cleaning lady, who does the shopping for me. But with her I'm OK. She's dumb as a post.

We see Anna, the cleaning lady with a broom in the back of the stage.

Peter: Is there any booze around?

Midge: Help yourself to whatever; you know where it is.

Peter: What's up with the vac?

Midge: Oh, I was just trying some … stuff with it.

Peter: What?!

Midge: When you learn how to use it, it's almost like being inside a woman.

Peter: Really?

Midge: Well, not really. It's far from the real thing, but it's better than nothing, right?

Peter: *(Toasting with his beer bottle.)* To Jeanette. May she come back to me. I'm going to see them tomorrow but first I have to figure things out …

Midge: There is another proven method to get a woman back.

Peter: What is it?

Midge: You put yourself in a box, tape yourself up, and mail yourself to her address as a package.

It's a bit risky, but clean. No magic there.

PETER: Package…?

MIDGE: By mail. To the addressee only.

PETER: That's bullshit.

MIDGE: You have to put your return address on it to let her know it's from you. Two days in a box,

that's survivable. Of course you have to have a water bottle, and a bottle to …

PETER: Wait a minute. You mean to say that you mailed yourself in a box to one of your women?

MIDGE: A friend of mine tried it once …

PETER: Bullshit. What friend?

MIDGE: You don't know him.

PETER: Come on, you don't have any friends.

MIDGE: But it really is a great method. No woman in the world can resist it. It's an attack straight on the heart. Here … heart. Get it?

PETER: You really mailed yourself in a box. I can't believe it! Who mailed you?

MIDGE: A mailman.

PETER: Why didn't you come to me?

MIDGE: You … weren't home … But it worked!

PETER: I thought that all your girlfriends left you.

MIDGE: This one was an exception. She left me only after she came back to me.

PETER: I think the whole thing is bull. *(He notices that the lower part of the drainpipe of the sink is missing and that it is not connected to the wall.)* What's up with the sink?

MIDGE: Oh, I was just trying some … stuff with it.

PETER: What the f…??!!

MIDGE: It can be used in … all kinds of ways.

Peter: A sink?!

Midge flips up the sink, which is specifically modified for his unholy activity. Peter is shocked.

Peter: Come on Midge!!! The whole thing is full of gunk and stuff!

Midge: Stop calling me Midge.

Peter: But it's disgusting.

Midge: The drainpipe is totally clean. I wash it daily.

Peter: You are totally screwed up … These aids of yours …

Midge: What aids do you use?

Peter: Me? Uh … just uh … normal … hand and stuff.

Midge: That's old …

Peter: Midge, I am really worried about you.

Midge: You don't need to worry about me. You should sort out your relationship with Jeanette first, then you can tell me what to do.

Peter: I will, don't you worry. I'm going to see her tomorrow, and I need to figure things out first. But you should really do some soul searching, Midge.

Midge leaves. Mother enters holding a blood pressure monitor. During the following conversation, she wraps the device around her arm, and with Peter's help begins to take her blood pressure.

Mother: You should really do some soul searching, Peter. I have no idea where we went wrong. We used to take you to the beach … We bought you the best vitamins … Are you even working?

Peter: I am.

Mother: Did you get the clippings?

Peter: I did.

Mother: So what do you think? It's horrible isn't it?

Peter: …uh …

Mother: You don't think it's horrible? An earthquake like that?

Peter: Sure … it's awful …

Mother: So many of those Georgians suffering! And it leaves you cold?

Peter: No it doesn't, but … You just keep sending so many of them, I have boxes full of them.

Mother: I send them to you, so that you'll know how things really are.

Peter: Please don't. You're constantly buying me stuff, sending me those newspaper clippings … I'm running out of space, Mother. I even had to get rid of my bed.

Mother: What?! You sold that beautiful bed from your grandmother?

Peter: I didn't sell it. I threw it out, Mother.

Mother: You threw out your bed?! You need to do some soul searching. You're thirty-five years old, and you can't even do your own shopping. You continue to refuse my advice; you don't know how to buy your shoes, you don't know how to buy pants …

Peter: But I do …

Mother: … Stop interrupting me. Not to mention that you can't even find a girlfriend. I was giving blood today, and I spoke with an acquaintance of mine. She was completely shocked. She found out that her son is a homosexual. She simply couldn't get over it. Poor thing, she couldn't even donate, her red cells turned thin from the shock. You aren't a homosexual, are you?

Peter: No.

Mother: So you are a homosexual.

Peter: I am not.

Mother: So why don't you bring home a girlfriend?

Peter: I can't find the right one.

Mother: Just bring one home, right one or not. Continue pumping.

Peter: Is this why you wanted me to come today? To tell me to get a girlfriend?

Mother: I wanted you to come because of your father. To enjoy him as long as you can.

Peter: What do you mean, "to enjoy him"?

Mother: He may not be with us much longer, and then what? He will get dementia, and we won't be able to speak with him at all.

Peter: Is he that bad?

Mother: I am giving him maximum two months. *(She points to her head.)* ... But not a word ...

Father enters.

Father: How much do you give me?

Mother: Two months. Maybe less.

Father: Hi.

Peter: Hi.

Mother: *(To Peter.)* He doesn't care about anything. He's not interested in the news, he doesn't care about the earthquake in Georgia; all he cares about are those beer bubbles of his.

During her speech, Father opens a beer bottle and begins his peculiar ritual: he pours the beer in his glass, but rather than drinking it right away, he continues holding the bottle, and warming the bottleneck with the palms of his hands, thus warming the air in it. The air in the bottle expands, freeing two or three additional beer bubbles, which otherwise would have perished inside.

Father: I am fascinated by the way you can warm the bottleneck, and see how the air inside expands and pushes up more bubbles.

Mother: You've been doing this for the past thirty years.

Father: And I am still fascinated by it.

Mother *(To Peter.)* Yesterday, I found him standing in the bathroom with a light bulb in his hand.

Father: I wanted to find out if I could fit a bulb in my mouth.

Peter: And...?

Father: I didn't try it. I was afraid I wouldn't get it out again.

MOTHER: And he is trying to change his voice. That's why he drinks. He's hoping that all that beer will change his voice.

FATHER: That's not ...

MOTHER begins to measure FATHER's blood pressure.

MOTHER *(To PETER.)* Last week he forgot my name. He had a friend visiting, and he wanted to introduce me but he couldn't remember my name. He kept calling me "my darling," "honey," and "bunny," "honey bunny"—yessir, not even "honey bunny" was off limits.

FATHER: Well, it wasn't that bad ...

MOTHER: At one point I thought he had Alzheimer's disease, but by now I am sure that it's old-age dementia. I can tell from the reaction of his pupils.

FATHER: She shines a flashlight in my eyes.

MOTHER: *(Proudly repeats.)* I shine a flashlight in his eyes. Because he refuses to be seen by specialists!

FATHER: I was there last week. They couldn't find anything.

MOTHER: Because each time you go, you manage to dupe them.

FATHER: How do I dupe them?

Suddenly MOTHER "barks" at him, as if to startle him. FATHER doesn't react.

PETER: Mom, do you have a wig or something?

MOTHER: A wig? But you just told me you aren't a ...

PETER: Anyways. Well, I guess I should be going.

MOTHER holds him back and shines a flashlight in his eyes.

MOTHER: You have a history of dementia in your family, and it will only get worse. His father had it too ... When you were small, your grandfather made all sorts of strange faces at you.

FATHER: But that was just for fun.

MOTHER: Yes, fun. That's how he imagined "fun." And then, my dear, one day they found him running down the street in his underwear.

FATHER: That's not ...

MOTHER: It is. Did they find him or didn't they! He was running up and down the street in his underwear!

FATHER: He just wanted to annoy grandmother.

MOTHER: Nonsense. *(MOTHER again "barks" at FATHER. Again, FATHER doesn't react. To PETER.)* Did you know that it's impossible to startle your father anymore? That's one of the symptoms of old-age dementia. Sometimes I hide behind the door and bark ... you see I barked at him twice already, and he didn't start at all. *(She "barks" at him, FATHER doesn't react.)* You see? He would like to be startled, but he simply can't.

PETER: I think I should be going, mom.

MOTHER: Aren't you happy here with us?

PETER: I am.

MOTHER: So stay here! Are you happy with us, or aren't you?

PETER: Not really.

MOTHER: I knew it. But the problem is in you. You don't have a girlfriend; you don't know how to relate to people ... And this, among many other things, is well demonstrated by the fact that you are refusing to spend time with your poor old father, who soon will no longer be with us.

(She cries, and then again in a normal voice.) Did you know that he doesn't even know how to use the phone any longer? Yesterday I made him dial a random number ...

PETER: Why?

FATHER: We bet whether someone will recognize my voice.

MOTHER: I thought he'd be happy to know that people still remember him from the time he narrated the weekly newsreels. He was the voice of the time, reverberating from the screen ...

FATHER: But I don't want people to remember me.

MOTHER: You see, he doesn't want it ...

FATHER: I am not going to call anybody!

MOTHER: First he didn't want to call, but in the end I made him do it …

MOTHER's story transforms into a real stage action.

MOTHER: I bet you that if you dial a random number, you'll bump into someone who will recognize your voice because they remember you from the weekly newsreels.

FATHER: A random number?

MOTHER: Uh-huh.

FATHER: Why would I do a thing like that?

MOTHER: So that you'll know how things really are.

FATHER: They'll think that I'm some sort of a pervert.

MOTHER: Don't try to talk yourself out of it.

FATHER: You really want me to do it?

MOTHER: Yes. We can bet if you want to. I say that people will remember your voice. In the store, for example, when we go shopping—people still turn when you say something.

FATHER: And will you leave me in peace for a while if I do it?

MOTHER: Then you can play with your bubbles again.

FATHER picks up the phone and blindly dials a random number. A woman's voice answers. FATHER wants to say something, but the woman on the other side of the line beats him to it. It is SYLVIA, an attractive woman of around thirty, now a bit at the end of her rope. She thinks the caller is the man who just left her today.

SYLVIA: Martin? Martin, is it you? Did you know what happened? Charlie was run over by a car!

FATHER: Charlie?

SYLVIA: Our dog!

FATHER is shocked. He doesn't know what to say. MOTHER continues to watch him skeptically. In her eyes, FATHER has once again failed. During the phone call, MOTHER makes remarks about the conversation, even though she can't hear what is being said on the other side of the line.

Father: Aah ... well ...

Sylvia: I was hoping you'd call. You shouldn't have left. I can't bear my life without you. I just wanted to say that I am awfully glad you called. I was afraid I'd never hear your voice again. I almost went mad without you.

Father: Right ... well ...

Mother: What "right ... well ..."?

Sylvia: Where are you?

Father: Aah ... Right now I am in ... sort of an apartment.

Mother: So...? Did they recognize you?

Sylvia: Are you calling from her place?

Father: Whose place?

Sylvia: That woman's place. Each time you call from there, you have this strange voice. You should stop living with that woman; she is a bad influence, really. I want you to be with me. Can you come here?

Father: Right now ... I don't think it's ... possible ...

Mother: What's not possible? Why shouldn't it be possible?

Sylvia: I am awfully glad to hear your voice.

Father: Good.

Sylvia: I love you, you know.

Father: Yes.

Mother *(Mockingly.)* Yes!

Sylvia: I really mean it.

Father: Sure.

Mother: "Sure!" Is that all you can say?!

Sylvia: I haven't been too well lately. I even swallowed a bunch of pills, did you know?

FATHER: Really?

SYLVIA: They had to pump my stomach. And then, in the hospital somebody stole all my money, and even my papers and my address book. I don't even have your number.

FATHER: Aah ... well ...

SYLVIA: Can you give me your number?

FATHER: I think I have to hang up now.

MOTHER: You have to hang up, and you haven't said anything!

SYLVIA: Say something nice to me.

FATHER: Well ... I don't know what to say.

SYLVIA: Tell me that you love me.

MOTHER: Say something in your voiceover voice.

Pause.

SYLVIA: Martin, are you still there?

FATHER: Yes.

SYLVIA: Please say that you love me, even if it isn't true. I just need to hear it.

MOTHER: Say some longer, continuous sentence.

FATHER: OK. I love you.

MOTHER can't believe her ears. She is speechless.

SYLVIA: I love you too.

FATHER: I have to hang up now ...

SYLVIA: You will call again soon, will you?

FATHER: Bye ...

He hangs up. For a while both he and MOTHER stand there, shocked. Then FATHER begins to behave as if nothing had happened.

MOTHER: David, I am really starting to think that it is Alzheimer's disease.

She leaves. FATHER *unplugs the phone from the wall and carries it away. Enter* PETER'S BOSS. *He is a forty-year-old, tall man in a business suit, with an honest face. He is a busy man with lots of responsibilities.*

BOSS: Are you happy with your work here?

PETER: Yes.

BOSS: Your work hours are suitable?

PETER: Yes.

BOSS: Do you get along with your colleagues?

PETER: More or less.

BOSS: Good. What is it you needed?

PETER: I need to take a day off tomorrow.

BOSS: Family troubles?

PETER: Something like that.

BOSS: No problem.

PETER: Thank you.

BOSS: Mister Hanek, since we are already talking ... there is something you should know about me. *(Pause.)* I like little boys.

PETER: I beg your pardon?

BOSS: Right. Somewhere between seven- and eleven-year-olds. I am fascinated by their little, barely pubescent po-pos ...

PETER: Ehm ...

BOSS: ... their little wrinkled weenies ...

PETER: I ... I don't know what to say.

BOSS. I suspected it for a long time, but last week it was confirmed.

PETER: I am sorry.

Boss: So am I. I'd prefer to like little girls or big guys, or as a matter of fact even big girls, but I like little boys. That's the worst combination.

Peter: Aah ... well ... *(Peter gets up and is about to leave. Boss holds him back.)*

Boss: But you don't need to think that I would somehow throw myself at them ... I just simply like them.

Peter: I understand.

Boss: I just thought that you should know this about me.

Peter: Thank you. *(Peter is about to go.)*

Boss: You are welcome. And could you please tell Mr. Pokorny to come and see me? No wait, not Mr. Pokorny.

Boss leaves. Music. Alex, a robust and serious man in his mid-thirties enters with two chairs—one for him and one for Peter. Even though the situation will slip out of his control later, he is completely in charge now. Jeanette stands nearby.

Alex: We are all adults here and we can reach some sort of an understanding. Sit down here.

Peter sits down.

Alex: What do you drink?

Peter: Double Scotch.

Jeanette: I begged you to stop drinking.

Alex: Come on, leave him in peace.

Jeanette: You may not realize how serious this whole thing is.

Alex leaves to fix the drinks.

Peter: I do. That's why I need a drink. *(Pause.)* First of all, I'd like to apologize to all of you. I am very sorry; I was drunk, and so on. And I guess I should especially apologize to Alex's aunt.

Jeanette: She won't come out. She's locked herself in her room and stopped talking.

Peter: And the kids?

ALEX: *(Coming back with the drinks.)* We had to take them away.

PETER: Did something happen to them?

ALEX: They were getting fits of laughter.

PETER: *(Pulling out wads of hair from his pocket.)* I brought back some of the hair. Maybe one could graft them back on, or …

JEANETTE: Are you trying to be funny?

PETER: Or maybe I could get her a wig, or something.

JEANETTE: The aunt is allergic to wigs.

PETER: I see.

JEANETTE: She can't stand artificial fibers. She needs a custom-made wig, which you will have to pay for.

PETER: No problem.

ALEX: Which you will have to pay for.

JEANETTE: Apart from that, she wants a public apology.

PETER: How public?

ALEX: Public.

JEANETTE: She wants you to apologize in a newspaper. That will of course cost you.

PETER: Sure.

ALEX: We don't know whether you have enough money. Otherwise we could lend you some …

PETER: That's all right.

ALEX: We are all adults here and we can reach some sort of an understanding. We are not out to exploit your misfortune.

PETER: What misfortune?

ALEX: You should do some soul searching, Peter. I have been watching you for quite some time now, and …

PETER: And what?

ALEX: ... And I just don't know.

PETER: What don't you know?

ALEX: Well, I don't know, I just don't know ...

JEANETTE: Forget about it.

ALEX: Can you please explain to us why you did it?

PETER: I'm not sure you'd understand.

JEANETTE: Why wouldn't he understand?

PETER: I thought she was Jeanette.

ALEX: I don't understand. You mistook my aunt for Jeanette?

PETER: I was disoriented. I needed her hair.

ALEX: Her hair?

PETER: So that I could boil it in milk.

ALEX: In milk?

PETER: And than dry it, burn it with ...

JEANETTE: *(To ALEX.)* Clearly, he and Midge were doing one of those stupid rituals of theirs. You are a couple of perverted bozos, you two, if you want to know what I think.

PETER: He is your cousin, after all.

JEANETTE: But you are a bad influence on him. Does he still have all those aids?

PETER: What aids?

JEANETTE: You know very well what aids.

ALEX: What aids?

JEANETTE: Forget about it.

PETER: Look Jeanette, I am doing all of this so that you'll come back to me.

JEANETTE: Don't start again.

PETER: I love you. I miss you. *(To ALEX.)* Alex wouldn't be upset, would you?

ALEX: Now wait a minute. You can't just barge into my house and try to get my wife to come back to you.

PETER: Your wife?

JEANETTE: We are getting married.

ALEX: We are getting married.

PETER is speechless.

PETER: You two?

JEANETTE: Sure.

PETER: When?

JEANETTE: Soon.

PETER: Whose idea was that?

JEANETTE: Who cares whose idea it was. Actually, if you really want to know, it was my idea.

ALEX: I thought that it was my idea.

JEANETTE: No. It was my idea! How on earth could it have been your idea?

PETER: Absolutely.

JEANETTE: What do you mean, "absolutely"? I see no reason why I shouldn't marry somebody whom I like and with whom I am happy.

ALEX: Exactly my words.

PETER: But Alex is far too simple for you. You need someone who will inspire you.

ALEX: Hey, hold you horses there, OK ...

PETER: *(To ALEX.)* No offense, but basically all you do is repeat what she says. You should try to listen to yourself sometimes.

JEANETTE: Don't insult him.

ALEX: Don't insult me.

ALEX realizes what he just said, and leaves.

JEANETTE: *(To PETER.)* I just want to lead a normal life. With you I felt that the whole world is full of madmen and psychopaths.

PETER: It's just my bad luck to be around strange people.

JEANETTE: It's not bad luck. You attract people like that, because that's exactly how you are inside.

JEANETTE leaves. Music. Peter is drinking ... Music fades back, and from behind the wall we hear insults and screams of a man and a woman, as well as the sound of falling objects.

GEORGE: Your mother is so stupid, she eats marinated cat farts!

ALICE: And your brother is so dirty, he can't tell his ass from a hole in the ground!

GEORGE: Leave my family out of this, you ... etc.

PETER sits up and listens intently. The noise goes on, so PETER bangs on the wall, and both of the voices die out. ALICE, age twenty-five, enters.

ALICE: Hi, I am Alice.

PETER: Hi, Peter.

ALICE: I heard some banging. Is something wrong?

PETER: No, no. I just heard some noise, and I thought ... you know ... if everything was OK, and stuff.

ALICE: Sure. Everything's fine. We just moved in a few days ago. We are still unpacking, and sometimes we drop stuff. You know how it is.

PETER: I see.

ALICE enters PETER's place and examines it. She behaves as if she were at home there.

ALICE: You don't look too good. Is something wrong?

PETER: No, no ... That's how I always look, it's normal.

ALICE: *(Nods in agreement.)* I get it. George isn't exactly well, either.

PETER: George?

ALICE: The guy I live with. My partner. He's a musician. Composes music. Hey, do you have some more booze around here? I'll help myself, OK? *(She pours herself a glass.)* Funny, your place is just like ours. You live with someone?

PETER: No.

ALICE: Cool. He is concerned about elevators.

PETER: Who is?

ALICE: George. He's suing a bunch of hotels for his music. They have been playing it for the past ten years all over this stupid country. Mostly in hotels. You've heard elevator music, right? Basically, nobody realizes that someone has to compose it. And if someone composes it, logically, he should get paid for that, no? That's pretty basic, right?

PETER: I guess so.

ALICE: But so far they haven't paid a penny. That's why he's suing them.

PETER: Listen ... Alice ... I sort of need to be by myself for a while ...

ALICE: Sure thing.

ALICE is about to go, but GEORGE enters. He is somewhere between fifty and sixty, and he looks like somebody who has lived a lot.

ALICE: *(To GEORGE.)* I just had a little drink here. *(She leads GEORGE in.)* This is Peter. This is George.

PETER: Hi.

GEORGE: Hi.

ALICE: He heard the noise. He thought that something might be wrong ...

GEORGE: You thought we were fighting, didn't you? Neither Alice nor I believe in violence. *(He winks at ALICE as if to confirm that this indeed was the case. ALICE agrees.)* We live in a country filled with violence and fraud, but we don't believe in any of that.

PETER: I am glad to hear it.

GEORGE: We could be cruel to each other, be vulgar, fight, and play all kinds of swinish tricks on each other, but that's not who we are. But let us show you how it would look like if we were like that.

As if in a sharp movie cut, Alice *and* George *suddenly change: They start throwing things at each other, and vulgarly insult each other. Their insults are highly stylized.*

George: Your mother is so stupid that she eats marinated cat farts.

Alice: And your mother smells like hell, and your sister's tits hang all the way down to her ass.

George: Leave my mother out of your dirty mouth.

Alice: Fuck your mother. Fuck your mother, and fuck your sister's hanging tits.

George *is strangling* Alice*; she kicks him between his legs … and so on. This goes on for a while. Then, as suddenly as it began, both calm down and return to their chairs. There is not a trace of hostility.* George *even starts picking up the objects they were throwing at each other during the "fight."*

George: This is what it would look like if we believed in violence. But we do not believe in violence. You want a beer?

Peter: Actually, that would be nice.

George: Alice, get us some beer, would you.

Alice *gets up to get the beer.*

George: Did Alice already tell you about …

Peter: Yeah. About the hotels …

George: I see … Basically, my problem's name is "copyright." Copyright is a relatively recent invention—a few hundred years at the most. It clearly didn't exist before the invention of the printing press, and I am convinced that it won't be around for much longer.

Peter: How much longer do you give it?

George: Ten years maximum. Copyright is the main reason why the world today is filled to the brim with crap that calls itself art. Every even minimally gifted nincompoop has a chance today to make tons of dough or even become famous because of copyright. So everybody and their brother makes art as if the world were on fire. And you know the worst thing about it all? That even people who under normal circumstances wouldn't even dream of making art because they have nothing to say, do what? They make art! Which is more or less my case as well. But all of this will go to hell, because sooner or later it won't be possible to protect all this self-indulgent crap with copyright. Protecting against the theft of art will end up being more expensive than making the art itself. People will simply stop paying for books, music, movies, and so on. You make art?

PETER: No.

GEORGE: Excellent. Even though you of all people actually could. You have good eyes. You wear contacts?

PETER: No.

GEORGE: Excellent. The real art comes from God, and it would be laughable to charge money for it. The only reason I am suing these bastards over my stupid tunes is because I don't have a very high opinion of them myself. I wouldn't claim that they come from the Almighty himself. But as long as good old copyright exists, I will insist that the swine pay for the right to play that garbage of mine in their fucking elevators.

He inhales deeply—he is tired. In the meantime, ALICE, wearing a dressing gown, has brought the beer. Everybody drinks.

PETER: Thanks.

ALICE: *(To GEORGE.)* Did you tell him?

GEORGE: I told him about the hotels, Pussycat.

ALICE: I see. So did I.

GEORGE: *(To PETER.)* As you can see, this whole hotel thing is pretty darn complicated. And as if that weren't enough, I got myself this pussycat here, who needs somebody to watch us when we do it. What's your take on that?

PETER: To tell you the truth, I don't know.

ALICE: We tried to do it just us two, alone, but it was awful, ugh ...

GEORGE: We have been trying all sorts of things. We even thought that Pussycat here might be a lesbian, which wouldn't be the worst scenario—but she's not.

ALICE: I'm not.

GEORGE: But it is awfully difficult to find somebody to watch us. You'd think it would be easy, but it's actually damn difficult. Have you ever noticed people's eyes here? No? They are burnt out, dead. We wouldn't mind if they were mad. Mad eyes are fine with us. But here, peoples' eyes are simply burnt out. They are set deep in the face, like ... cherries in some sort of dough.

PETER: What kind of dough?

GEORGE: The kind of yeasty dough that rises and gradually swallows everything in it. We need somebody with eyes right up front, eyes that one can see. Somebody like you.

In the meantime, ALICE takes off her dressing gown, revealing sexy underwear.

ALICE: He's really got beautiful eyes.

GEORGE: Are you getting hot?

ALICE: I am.

GEORGE: Bitch in heat!

ALICE: Don't call me a bitch!

GEORGE: Sorry, Pussycat.

He drags ALICE onto a sofa offstage. They start making love. The audience can't see them, but from the expression on PETER's face and from the sounds of ALICE's moans it can well imagine what is going on. PETER doesn't know how to react, but when he tries to look away, ALICE starts screaming.

ALICE: That bastard's not watching us!

Bravely, PETER turns their way again and watches. After a while they both achieve a tremendous orgasm. GEORGE starts dressing. He is tired and he can barely walk. He takes out a wad of money and wants to give it to PETER. PETER refuses.

GEORGE: Thanks, you were a great help.

PETER: No, really ... I was just watching.

GEORGE: Come on, take it. It's not easy to find someone to watch us. You have inquiring eyes.

ALICE: Should you ever feel lonely, just bang on the wall again.

As they are leaving, they again reaffirm their satisfaction with PETER.

ALICE: He is goood.

GEORGE: Yeah. He is good.

ALICE and GEORGE leave. PETER stands alone looking at the money in his hand. Never in his life has he earned money in such a way. Music.

PETER makes his bed out of boxes filled with about fifteen years' worth of newspaper clippings from his mother. He is about to lie down to sleep. At that moment the blanket on his improvised bed slowly begins to rise all by itself. Peter notices and starts. He runs to the phone and dials a number.

PETER: Jeanette ... This is Peter.

We see JEANETTE on another part of the stage in a nightgown. She is sleepy.

JEANETTE: Are you completely out of your mind?! It's three o'clock in the morning.

PETER: Something just happened to me. My blanket came alive. I'm sort of in shock. I need to hear a real human voice.

JEANETTE: Peter, I don't think that you should call here anymore.

PETER: Wait! Jeanette, I am not making this up. I am thinking of you constantly, day in day out, and maybe I'm losing my marbles ... I am now seriously considering having myself sent to you as a package ...

JEANETTE: What package?

PETER: By mail.

JEANETTE: Now, that would be romantic ... certainly much better than the hair thing.

PETER: Do you still want to marry Alex?

JEANETTE: Yes. Good night.

PETER: Jeanette, please, I need to hear something nice.

JEANETTE: Call another time.

PETER: But I need it now, I need to hold your hand, I'm scared that strange things are happening around me ...

JEANETTE: But it's not what's happening around you. It's what's inside you, Peter.

PETER: That's exactly what I am scared of, that it's inside me.

JEANETTE: There you go. It's inside you. Good night.

Lights up. Enter FATHER looking around PETER's studio.

FATHER: I haven't been here for a while. This is a nice place you have.

PETER: Mom was telling me that you never go out.

FATHER: I don't, but I had to leave the apartment for a while. Your mother behaves like a madwoman. She keeps moving things from one room to another ... she keeps looking for things. She hustles and bustles all over the place. I'm scared for her. She takes things too seriously; she carries the weight of the world on her shoulders. It's bad.

PETER: She's concerned about you. She told me you hid the phone.

FATHER: Oh well ... She's concerned about you too.

PETER: Oh well ...

FATHER: Hmm ...

FATHER opens a bottle of beer, which he brought along. He pours himself a glassful, and with his palms frees a few additional bubbles from the bottle.

FATHER: There was one thing I meant to ask you. The last number you dial—does the phone remember it?

PETER: It depends on what kind of the phone you have.

FATHER: Assuming it's similar to the one we have at home.

PETER: How similar?

FATHER: Pretty similar.

PETER: You mean exactly the same?

FATHER: Well ...

PETER: If what you are saying is ...

FATHER: It's the same phone.

PETER: In that case, I think that your phone does remember the last number. Why do you want to know?

FATHER: Well … It's nothing important. I'm not a technical genius. You know me. *(He drinks some beer.)*

PETER: I have a question for you, too. Is it possible for your own blanket to sort of peek at you all by itself?

FATHER: Well … If it's a perfectly normal blanket … then no, that wouldn't be possible.

PETER: I thought so.

FATHER: Right … and is there a way to dial the number again?

PETER: Your phone has this "R" button. When you push it, the phone redials the last number.

FATHER: You just push the "R"?

PETER: Right. That's what I'm saying.

FATHER: This "R"?

To PETER's great surprise, FATHER pulls out the missing phone from his bag.

FATHER: I have it with me, just in case … Can I plug it in here?

PETER: You can use my phone.

FATHER: This one has the number in it …

PETER: What number?

FATHER: The last one. It belongs to someone who may need help.

FATHER plugs in the phone. He hesitates, and practices his introduction before dialing the number.

FATHER: Good afternoon. This is Hanek speaking … Good afternoon. Hanek speaking.

PETER watches him intensely. He realizes that his father has really gone mad. Finally FATHER pushes the "R" button, and the phone dials SYLVIA's number. We see SYLVIA on another part of the stage working on a clay sculpture. She picks up. During the conversation, PETER quietly removes himself.

FATHER: Good afternoon. This is Hanek speaking.

SYLVIA: Good afternoon.

FATHER: We spoke recently … about a week ago.

SYLVIA: Ah, you must be the insurance guy?

FATHER: No … I am the one, who you thought was somebody else calling …

SYLVIA: Somebody else?

FATHER: Martin.

SYLVIA: Which Martin?

FATHER: Your Martin. You thought it was him calling, but it was me.

SYLVIA: Who "me?"

FATHER: Me. Hanek.

SYLVIA: So you, like, dialed a wrong number?

FATHER: Well … more or less.

SYLVIA: I get it. But how come I didn't recognize that it wasn't his voice.

FATHER: You wouldn't let me talk.

Pause.

SYLVIA: And now, you're calling because … why?

FATHER: I only wanted to find out if you are OK.

SYLVIA: You mean if I am in the same shape I was in last time?

FATHER: Yes.

SYLVIA: No. I'm fine. I just had a little crisis. That could happen to anybody.

FATHER: You wanted to swallow pills.

SYLVIA: Pills? Really? You're kidding me? *(SYLVIA takes a sip from a water bottle and spits it on the clay.)*

FATHER: What was that noise?

Sylvia: I moistened my clay.

Father: Is somebody with you? Am I disturbing you?

Sylvia: No. I'm just in a good mood, so I make art.

Father: Well … I guess I should be going.

Sylvia: Wait … Was I crying on the phone?

Father: Well … Not much.

Sylvia: I really hated myself for crying in front of Martin. Actually I am glad it was you. It's not like I wanted to cry in front of you, but … you know what I mean …

Father: How about the dog?

Sylvia: What dog?

Father: Charlie.

Sylvia: What's with him?

Father: It must have been horrible for you.

Sylvia: What…?

Father: I thought he was run over by a car.

Sylvia: Is that what I told you? I made it up.

Father: *(Sadly.)* I see.

Sylvia: I am sorry I lied to you, but I wanted to move that little bastard to tears …

Father: Well … I was moved by it.

Sylvia: You were moved?

Father: Well …

Sylvia: I am so sorry.

Father: Don't worry. I liked being moved.

Sylvia: That's very nice of you … that you know how to be moved.

Pause.

FATHER: Well … I guess I should be going … I am glad that you are OK, that Charlie is OK …

SYLVIA: Why don't you come by one of these days?

FATHER: I don't think so. Well … I guess I should be going. Goodbye …

FATHER hangs up, unplugs the phone, and leaves. Enter MIDGE and PETER. They are watching the blanket, now on the floor in front of them.

MIDGE: Is this it?

PETER: Right.

MIDGE: When did it happen?

PETER: Last night. First I thought it was a dream, but I was wide awake. I was pinching my hand like crazy. It lasted for about five minutes. Then it played dead again.

MIDGE: Nothing since?

PETER: Nothing.

MIDGE: Did it talk?

PETER: No. It just kept sort of peeking at me.

MIDGE: In any case it looks like you have a serious problem here.

PETER: I sure do.

MIDGE: One shouldn't underestimate these things.

PETER: Could it be from alcohol? I really wouldn't like to give up drinking because of that. It's the only thing that's keeps me from going under.

MIDGE: It all because you are without a woman. That's why you are going nuts. I knew I was over the edge when my sink started winking at me.

PETER: But I do have a woman.

MIDGE: Jeanette?

PETER: Right …

MIDGE: Sure you do.

Peter: I know it's inside her somewhere. Our relationship is still there.

Midge: "Relationship"?

Peter: Granted, we may have a sort of a strange relationship ... one might not even call it a ... relationship, but somewhere inside she still likes me.

Midge: She is marrying Alex.

Peter: It's just out of spite. That's the worst thing about women. They do things out of spite, and then there's no turning back. I see you fixed your sink.

Midge: I'm definitively done with that nonsense.

Peter: But the vacuum hose looked pretty promising.

Midge: Look, when you are without a woman, then no matter how much you try to explain why, or how many platitudes you blabber about it, the basic fact is always the same: you are without a woman. But when you are with her, then you travel to another world. Then you are in contact with the Creator of the Universe.

Peter: You are in contact with the Creator?

Midge: Annie resurrected me.

Peter: What Annie?

Midge: She is beautiful, young! And she loves me.

Peter: Wait a minute, that's the stupid girl who does your shopping, right?

Midge: Not stupid. We live together now. Tonight we are going to see a ballet. You could come with.

Peter: Ballet? You've never seen a ballet in your life.

Midge: I started because of her. She'd explain the meaning of different steps and positions. *(Demonstrates different gestures and positions.)* Jealousy, wedding, baby. She leads this tremendously cultured life, so we go out almost every night. And I am being very generous with her. I don't want her to keep cleaning houses like some sort of a cleaning woman.

Peter: But she is a cleaning woman, isn't she?

Midge: She is an angel. She is a genius, a Goddess! I want a train to cut off her legs so that I could carry her in my arms! You see, I am mad, but I don't mind. I pay her lost wages. You'd be surprised how much money a cleaning woman makes …

PETER: So what do we do with the blanket?

MIDGE: I'd prefer you not leave it here.

MIDGE picks up the blanket and gives it to PETER.

MIDGE: As far as I am concerned, the blanket is a sign.

PETER: What sign?

MIDGE: What's the first thing that comes into your mind when you hear the word "blanket"?

PETER: Bed…?

MIDGE: There you go.

PETER: It's a sign that I should buy a bed?

MIDGE: It is a sign that you should find yourself a normal woman.

MIDGE leaves. Enter ALEX.

ALEX: I expect you not to call here anymore. You are a bad influence on Jeanette. I am very serious about her.

PETER: Jeanette is too insane for you. You have no idea what you are getting yourself into.

ALEX: We have a very nice relationship.

PETER: And we have this very nice unwritten agreement. Or maybe it's only a sort of a nasty habit. Whenever one of us does something crazy, like for example cutting off your aunt's hair, then the other one has to do something even worse. Do you know what I mean?! That's how it worked when we were together, and that's how it still works.

ALEX: I don't know whether she told you about it, but our first meeting was arranged by the hand of providence. As opposed to yours.

PETER: Our first meeting was completely ordinary, which is exactly what made it beautiful.

ALEX: I firmly believe in those things. The world might be full of madmen like you, but there still exist a few islands of happy coincidences. These are moments when God reaches into our life and turns it in the right direction. That night I was walking down the street, it was very late ... I passed a phone booth, and suddenly the phone starts ringing. I hesitated for a moment, but I summoned my courage and I picked up the receiver. There is something like ... incredibly magical in it, right? A lonely street at night, a lonesome phone booth, and in it a ringing phone. Do you know who it was?

PETER: Jeanette.

ALEX: Right ... How did you know? Anyhow, she misdialed. Coincidence. We talked for a while—just normal, everyday stuff, but something ... ignited between us.

PETER: Let me guess—a spark.

ALEX: Exactly, a spark! She invited me up for a coffee, because ... now get this—and this is yet another "coincidence"—she lived nearby! The entry gate was locked; she came down to open it ... Here is the bill for the wig. *(He gives PETER a receipt for a new wig. PETER takes the receipt.)* We did it right in the elevator ...

ALEX leaves. PETER exits to the other side. SYLVIA enters with a modeling stand, clay, little side table, and a stool. FATHER watches her.

SYLVIA: If you want, I could sculpt your head from clay. It would be called: "An Unknown Man Calling a Woman On the Verge Of a Nervous Breakdown."

FATHER: What would I have to do?

SYLVIA: You'd just come by a few times. I don't know what your time situation is like.

FATHER: I have enough free time, it's not that ... but I am ... bashful.

SYLVIA: You saved my life. Without you I would have swallowed the pills and died.

FATHER: Can I think it over first?

SYLVIA: Are you afraid that I'm unstable? That you will get mixed up with someone psychologically unstable? All men are terrified by unstable women.

FATHER: I don't know much about women.

SYLVIA: Martin hated it when I was unstable. When I had to cry, I did it in secret and fast. In the end I managed to cry myself out in less then two minutes. I would sit down like this, and ... *(Suddenly she collapses and cries, maybe even moans.)* Martin, oh my dear, dear, dear Martin ... please don't leave me!!! *(Suddenly, completely matter-of-factly.)* See, that's want I learned from Martin. But don't worry, I am not unstable.

FATHER: It's more about me. I seem to have Alzheimer's disease, or maybe old-age dementia—I'm not sure yet. But in any case I do have something ...

SYLVIA: *(Offers him a joint.)* This is good medicine.

FATHER: This is medicine for old-age dementia?

SYLVIA: You bet.

FATHER takes the joint, examines it, and takes a drag.

FATHER: Did you know that I can't even startle any longer. For example, my wife tries to startle me, but I don't start. Not at all.

SYLVIA: Wow! She really startles you? What does she do?

FATHER: For example, all of a sudden she'll hit the table with her fist. Or she yells "whuff" But nothing happens. Because of that disease.

SYLVIA has to laugh at such an image. FATHER notices a business suit hanging over the back of a chair. SYLVIA spits water on the clay to moisten it.

FATHER: Do you live with someone?

SYLVIA: No ...

FATHER: I see a man's suit here.

SYLVIA: That used to be Martin's. I thought that if I put on his clothes I might somehow empathize with him.

FATHER: Really? And what did you find out.

SYLVIA: I found out that he doesn't like me.

FATHER: I see. And the one with polka dots?

SYLVIA: That one is mine.

FATHER: It's a lovely dress. Maybe if I put it on, I might empathize with you.

SYLVIA: I think it should be the other way, I should try to empathize with you.

FATHER turns. SYLVIA "barks" at him. FATHER has a horrible start.

FATHER: Jesus Christ!!!!

SYLVIA: You do start!

She seats FATHER onto the stool and starts measuring his face using a pair of special tongs.

SYLVIA: What did you do?

FATHER: You mean my profession?

SYLVIA: Yes.

FATHER: It's nothing I should brag about.

SYLVIA: Come on, out with it.

FATHER: I narrated weekly newsreels. Mostly in the seventies.

SYLVIA: Wow! Do you still remember some of them?

FATHER: It was just a bunch of communist nonsense. "Today, comrades, farmers mounted the harvesters," and stuff like that. You know.

SYLVIA: No I don't. Tell me more.

FATHER: I am ashamed of it ... It always bothered me that people associated my voice with the news from that time. When I retired, I tried to change my voice, but it didn't work.

SYLVIA: You have a lovely voice.

FATHER: Thank you. That's very nice of you to say so. Do you have something to eat?

SYLVIA hands him a plastic cup of yogurt, and continues working with her clay. FATHER watches her. At one point they look at each other.

FATHER: I remember this yogurt used to be sold in those handy little glass jars. Nowadays everything is in plastic.

He struggles with the cup, unable to peel off the lid. He keeps turning to SYLVIA even though she is modeling his nape, and needs to see him from behind. During the following conversation, SYLVIA continues to try to readjust FATHER's position.

FATHER: Slowly but surely, glass is on the decline. We have wine in wax-paper boxes, caviar in tubes, yogurt in plastic, milk in paper, and so on, but glass is nowhere to be seen. We used to be a glass-based culture; we could have entered history as a culture based on glass. But today, we are a culture of paper and plastic. The only things made of glass are light bulbs. Have you ever tried to put a bulb in your mouth? No? Neither have I. I'm afraid I'll get a cramp in my face muscles and won't be able get it out again.

SYLVIA: I can see that you care for glass a great deal.

FATHER: Do you remember what happened in ninety-three?

SYLVIA: What?

FATHER: Overnight, they introduced the Euro bottles. You remember?

SYLVIA: Not really.

FATHER: I am sure you will remember. It came absolutely out of the blue. All of a sudden the old beer bottles lost their return value; you couldn't bring them back. It was a shock. People would pave their garden paths with them. Some would even break them. Broken glass everywhere, shards. Thousands of injuries. Blood all over garden paths … *(Emotional gesture.)*

SYLVIA: I see.

FATHER: And after two years it was all over.

SYLVIA: What was?

FATHER: They did away with the Euro-bottles and came back with the good old beer bottles. Naturally because they were better. They had thicker glass than the Euro-bottles, and they had a better grip.

SYLVIA: So why did they even bother with the Euro-bottles?

FATHER: Because the whole thing was one big fraud. They wanted to revive the failing glass factories. It happened all over Europe. It was then that I first realized that something was wrong. *(SYLVIA starts crying silently.)* Basically everything is wrong. Somewhere around that time I stopped caring about what was happening around me. Somehow it even affected my family. I lost contact with people whom I cared about. With my wife, with Peter … I stopped buying newspapers …

SYLVIA: *(Suddenly matter-of-factly again.)* You don't read the papers?

FATHER: What would I read them for? They are full of anonymous news, and that's it. You could browse through them for hours and you wouldn't find out anything. *(He opens a newspaper and begins turning the pages.)* Nothing ... nothing ... nothing ... boring ... nothing ... and the Sunday magazine ... nothing either ... Here is something. They are writing about Peter, my son. No actually they don't ... he's written it himself. He is apologizing to some woman for cutting off her hair while she slept ...

SYLVIA: He cut off her hair?

FATHER: That's what is says here. What do you think about that?

SYLVIA is looking at the paper, coming very close to FATHER. Maybe too close. FATHER interrupts the intimate moment with his recitation. We hear the typical weekly newsreel music of the 1970s. FATHER climbs on the stool, and starts reciting the contemporary news. SYLVIA is excited and she sculpts FATHER's profile.

FATHER: In the course of his two-day visit in the Northern Moravian region, the General Secretary of the Central Committee of the Communist Party of the Czechoslovak Socialist Republic, Gustav Husak, along with the Party Secretary, Joseph Kempny, and the Chairman of the Governing Council the Czech Socialist Republic, Jaroslav Kotscharek, arrived in the city of Ostrava. In the morning hours the Comrades also visited the State Enterprise "Technoplast" in the neighboring town of Chropynie, where they took part in the festive launching of a new production line for artificial leather, which is being introduced into the market under the trade name BAREX. In the center for material surface preparation at the BAREX factory they witnessed the happy occasion of the workers celebrating the production of the millionth square meter of this poro-metric leather.

Music fades. SYLVIA applauds. She is euphoric. FATHER is embarrassed.

SYLVIA: That was beautiful. When did you do that?

FATHER: July 15, 1973.

SYLVIA: You remember the exact date?

FATHER: Somehow this one stuck in my mind.

SYLVIA: You could recite it at parties ...

FATHER: I don't know about that.

SYLVIA: It's sort of poetic, like a nursery rhyme or something.

FATHER: You think so?

SYLVIA: People have this sort of nostalgia for those times. There is a kind of ... tenderness in it ... I don't know how to say it ... Or maybe the tenderness is in you ...

FATHER drops the papers. Blackout. We hear the amplified sound of a blood-pressure gauge cross-fading into a real sound of the same on stage. Lights on. PETER is taking his blood pressure, MOTHER stands next to him.

MOTHER: Our family did not turn out the way I hoped ... I always hoped to see your name in the papers, but not like this. Did you really cut off some woman's hair?

PETER: It was a misunderstanding.

MOTHER: What I would like to know is, will you ever apologize to "us"?!

PETER: For what?

MOTHER: For disappointing us. Or do you think I should be happy with the way you live? I have no idea where we went wrong. We used to take you to the beach ... We bought you the best vitamins ... What are you doing?

PETER: I am taking my blood pressure.

MOTHER: You are taking your blood pressure? What's gotten into you?

PETER: I am not sure ... I may be sick.

MOTHER: You are sick, but it has nothing to do with your blood pressure. The other day I found an old notebook of yours filled with names. The handwriting is yours when you were a child, and your dad's. Does it look familiar?

She hands him the notebook. PETER examines it.

PETER: Those are the politicians that dad and I shot dead.

MOTHER: What are you talking about?

PETER: We used to go to see their motorcades on the way from the airport. And when they approached and went just by us, we shot them with our finger.

MOTHER: Is that how you and dad amused yourselves?

PETER: I took it seriously. Dad told me that if we shot them all, everything would turn out well in the end. We wrote down their names so that we wouldn't shoot any of them twice.

Mother: There you go. I know nothing about either of you. Maybe I never did. Maybe I just deluded myself my whole life. Do you know what he did yesterday? He put on my clothes. I walked into the kitchen, and there he was sitting in a chair wearing my dress that I bought twenty years ago in Bulgaria … I couldn't even recognize him.

Father enters, wearing Mother's dress from Bulgaria. He sits down with his beer, and, as is his habit, he forces a few additional bubbles from the bottle. Mother's story becomes a real stage action.

Father: That was a nice one …

Mother: Who is it?

Father: It's me.

Mother: I didn't recognize you. What is the meaning of this?

Father: Well … It's your dress.

Mother: I can see that it's my dress. Why are you wearing it?

Father: I was just trying some … thing …

Mother: What were you "trying"? *(She approaches him.)* David, I am giving you no more than two weeks. *(Pause.)* Could you please explain to me what it is exactly that you are doing?

Father: I thought that it might help me to empathize with you.

Mother: So you have the need to "empathize" with me?

Father: Yes.

Mother: By putting on my dress?

Father: Right.

Mother: For that, you would have to approach it from the inside out, honey-bunny. For that, you would have to feel the burden in here. *(She points to her chest.)* That blood I give … Take it off, and stop playing the fool. David, I am really concerned about you, scared. We have been living together for forty years; I gave you my best years, and I don't want to live to see your dementia.

FATHER: It occurred to me that we know nothing about each other.

MOTHER: Is that what "occurred" to you? And whose fault is that? Is it my fault? Is it your fault? No.

We simply don't know each other. But that most certainly is not a reason for you to wear my dress. *(Pause.)* What exactly do you need to know about me all of a sudden?

FATHER: *(Shyly.)* I wanted to know whether you love me.

MOTHER: *(As if this statement were THE symptom.)* David, David, I am coming to the conclusion that this is old-age dementia after all.

They leave. Music. A FEMALE DANCER on "stage" far upstage. In the "audience," with their backs to us, sit MIDGE, his cleaning woman ANNA, PETER, and a MAN. ANNA watches the ballet as if it were a thrilling TV show. MIDGE sits with his arm around her shoulders, and eagerly listens to her explanations. He watches the ballet and ANNA's reactions to it with an expression filled with love.

PETER: Did you see that?!

MIDGE: She fell.

ANNA: That's peripeteia.

PETER: Peripe … what?"

ANNA: The reversal in the plot. Duh! *(Pause.)* I hate people who go to see a ballet without knowing anything about it. Every movement has a meaning. *(Pause.)* I once dated a dancer. *(Pause.)* He taught me the language of the body.

Pause.

PETER: Can you dance Alzheimer's disease?

ANNA: There isn't anything you couldn't express by dance.

PETER: What's going on now?

ANNA: She is unhappy. *(Pause.)* Her boyfriend left her. *(Pause.)* He was an alcoholic. *(Pause.)* But she loved him in spite of it.

PETER: How do you do "alcoholic"?

MIDGE: Stop it.

PETER: I'm just asking.

MIDGE: Did you study ballet? ... You didn't, so shut up!

ANNA: Now she says that her heart is bleeding.

PETER: How do you do "heart"?

ANNA: *(Demonstrates a movement.)* Like this ...

PETER: But she did this ... *(Demonstrates another movement.)*

They bicker about the dancer's exact movement. The MAN in the audience can't hold back any longer.

MAN: Can't you move your conversation somewhere else?!

PETER: I'm sorry.

Pause.

ANNA: I'm just explaining things to him. He has no idea about ballet. But I am sure you know it well. Also, your seat is better. *(She climbs into his seat, virtually falling over him.)* You are a connoisseur. If you want I could clean your house.

MAN: I beg your pardon?

ANNA: I am a cleaning woman. Right now I clean his house, but if you want I could clean yours.

MAN: For Christ's sake ...

ANNA: I don't want to impose, but ...

The MAN gets up and runs away. ANNA, and then MIDGE, run after him. PETER is alone ... He starts repeating the ballerina's movements, getting more and more frantic until he falls on the floor. Lights up, the ballet is over. ANNA and MIDGE are watching PETER on the floor. Peter gets up apologetically and leaves.

ANNA: Is he like a ballet student, or what?

MIDGE: No way.

ANNA: I found him pretty strange.

MIDGE: He is kind of losing it. He hasn't had a woman for ages. There were times when I almost lost it myself ... I would lock myself in here and experiment with my vacuum cleaner ... But it's all history ... Because of you.

ANNA: But really, there are so many things you can express by movement.

MIDGE: Absolutely.

ANNA: Do you know the oldest ballet in the world?

MIDGE: No. Let's go to bed.

ANNA: It's a Native Indian dance. If his wife left him, the Indian would dance it. Well, in those times it actually meant that his wife died, right? They found the dance in one of those cave paintings.

MIDGE: One day we could travel there to see them.

ANNA: It's called "The Dance of the Abandoned Indian." It's only a couple of basic steps ...

She demonstrates.

ANNA: This step means "the heart." This one is "blood." When you put them together ... like this ... it means that your heart is bleeding.

MIDGE: Absolutely. Why don't you take off your shirt?

He starts to undress.

ANNA: Just wait. Now this is "death" ... Go on, try it.

She forces MIDGE to repeat the movements. MIDGE is quite clumsy.

ANNA: This is "eyes," and this ... this is "eyes filled with sadness." Ok, all together now. Ready?

MIDGE: Oh, darling.

ANNA: The reason for the dance was, basically, to keep dignity in a moment of great despair. Go on.

MIDGE dances according to her instructions. He is getting better.

ANNA: Here you go. That's much better.

Suddenly MIDGE stops.

MIDGE: Why are you teaching it to me?

ANNA: Because ... I'm not coming tomorrow.

MIDGE: Are you busy?

Anna: Well, you see … I won't be coming anymore.

Midge: Wait a minute … What do you mean you won't…? But what about our future?! What about our relationship?

Anna: What "relationship"?

Midge: I love you.

Anna: Basically, you're sleeping with me, and you pay me for it.

Midge: But I don't pay you for it!

Anna: You don't?

Midge: I pay for your lost wages.

Anna: What do you mean?

Midge: So you don't need to clean peoples' houses.

Anna: *(Thinking hard.)* Oh, I thought you paid me for sleeping with you.

Midge: Oh my god … Annie! Please don't do it … You and I together—it's a miracle.

Anna: *(Thinking hard.)* Really?

Midge: Sure thing! I put an ad for a cleaning woman, and it was you who came. You are an angel, a messenger from God …

Anna is confused, she doesn't really understand.

Anna: Maybe I'll call you one of these days.

Midge: Sure thing. Call me anytime, Annie, darling …

Anna kisses Midge on the forehead and leaves. Aggressive Music. Midge starts dancing the "Dance of the Abandoned Indian," which gradually turns into a love dance, a sort of "mating ritual" with his ceramic sink. He approaches the sink as if it were a sacrificial victim, picks it up, and carries it offstage. Suddenly we hear a noise—something horrible has happened.

Midge: *(Offstage.)* Aaaaaaaaah…!!!

Midge staggers onto the stage. The bottom of his shirt is bloody. He is holding the wound on his belly, moans, and crawls to the phone. He dials.

MIDGE: Peter … I'm dying, help! … Annie left me … Don't call her that! … What neighbors? … No, I can't call back later. I'm bleeding! … No, I am really bleeding; I don't mean it as a figure of speech … I mean concretely, I am dying! Please come here, I need to tell you something.

He hangs up. Peter runs into MIDGE's apartment. He sees what's happening.

PETER: Did she try to kill you?

MIDGE: No, why?

PETER: So what's all this blood?

MIDGE: I was dancing the "Dance of the Abandoned Indian." The sink came loose, and …

PETER: I told you!

PETER examines the ceramic shards of the sink.

PETER: Somebody's tampered with this.

MIDGE: Probably Annie. She didn't approve of my experiments. I think she was jealous of the sink.

PETER: Do you have any bandages around here?

MIDGE: Forget about bandages. I'm dying. Listen to me!

Peter goes to look for bandages.

MIDGE: When a woman like her leaves you, it's as if an angel has departed.

PETER: *(Offstage.)* She was awful.

MIDGE: It's not just that a woman leaves you; it's like God is trying to tell you something. And this is clearly a sign from God. He is telling me: "I gave you a chance, and you fucked it up. I am finished with you."

PETER: *(Offstage.)* But she was a cow.

MIDGE: "I sent you my angel, the best angel I had. But you fucked it up, and that's the end. No more chances for you." That's the worst thing about women—God talks to us through them … They are part of God's language.

PETER comes back with a roll of toilet paper.

PETER: I found some toilet paper.

MIDGE: When a woman leaves you, it means that you fell from God's grace. I am not a believer, but this is really hard to bear. This would be a blow even for a strong man, but for a weakling like me it's fatal.

PETER begins to unroll the toilet paper to use it as an improvised bandage, but he notices there is writing on it.

PETER: Look at this, there is some sort of list here … some names, things … it goes on and on. Is it some sort of a poem or something?

MIDGE: Give it to me …

PETER: This is like a real poem.

MIDGE: No … I was just bored sitting on the pot once, so I started to write down a list of all the objects that women have thrown at me.

They go through the long roll of paper examining it.

PETER: It's a pretty long list.

MIDGE: What would you expect?

PETER: But it seems that some things are missing …

MIDGE: Which ones?

PETER: Don't tell me that no woman has ever thrown a screwdriver at you?

MIDGE: Roll on.

PETER: Right, I see … here … a crescent wrench, screwdriver … Well I guess I better stop here. It could be a pretty good poem, though. Listen, don't you have anything here I could use for a bandage?

MIDGE: Just let me die.

Peter begins to drag MIDGE towards the door.

MIDGE: What are you doing?!

PETER: I'm bringing you to the hospital.

MIDGE: I can't go to the hospital like this.

PETER: And how would you like to go there? You've lost gallons of blood.

MIDGE: They'll laugh at me.

PETER: Who cares? *(He continues dragging him across the room.)*

MIDGE: It's going to be a terrible embarrassment. I can already see the headlines: "A late-afternoon masturbation session slipped out of John M's hand," "Ill-fated Hand-job," "Thirty-two-year-old John M. from Prague became the tragic victim of his own self-gratification..."

PETER: We'll tell them you fell through a glass door.

MIDGE: Nobody falls through a door like this. I'd have to have cuts on other body parts. I once saw a guy tossed out of a bar through a glass door. He had cuts all over his stomach, but also on his hands and arms.

PETER. So what do you want me to do?

MIDGE: If you want to bring me to the hospital, you have to cut my hands.

PETER: Are you totally out of your fucking mind! I'm not going to participate in your perverted plans!

MIDGE: I'm not afraid. Do it! Hands, cut my hands! Cut me before I bleed to death!

PETER is about to do it, but he hesitates. He holds a piece of broken sink in his hand looking at MIDGE.

PETER: I can't do it. I never did anything like this; I can't just cut you to pieces.

MIDGE: Do it gently. Just take the shard, and gingerly pull it across my hand.

PETER puts the shard on MIDGE's hand, and is about to make a very careful move with it. In that moment JEANETTE enters.

JEANETTE: *(Screams.)* Aaaaaah.

PETER jerks, and makes a humongous cut across MIDGE's hand.

MIDGE: *(Screams.)* Aaaaaah! Shit, you cut off my arm!

JEANETTE: What going on? Jesus Christ, are you two doing those stupid rituals of yours again?

PETER: He cut himself on the sink.

JEANETTE: Midgie, what happened to you?

MIDGE: Please, don't call me "Midgie."

JEANETTE: Where did you cut yourself?

MIDGE: Here, on my hand … mostly.

JEANETTE: So why are you bleeding from your belly? Did you call the ambulance?

PETER: No. He's ashamed to go to the hospital.

JEANETTE: You, of all people, are ashamed?

MIDGE: I don't want people to think I'm crazy.

JEANETTE kneels down to MIDGE.

JEANETTE: *(To PETER.)* Get the elevator.

PETER calls the elevator. They move MIDGE into it, JEANETTE pushes the button, and the elevator begins to go down.

MIDGE: What are you gonna tell them was the cause of my death?

PETER: You were killed by women. Just like most other guys.

JEANETTE: For crying out loud! What woman ever tried to kill you?

PETER: I know of one.

MIDGE: There was one that really almost got me. *(He pulls up his shirt.)* You see this scar? Stabbing wound.

JEANETTE: Where is she now?

MIDGE: Still locked up. Locked up, the bitch.

JEANETTE and PETER sit down on the floor next to MIDGE. The atmosphere calms down. JEANETTE smokes. MIDGE passes out, but from time to time he comes to and moans. His occasional moans accentuate the following dialogue between JEANETTE and PETER.

JEANETTE: I wanted to tell you … the thing you made up with the blanket … I thought it was really charming.

PETER: I didn't make it up. It really happened.

JEANETTE: This is why I like you—all these crazy ideas of yours. *(She strokes him gently.)* In spite of everything that's happened, I wouldn't want to lose you as a friend.

PETER: That's very nice of you.

JEANETTE: Sometimes I remember when we were together. It wasn't so bad after all ... We used to visit your folks. Does your mother still give blood?

PETER: All the time.

JEANETTE: And how's your dad?

PETER: He's seeing another woman. She does his head in clay.

JEANETTE: I remember how he would force those bubbles from his bottle. I used to say to myself, as long as he manages to force up at least two of them, we will be fine.

PETER: Maybe he should have managed three.

JEANETTE: Will you kiss me?

PETER: I don't think this is a good idea. Jeanette ...

JEANETTE embraces him tightly. They kiss, until PETER frees himself from her embrace.

PETER: I should pay you for the wig.

JEANETTE: There's no hurry.

PETER: I have some money right now ... I'm sort of moonlighting a bit ...

JEANETTE: Where?

PETER: Just, like ... at my neighbor's.

JEANETTE is immediately suspicious. MIDGE moans and groans.

JEANETTE: What do you mean, "at your neighbor's"?

PETER: There is a musician living next door. He's a nice guy.

JEANETTE: And...?

PETER: Well ... he has this girlfriend who needs somebody to watch them when they make love.

MIDGE passes out again.

JEANETTE: And what's your role in it?

PETER: I am the spectator.

JEANETTE: And they pay you?

PETER: Right.

JEANETTE: Come on Peter! Nobody would pay you just for "watching."

PETER: It's a job, just like any other.

JEANETTE: I really doubt that!

PETER: But it's true.

JEANETTE is shocked.

JEANETTE: It's true, yeah? OK. So listen, I also have something to tell you.

PETER: I'm not sure I want to hear it.

JEANETTE: Oh, you do. It's quite interesting. When we broke up, it sort of broke me too. I kind of lost it a bit, and I started sleeping around with all kinds of characters.

PETER: I know I don't want to hear it.

However, in the tight elevator there is no escape from JEANETTE's stories.

JEANETTE: Do you remember the phone booth in front of my apartment?

PETER: You mean our phone booth?

JEANETTE: Suddenly you call it "our booth." It's a perfectly normal public phone booth. I wrote down the phone number, and late at night, I would look out the window, and when a decent looking guy would pass by, I'd call the booth.

PETER: By phone?

JEANETTE: Of course by phone. Duh ... Well, most of the guys would pick up.

PETER: Sure.

JEANETTE: You'd pick up too. There is something magical in it, and you men are so susceptible to things like that. A lonely street at night, a lonesome phone booth, and in it a ringing telephone. You think that it must be nothing less than the Creator of the Universe, who at this very moment wants to tell you something.

MIDGE moans quietly.

PETER: I get it. So what did you do?

JEANETTE: I'd pretend that I'd dialed the wrong number, which the guys of course found awfully romantic. We would talk for a while, and then I'd invite them up for a cup of coffee at my place. Mostly we did it right in the foyer or in the elevator.

PETER moans. MIDGE also moans.

PETER: Uuuuuuuh ...

JEANETTE: Some of them caught on pretty fast, and gave me money for it, but some really bought it.

PETER: How many were there?

JEANETTE: About twenty.

PETER: Uhmmm. In what sort of a time span?

JEANETTE: Well, in a sort of a short time span. I was looking forward to telling you all about it, but somehow it slipped my mind or something.

PETER: Come on, Jeanette! I know for a fact that you've made it all up.

JEANETTE: I didn't.

PETER: Alex told me a different version.

JEANETTE: Alex was one of the guys. He was one of the dumber ones, who didn't get it. Actually, he was the only one who didn't get it.

PETER: And that's why you want to marry him? Did you tell him about this?

JEANETTE: No.

PETER: Of course not. Because the whole thing is made up.

JEANETTE: It is not. I could tell you the details ...

PETER: Sure. Tell me the details! Come on!

Jeanette: OK … If that's what you want … here we go …

Midge comes to. It is as if their conversation woke him up.

Midge: This is a long elevator ride. What's going on?

Jeanette: We are not moving. We are stuck, Midgie.

She pushes the button, and the elevator starts moving again.

Intermission

Lights up. Alice and George. Alice holds up a soda-siphon bottle in George's face. She is packing her belongings in suitcases and bags—she carries stuff from place to place, and there is a general sense of her agitation.

Alice: I can't believe you did something so horribly tasteless.

George: It was the only reasonable thing to do.

Alice: Reasonable??!! You find it reasonable to stand up in the middle of a court room after the verdict and spray the entire court with a pressure bottle?!

George: With a soda-siphon bottle.

Alice: How would you like it if somebody did it to you?!

George: But they DO do it to me. My whole life they've been doing it. Can't you understand it? This state is urinating on us from hundreds of siphon bottles every day. And we are just standing there, in the stream of piss, and say that it's raining and that the sun will come out again … Did you see the judge's eyes? They were completely burnt out.

Alice: They were not burnt out.

George: No? So how were they?

Alice: Her eyes were filled with pity.

George: Well, I didn't notice that.

Alice: They all had eyes like that. When you finished your little "presentation," everything went quiet for few seconds. Like after some sort of an explosion. In that silence, I looked at the people you sprayed. I expected to see hate or shock, but instead I saw eyes filled with pity. They were sorry for me, because they knew I was with you.

George: You can't take them seriously. They were not real women. They were judges. Magistrates.

Alice: I don't want people to pity me because I live with you.

George: Are you ashamed of me, Pussycat?!

Peter enters.

Peter: I heard some noise. I thought you might need some help.

George: Not today. We had the trial, and …

Peter: Did you George: That depends how you look at it. I personally did.

Alice: Do you want to know what our "winner" did? He "victoriously" stood up, and sprayed the entire panel of judges with his own urine from a pressure bottle.

George: Soda-siphon.

Alice: I thought I'd die of shame! All of those festively dressed people, the stenographer, oak paneling on the walls … I could like totally feel the presence of justice in the air …

George: The presence of what?!

Alice: But you get up and pull out of a bag this spraying device of yours!

Peter: There are plenty of people would do the same.

George: It's quite easy. A dash of urine, a little CO_2 gas, a smidgen of despair, and you're ready to go.

Alice: I see. You men always need to stick together.

George: Pussycat had hoped I'd win.

Alice: I thought that you'd fight …

George: But I did fight. That's exactly what I am trying to explain.

Alice: You should have hired a lawyer. Prepared for the trial, or something. But the only thing you prepared was this …

George: I attacked from behind. Like a guerrilla. *(To Peter.)* Do you know how to keep a woman?

Peter: I tried it only once. I couldn't do it.

George: I started to write a book about it a long time ago.

Alice: You never told me about that.

George: You wouldn't like it. *Memoirs of an Old Guerrilla.* Basically it had no real story to speak of. It was more sort of a running list, something like, "What Are the Things One Is Willing To Do In Order To Hold Onto a Woman?" Plus or minus five-hundred pages. Well, I stopped writing on page twelve. You make art?

Peter: No.

George: Excellent. The main recipe for holding onto a woman was based on staying in open political opposition against the state. That, however, doesn't work any longer, so I stopped. Nobody admires you today because you are in political opposition. That's why Pussycat here is leaving me. Which basically means that it's sort of over for you, too.

Peter: But you were a pretty good couple.

George: Thanks. In a sense, I brought my own nakedness to the altar of our relationship. My sexual life is a satellite that circles around me without my own doing. But one thing is supremely important. My girlfriend must not ever be ashamed of me. I remember the times when women would never be ashamed of us. We were persecuted, we were poor, we never knew what tomorrow would bring, but women admired us for it. They stood by us at all times, like … lighthouses.

Alice: What kind of "lighthouses"?

George: The kind we saw on those little islands in Greece. I forget their name. We bumped into that nice fisherman there … His eyes were a little like Peter's … *(He breaks down.)* Pussycat, oh shit! Were you ever unhappy with me before?

Alice: I thought you were wonderful.

George: *(To Peter.)* There you go. In the old days no woman would leave you just because you didn't succeed at something. People say that the main difference between now and the Communists is more cars, or that we are free to travel abroad. However, the fundamental difference is that our suffering brings us neither inspiration nor the admiration of women anymore. It's possible that we were dissidents only because women found it attractive. It's hard to keep those two apart. But on some level, because of that, we believed that God was on our side. It's quite possible that we took our favor with women for God's grace, but I see no problem with that. In any case, the most difficult thing is to remain true to yourself even if women don't like it.

ALICE leaves. GEORGE is exhausted, and is about to leave as well.

PETER: Those twelve pages. Do you still have them?

GEORGE: What twelve pages?

PETER: About how hold onto a woman.

GEORGE: I meant it as a figure of speech. All I have is couple of notes. *(He goes to retrieve several pieces of paper and gives them to PETER.)* Here, you can finish it yourself. *(GEORGE is about to leave, but suddenly he remembers something.)* And give my regards to your dad. He's a good man.

PETER: You know him?

GEORGE: He's got your eyes. He came by a few days ago, but you weren't home. Somehow, Pussycat felt like doing it exactly then and … well … whatever. Bye.

GEORGE leaves. Music. PETER stares at the notes. Enter MIDGE with an inflatable swimming pool armchair.

MIDGE: When you moved me in the elevator … I had a vision.

PETER: It was a coma, not a vision.

MIDGE: No, it was a vision. It was a vision of God.

PETER: What did he look like?

MIDGE: Like a sort of a big blue armchair. He said: "John …" He didn't call me Midge or Midgie, or something like that, but "John … the relationship between man and woman is something sacred. I created you as a small human being with two hands, two legs, one head, and plenty of problems, but I gave you the yearning for something higher. Something that is bigger than you. Remain open."

PETER: And what did you say?

MIDGE: I said, "OK, I'll be open."

PETER: And what did God say?

MIDGE: God said: "I am sending you one of my angels."

PETER: Another one?

MIDGE: "The best one I have. All of my previous angels weren't real angels. But this time I am sending an angel who is real."

PETER: You mean to say that you've found yet another woman, right?

MIDGE: Well, It's not ... exactly a woman ...

PETER: Come on, is it a woman or is it not? Is it a guy?!

MIDGE: It's ... you know ...

PETER: Who?

MIDGE: It's a bit ... sort of ... a mannequin ...

PETER: It's a ... What did you say?!

MIDGE: A mannequin.

PETER: You live with a mannequin?! Where is it?

MIDGE: Over there, in my bedroom ... Eve, you can come out now!

PETER: What do you mean "Eve, you can come out"?!

MIDGE goes to his bedroom.

MIDGE: I know that she can't come out. I just said it like that. You see, I'm carrying her. *(To the MANNEQUIN.)* Look Eve, Peter is here.

He carries in the MANNEQUIN, covered by a cloth.

PETER: Where did you get her? You stole her, didn't you?

MIDGE: I bought her. I can show you the receipt if you want.

PETER: I'm sure you can! *(He unveils the MANNEQUIN. He is horrified.)* Midge, fuck, you are much worse off than before.

MIDGE: Don't call me Midge!

PETER: You are completely screwed up. This thing is plastic! Made out of man-made material. Does it talk? Does it walk? Come on! And you said: "look" to it!

MIDGE: I know that she's not alive. I use her to practice communicating with women.

PETER: Use me to practice, if you need to, but not …

MIDGE: I didn't want to risk yet another unsuccessful relationship. All the other women … I felt ridiculous with them.

PETER: And now you are not ridiculous, right?

MIDGE: I need to regain my dignity. Eve is helping me.

PETER: Wouldn't you prefer a woman?

MIDGE: Women are too dangerous for me.

PETER examines the MANNEQUIN. He touches the earrings in EVE's plastic ears.

PETER: How much were they?

MIDGE: I'm not stingy with things like that.

PETER: Look, I don't mean to pontificate here … You know that I'm the last one to judge people or to tell them how to lead their lives. But you should realize that if you are living with a mannequin, then you are in serious trouble.

MIDGE: But I've always been in trouble. In the last seven years I've had eighteen girlfriends. I loved them all. On average they all left me after about three months. I've never been unfaithful to any of them, which by the way is something I can't say about them.

PETER: All right. I know it's not fair, but that's life. You deserve a wonderful woman, just like the rest of us, but you can't find her. You might never find her, but that's how it is. You have to get over it. You must fight! We simply cannot allow women to drive us into madness.

MIDGE: Fine. But this arrangement has simply too many pluses … Eve doesn't bother me with her problems. She really listens to me. She is great in bed … She doesn't lie, doesn't cheat on me. She has no past. She can't compare me with other guys. And, she can't leave me. *(He thinks.)* The other advantage is that I don't need to go out with her.

Peter: Right, that's a good thing.

Midge: Though tonight actually I thought I'd take her to a party.

Peter: Jesus Christ!

Midge: We've been together since I came back from the hospital, and I haven't taken her out yet.

Peter: If I were you, I wouldn't do it.

Midge: You don't think so?

Peter: Some people might think that you are crazy.

Midge: Why?

Peter: Because normal people don't go to parties with mannequins.

Midge: I couldn't care less what normal people do. *(He wants to take the Mannequin but Peter stops him.)*

Peter: Right … Neither could I, but I still think that you shouldn't take her anywhere. Leave her here.

Midge: Why?

Peter decides to accept Midge's way of thinking. He is trying to come up with an acceptable argument.

Peter: I think … she'd be bored.

Midge is very surprised.

Midge: Peter … It's only a mannequin. Mannequins can't be bored.

Peter: Right … sure … I completely forgot.

Midge: No, I get it. You are afraid …

Peter: I'm afraid … Right … Maybe I should take her to my place. I'd take care of her, and you could come to see her whenever you felt like it.

Midge: Why would I leave her with you?

Peter: Just an idea.

Midge: I'll think about it.

Both walk over to the edge of the stage. They watch, and eventually become part of the party that is about to begin. Enter SYLVIA. She talks to an audience of six to ten people who are slowly filling the stage during her speech.

SYLVIA: Good evening, friends. Tonight, I would like to introduce to you my friend ... well a friend of mine. He is a man who recited ... I mean, narrated the weekly newsreels in the 1970s. And to this day, he still remembers them all. For me, there is a sort of tenderness in it ... or maybe the tenderness is in him. Ladies and Gentlemen, David Hanek ...

Spot on FATHER ... Party guests applaud.

FATHER: *(To SYLVIA.)* Should I do the one about Haná?

SYLVIA: Do the one about the leather.

FATHER: Not the leather one. *(To the party guests.)* I never spoke to more than two people at one time. I also never imagined that I would speak the following sentences again in a place other than a sound studio with a microphone. At that time I was embarrassed about it. Today, I am embarrassed again. For different reasons. So in the end, not much has changed. With the exception that I suffer from Alzheimer's disease ...

He discovers PETER and MIDGE with his MANNEQUIN in the audience.

PETER: ...Hi.

FATHER: ... Hi.

Music.

FATHER: In the course of his two-day visit in the Northern Moravian region, the General Secretary of the Central Committee of the Communist Party of the Czechoslovak Socialist Republic, Gustav Husák, along with the Party Secretary, Joseph Kempn, and the Chairman of the Governing Council of the Czech Socialist Republic, Jaroslav Kotscharek, arrived in the city of Ostrava. In the morning hours the Comrades also visited the State Enterprise "Technoplast" in the neighboring town of Chropynie, where they took part in the festive launching of a new production line for artificial leather, which is being introduced into the market under the trade name BAREX. In the center for material surface preparation at the BAREX factory, they witnessed the happy occasion of the workers celebrating the production of the millionth square meter of this poro-metric leather.

Tumultuous applause. Sylvia kisses Father on his mouth. Father introduces Sylvia to Peter.

FATHER: This is Sylvia. This is Peter.

SYLVIA: Hi.

PETER: Hi.

SYLVIA: I'll leave you two alone.

SYLVIA leaves.

FATHER: I'm glad you could make it. You want a beer?

PETER: Thanks.

FATHER: I brought some along with me since I didn't know what sort of party this would be. I don't know anybody here. Sylvia brought me here.

PETER: Right ... Sylvia.

FATHER offers PETER some beer, and both sit down on the floor.

PETER: How's the head coming?

FATHER: Good. It's almost finished.

Pause.

FATHER: I dropped by a few days ago, but you weren't home.

PETER: You should have called first.

FATHER: I wanted to surprise you.

PETER: Oh well ...

FATHER: Fortunately, those people who live next door were there ...

PETER: You mean the neighbors.

FATHER: You seem to know each other, am I right?

PETER: A little.

FATHER: Nice people.

PETER: That's right.

FATHER: If there is something you need to tell me … you can, you know.

PETER: Sure.

FATHER: But if you don't want to tell me anything, you don't need to … You know what I mean.

PETER: Sure. *(Pause.)* If you need to tell me something, you could tell me too …

FATHER: Oh well …

PETER: Oh well …

FATHER: You don't have it easy, you know.

PETER: You don't have it easy either.

FATHER: That's life.

PETER: If you ever need some help, just …

FATHER: Well, there is one thing I would need help with.

PETER: What is it?

FATHER: It's something that's been on my mind for a long time. Do you think that you could fit a light bulb in your mouth?

PETER: What…?!

FATHER: I always wondered about it.

PETER: Why don't you just try it?

FATHER: I am afraid that I would get a cramp in my face muscles and wouldn't be able to get it out again.

PETER: Let's try it now.

FATHER: Now is not too good.

PETER: Why not?

FATHER: There are no bulbs around here.

He looks around, and sees two naked light bulbs hanging from the ceiling.

Father: We'd have to let them cool down.

Both get up, each goes to one of the bulbs and unscrews it using his handkerchief. Lights out. Prolonged silence.

Father: Can you see anything?

Peter: No.

Father: I forgot where I put my beer.

Peter: Here.

Clinging of glasses. Then suddenly, as if the darkness had freed them to do so, both start talking furiously, almost stepping on each other's lines.

Father: Do you go to those neighbors for money?

Peter: They forced me to take it. They didn't pay you?

Father: Why do you take it?

Peter: I live on it.

Father: You go there regularly? I can't believe it.

Peter: It's over now.

Father: And what's with that hair?

Peter: And what's with that Sylvia of yours? You sleep with her? She's thirty years younger than you.

Father: It's platonic.

Peter: You have plans with her?

Father: She's doing my head. That's all.

Peter: And why do you wear Mom's dresses?

Father: I only wanted to annoy her a bit.

Peter: But you have to admit that it's not normal.

Father tips over his beer. Everything quiets down.

FATHER: *(Speaking very slowly.)* The way Mom and I live is one thing. Mostly, there is nothing much to be done about it. But we two shouldn't lose contact. Your mother is right about that.

PETER: Let's do it.

FATHER: I don't want to end up a lonely man.

PETER: Now.

We can only hear some incoherent mumbling and huffing from the darkness as they attempt to put the light bulbs into their mouths. We can only imagine what is really going on. Enter SYLVIA. She is tipsy. Lights come up and discover FATHER and PETER. Both turn their backs to her.

SYLVIA: Are you boys having a good time? David?

FATHER: Hmmmm.

PETER: Hmmmm.

SYLVIA: OK. I'll be next door.

She leaves. Lights out again. Peter lights a lighter. He takes the bulb from his mouth. FATHER is trying to do the same, but it doesn't work—he has a cramp in his face muscles. PETER is trying to help him. He starts to massage his FATHER's jaws. They freeze in that position. Music. Enter MOTHER in a nightgown.

MOTHER: I had a dream. A soldier came to me. He was Russian. Fought in Chechnya. He was wounded and he died. He got a blood transfusion, but it didn't help. He told me he could have survived. But he died, because my blood was not good enough. *(We see the SOLDIER in another part of the stage.)* He said:

SOLDIER: "I died, because your blood wasn't good enough, young lady."

MOTHER: He called me "young lady."

SOLDIER: They pumped it into my veins, but there was no strength in it. I became weak, and I was horribly cold, and then I died. That's what I wanted to tell you.

MOTHER: And then the dream continued. My husband came to me, and he said: "I have another woman. She resurrected me. I have become interested in the world around me again. Because of her, I've started to like my voice again."

FATHER with the bulb in his mouth is still on stage. SYLVIA takes over from PETER massaging FATHER's jaws.

MOTHER: But he didn't know what to do with it. He said that he only pushed the "redial" button, and now he didn't know what to do, he said. The woman advised him to put on my dress, and he did it, and indeed he managed to empathize with me. And he was surprised to find out I didn't like him the way he thought I did. We lived together for forty years, and he knew nothing about me. Nor I about him. Then the dream ended. WHOOF!!!

Everybody runs off. Only PETER stays. Enter JEANETTE. She starts cleaning up after the party, rolling up a small carpet, etc.

JEANETTE: In the end, everything turned out fine ... The way you destroyed Auntie's hair ... well, finally she decided to get a buzz cut, and she looks great. So I'll return the money for the wig. She even got together with some guy ... finally gained some confidence ... And how about you? You live with someone?

JEANETTE is about to put away a carpet, but PETER blocks her way.

PETER: Don't put it there ... It's not where it belongs.

JEANETTE: It doesn't? Well, you go and put it in its proper place.

PETER leaves with the carpet. JEANETTE immediately discovers what PETER was trying to hide. It's the MANNEQUIN.

JEANETTE: What is this?

PETER: A mannequin.

JEANETTE: I can see that. *(She finds the MANNEQUIN suspiciously good-looking.)* Where did you get it?

PETER: It's Midge's. He left it with me for a while.

JEANETTE: Midge? What would Midge do with a mannequin?

PETER: I don't know. He hangs his clothes on it before he goes to bed.

JEANETTE: Right ... Knowing our Midgie, I'm sure that's all he does. Give me a break!

PETER: Well ...

JEANETTE: And how about you? What do you do with her? You hang your clothes on her too, before you go to bed?

PETER: Sure ...

JEANETTE begins a more thorough examination of the MANNEQUIN. One may even say, a rather intimate examination.

PETER: Hey, hey, hey…! What are you doing to her?

JEANETTE: It's a mannequin, right?

PETER: Granted … but at the same time you should follow at least the basic rules of decency.

They play a tug of war with the MANNEQUIN. Then JEANETTE grabs the MANNEQUIN between the legs. She finds out that down below, it is "fixed."

JEANETTE: Are you two sleeping with her?!

PETER: Ah, come on!

JEANETTE: You asshole!

PETER: Is this why you came here? To call me an asshole?!

JEANETTE: If you are sleeping with this plastic cow, than you are an asshole.

PETER: And even if I am, what business is it of yours? Actually, I just remembered … yes, I live with a mannequin … but you live with Alex.

JEANETTE: I don't any longer.

PETER: You don't?

JEANETTE: I told him everything.

PETER: Everything what?

JEANETTE: Everything. How we got to know each other … how the whole phone booth thing was not exactly a coincidence, and so on. He had a fit and we broke up. That's why I came to see you.

PETER: Why?

JEANETTE: Because I want to live with you.

PETER: And what about those twenty guys?

JEANETTE: I did it because of you!

Peter: Right. I forgot. I am really touched. *(He begins to sniffle.)* Eve, did you hear it, she did it all because of me.

Jeanette: All right. So I am a whore. But I'm not a pervert.

Peter: And I am a pervert, but I'm not a whore.

Jeanette: What do we tell the kids?

Peter: What kids?

Jeanette: Our kids.

Peter: Do we have kids?

Jeanette: No. But we could have them, if we lived together.

Peter: But you and I can't live together.

Jeanette: Right. We can't.

Peter: Right. We can't.

Jeanette: But it's a pity, isn't it?

Peter: I guess so.

Jeanette: Where did we go wrong?

Peter: I don't know.

Jeanette: I don't think it was because of the twenty guys.

Peter: I don't know.

Jeanette: Or because you cut off Auntie's hair.

Peter: I guess not.

Jeanette: Or because you barfed all over my uncle's dog …

Peter: Now, wait a minute …

The shared memory of that little incident brings them nearer to each other. Pause. Peter points to Mannequin.

Peter: I don't sleep with her.

JEANETTE: You don't?

PETER: No. I took her here to keep her away from Midge.

JEANETTE: Aha.

PETER: We just talk a bit.

JEANETTE reacts.

PETER: I pretend she is you. I practice my behavior towards you using her.

JEANETTE: Practice it on me, if you need to, but not …

PETER: I'm not ready for it yet. But when I am with Eve, I do think of you. I know that my behavior towards you hasn't always been good, but I am working on it. Once I learn how to behave better, I'll call you …

JEANETTE: Right … You call me then …

She is leaving uneasily.

PETER: *(Maybe a little bit to himself.)* I'm not ready yet. I'm not ready yet.

Enter MOTHER. She is dressed in FATHER's clothes—corduroys, shirt, etc. In her arms she carries FATHER's clay bust. She puts it on the table.

MOTHER: I decided to stop whimpering. It's not the end of the world. Things like that happen. I came to tell you that you don't need to worry about me.

PETER: Right.

MOTHER: *(Presenting the bust.)* What do you think? It's a perfect image … talented woman, this … her name is Sylvia. She could do our whole family. A sculpture called: "A Family That Went Wrong." I don't mean it against you.

She winks at him conspiratorially. PETER stares at her clothes.

MOTHER: Do you know what they did to me? They refused to draw my blood. I have been going there for the last twenty years, and suddenly the nurse says: "Miss Hanek, you don't need to come anymore. Your blood doesn't fulfill the requirements for blood donations." So I ask her, if she knew what was happening in Chechnya. Whether she was sure that they didn't need my blood over there … You'd draw my blood, wouldn't you?

Peter: Me? Why me?

Mother: Because you are my son. You could draw it, and we would send it somewhere. Just you and I. To someone who needs it. Oh, don't worry, I am just joking. I'm not crazy. Besides, you couldn't even draw my blood, because my red cells turned thin from all that agitation with your father. That's perfectly clear. Can you see what I am wearing?

Peter: Dad's clothes.

Mother: Exactly! You probably think that I am already deranged, and that I put them on by mistake?

Peter: Well . . .

Mother: I wear them on purpose. When you dress in somebody else's clothes, you learn how to empathize with them. Did you know that?

Peter: I didn't.

Mother: So now you do. I need to find out what Dad should do with that Sylvia. I am worried about him. He's never had another woman, he's not used to people, and I'm not sure he can make the right decisions. What would you advise him to do?

Peter: Well . . .

Mother: I even put on his underwear. So as not to get a cold in my liver.

Peter: Mother, please!

Mother: After all those years, I don't seem to be able to advise him in such a fundamental situation. Advise me how I should advise him.

Peter: Dad is leaving you for another woman, and all you worry about is that you are not able to give him good advice. You are strange, Mom.

Mother: But he is leaving me exactly because I can't advise him.

Peter: Dad is leaving because you don't love him. That's why our family lost all its meaning. Because it was based on "good advice."

Mother: And what do you want to base a family on?

Peter: On love.

Mother: Oh for crying out loud!!! How can you base a family on love? Do you love me? Does your dad love me? You men constantly prattle on about love, but you know nothing about it. Am I a cynic? No, I'm a practical human being. For me a family is a place where you can come and ask what you should do in life. Family is supposed to give you an answer. Don't you remember how much good advice I gave you and your dad?

Peter: I don't.

Mother: You don't?

Peter: No.

Mother: So what do you remember?

Peter: I remember that it was always strange at home. That nobody ever came to visit, because you advised him to break up with all his friends …

Mother: That's what I advised him, that's true. Because they used him.

Peter: … how he started to be afraid of his voice, because you advised him to do those newsreels … You made him into a lonely human being, and now you want to play the sensible woman who understands him.

Mother: Look at that. Aren't we a chatterbox.

Peter: Normal people are supposed to complement each other, but you've always sort of subtracted from each other.

Mother: *(Calmly.)* Because you never liked us. That's exactly what I am saying.

Peter: I did like you. But each of you separately. Together you were a nightmare. And that won't go away even if you put on dad's clothes or if you keep on giving blood …

Mother: You think I'm a bit of a nutcase, don't you?

Peter: That's not …

Mother: Well, you aren't completely together either. These people that you surround yourself with, those blankets that come alive … all this is a sign that you are at a kind of crossroads. You are at a crossroads, my dear, that's for sure.

Peter: OK. So I am at a crossroads, so what!

MOTHER: But at a pretty big crossroads.

PETER: Well? And you aren't at a crossroads?!

MOTHER: I might be, but you don't know what road to take, you have no plans. You are thirty years old, and you don't know what will happen in a year, in two years, you don't have any lasting relationships with people, all you have is this deranged Midge character ... oh yes, don't interrupt me ... he is deranged that Midge of yours, you don't have a woman, you don't know what to think, you don't know what to believe, you drink ... You cut off people's hair, and then you publicly apologize for it. People use you, because you are like a sponge that absorbs everything around it, and this is all because of your eyes. You have your father's eyes. He had the same problem—people used to confide in him all the time, but I helped him to get rid of it. Otherwise he would have ended up just like you. Like a tired man-sponge, who refuses to take his old mother's blood, when she begs him to do it.

MOTHER begins to rummage through the boxes with newspaper clippings. There really are very many of them.

MOTHER: And those boxes of clippings of yours are also a symptom of something, if I may say so.

PETER: They are all from you.

MOTHER: Nonsense. How could I have ever managed to send you so many?

PETER: You could.

MOTHER: I sent you some, that is true, but the rest ...

PETER: What's with the rest?

MOTHER: You must have mailed them to yourself, my dear.

PETER: Come on, mom.

MOTHER realizes that it is possible that over the years she actually might have sent them all.

MOTHER: Why didn't you throw them out?

PETER: I simply didn't. I don't know why not. Because I am a sponge. I drink, so I don't have the strength to get rid of them. I don't have a woman to help me with them! I don't have a mother to advise me how and where to get rid of them.

Pause.

MOTHER: You didn't throw them away, because after all you do love me.

PETER: Not really. I don't.

MOTHER: Come, don't be afraid to say it. You love me.

PETER: Of course I love you.

Pause. Maybe they even touch or embrace somehow. However, MOTHER immediately changes the mood by returning to the theme of her blood donation.

MOTHER: If you really love me, then take my blood. I brought the tools with me …

PETER: I don't know how to do it, Mom! I can't just take your blood like that.

MOTHER: Why not? What are you good for, if you can't even take your own mother's blood.

PETER: Is that something any parent's child should know?

MOTHER: Of course. What did they teach you in school?

PETER: In what school?

MOTHER: I don't know what school you went to. A school. This is the only thing I'm asking you to do. To take your own mother's blood. We won't tell anybody. It will be our little secret. We'll hide it, and if there's ever a need for it anywhere, we'll have it …

PETER: But nobody needs your blood! Didn't they tell you clearly enough?! Nobody wants your blood or your advice.

MOTHER: Don't you know what is happening in Chechnya?!

PETER: What Chechnya?

MOTHER: They need blood in Chechnya!

PETER: But nobody would send it there.

MOTHER: We'll send it ourselves.

PETER: And how, might I ask?

MOTHER: I don't know.

PETER: Right. I can already see us chartering a flight to Chechnya just to carry your half-pint! Or should we maybe take the car?

The fight calms down. MOTHER takes out her paraphernalia.

MOTHER: Hurry up.

PETER: You really brought it with you?!

Glorious, majestic Music slowly fades up. MOTHER empties one of the cardboard boxes filled with newspaper clippings. She sits in the box, and PETER is about to take his mother's blood.

MOTHER: Your hands are shaking; you should get a drink. That's an early symptom of Parkinson's. You don't have Parkinson's do you?

PETER: You don't have any veins there.

MOTHER: I don't have any veins? And how do you think it circulates?

Their conversation fades under the Music. PETER takes his mother's blood. When he is finished, he pushes her offstage in the box. PETER returns holding a syringe with his mother's blood. He stops by the pile of newspaper clippings on the floor.

PETER: *(Even though he doesn't look at her, he is probably speaking to the MANNEQUIN.)* I yelled at her. I shouldn't have done it, I know. But she drove me up the wall. I am at a crossroads. So what. So I'm at a crossroads … Who isn't at a crossroads, after all? A human being needs either advice or love, that's pretty clear. But: Is it possible to get the wrong advice from a person who loves you? That is the question. Or: Is good advice from someone who doesn't love you worth it? That's another question. Too many questions … In any case, the most important thing is to be true to yourself, even if women don't like it. I am sorry to trouble you with all these problems of mine.

EVE THE MANNEQUIN comes alive.

EVE: That is quite all right.

It takes a little moment before PETER realizes that the MANNEQUIN spoke. He does a double-take, and than he turns to her.

PETER: Did you just say something?

EVE: I said that it was quite all right.

Now, EVE even gets up. PETER is completely flabbergasted.

PETER: So … a mannequin … right …

EVE: I am not a mannequin.

PETER: What am I supposed to do?

EVE: I don't know. I am not here because of you. I have to speak with Midge.

PETER: I haven't really seen him for quite a while.

EVE: In that case, I will go out for a while. May I take a walk?

PETER: You mean, like walking? By foot?

EVE: By foot.

PETER: Sure, sure … You take a walk.

EVE leaves. MIDGE bursts in.

MIDGE: Where is she?

PETER: Who?

MIDGE: I know everything. Jeanette called me! Where is she?!

PETER: Who?

MIDGE: Eve!

PETER: She's taking a walk.

MIDGE: I asked you about Eve.

PETER: And I am telling you. She's taking a walk.

MIDGE: Eve's taking a walk?

PETER: Yeah.

MIDGE: Jeanette broke her, right?! She thought you were having an affair with Eve, and she destroyed her. Is that it?!

PETER: It isn't.

Midge: You fought over her, broke her to pieces, and then you threw her away. Am I right?

Peter: No.

Midge: So where is she?!

Peter: Are you listening to me at all?! For the hundredth time, I'm telling you. She is taking a walk.

Midge: Listen, if you believe that Eve is taking a walk, then you are definitely over the edge. You should catch a cab to the funny farm right away.

Peter: You remember that blanket thing.

Midge: Sure.

Peter: How it came alive ... The same thing happened with Eve today.

Midge: With my Eve?

Peter: With our Eve ... I mean your Eve ... A situation occurred here, that Eve was originally a mannequin, but then she started talking and went out for a walk.

Midge: Right. And how about the blanket?

Peter: What blanket?

Midge: The blanket took a walk as well, right? And the chair, what did it say? Nothing? That surprises me. A "situation" like that, and the chair has nothing to say about it. The chair just sits here as if nothing happened.

Peter: You think I'm crazy, eh?

Midge: OK. I am going to take a walk as well. I'll be back in an hour, and if Eve isn't here when I come back, you are in for a surprise.

Peter: Wait! Don't leave me here. I've been traumatized. I can't stay here alone.

Midge: You've been traumatized?! You were supposed to take care of her, and now you've lost her ...

In that moment EVE enters. She smiles at Midge. It takes a moment for Midge to recognize her, and to admit to himself that something like that is actually possible.

Eve: Hi.

MIDGE: Hi. Did you just come back from a walk?

EVE: Yes …

Slowly they walk towards each other, they kiss, and they leave together. MIDGE waves goodbye to PETER. A trap door opens, and GEORGE climbs out. He is dressed in overalls with lots of pockets; in his hands are gas canisters and a lighted flashlight. He looks like Robert DeNiro in Brazil. *He flips up a sort of a metal construction and begins to measure it with his tape measure. His monologue is to PETER.*

GEORGE: Plenty of people kid themselves into believing that they are insane, but their secret is that they are completely normal. When you look around, you see plenty of would-be crazy people, but nobody who's truly mad. You know what I mean. You won't see anybody running up and down the streets in their underwear. Nobody who really is deranged, who's totally lost all their good old marbles. Plenty of people here want to be mad, because madness brings with it a state of complete freedom. Madness would allow them to behave honestly again. But they are out of luck, because that state simply isn't coming. Which is basically my case as well. I'd like to slip over that edge, and bear no responsibility for what I am about to do. But I don't think it will work out. Real insanity is as rare as genius or perfect pitch. I'm about to do an insane deed, but I'll do it fully conscious.

PETER: What are you planning?

GEORGE: Can't tell you. The majority of people won't understand it. Women won't admire me for it. So be it. I'm not doing it to win favor with women, or even with men. I am simply doing it, because I need to take justice into my own hands. And I am not even sure if God is on my side or not.

GEORGE packs up his tape measure, grabs the gas canisters, and leaves.

FATHER: *(In a spotlight on another part of the stage.)* Hi Peter. It's Dad.

PETER: *(Picks up the phone.)* Hi.

FATHER: I'm calling you …

PETER: Did something happen?

FATHER: No, everything is fine.

PETER: Is it because of Mom?

FATHER: Well … it's just a … sort of a trifle …

Peter: What's with her? Is she OK?

Father: She's had … sort of a small … accident …

Peter: Was she run over by a car?

Father: No, no. You always imagine the worst. Nothing like that. They basically found her … on Wenceslas Square …

Peter: Heart attack?

Father: No. She was running around …

Peter: She was running around in Wenceslas Square?

Father: Well … In my long johns … she was running around in them …

Peter: She went mad, didn't she?

Father: Not really. She was just trying to startle people …

Peter: What do you mean, "startle"?

Father: She barked at them.

Peter: With that "whoof" of hers?

Father: With her "whoof."

Peter: She's been running around Wenceslas Square doing her "whoof" at people?

Father: Right. But she's fine now. I was just thinking that maybe we should go visit her.

Peter: She's not at home?

Father: No.

Peter: So where is she?

Father: She's in a psychiatric clinic.

Peter: Jesus …

Music. Father and Peter leave. Enter Midge with a vacuum cleaner. He is getting rid of his old sexual aids. Alex bursts in. He is distraught, his face is flushed, and he is hyperventilating. Occasionally, he inhales and exhales using a paper bag.

ALEX: I'm finished. For a week now, I've been walking around that phone booth. I can't sleep. I stopped eating. My mind is like a roller-coaster … thoughts, memories of Jeanette … I tried to get drunk, but it didn't help. I should blow up that booth, but I'm not insane enough to do it. Maybe Jeanette would come back to me if I were crazy enough to blow it up.

MIDGE: Is that what she told you?

ALEX: She lied to me, but I still love her. Do you think I still have a chance?

MIDGE: Well …

ALEX: Maybe you could put in a word for me … I know. I talked badly about you. I said that you were a pervert, and a psycho, and stuff like that. But I didn't mean it. You know me. I only repeat what others are saying. I'm an imbecile.

MIDGE: Well, I wouldn't …

ALEX: Did you know that I was the only one of all the twenty guys, who actually bought it? I was the only one who believed that the whole phone thing was really an accident. What does that mean? How does it reflect on me? What does it prove?!

MIDGE: That you are a romantic.

ALEX: That I am an idiot.

MIDGE: Naïve romantic.

ALEX: I'm an imbecile. I always had a suspicion, but this definitely proved it.

He starts crying. Then he notices the vacuum cleaner.

ALEX: What's up with the vac?

MIDGE: I used to try stuff with it. You can have it if you want.

ALEX: You stopped vacuuming?

MIDGE: I never vacuumed.

ALEX: So why do you have it?

MIDGE: When you learn how to use it, it's almost like being inside of a woman. Do you want it?

ALEX: *(With an air of superiority.)* You really think that I would stoop that low? *(He breaks down.)* Jesus Christ, I couldn't stoop any lower! *(He grabs MIDGE's hand like a small child.)* When that phone booth thing happened ... when Jeanette and I first met ... it was such an incredible coincidence that I considered it a miracle. I couldn't explain it any other way. I became, almost a believer ... I know that the world is full of madmen like you and Peter, but at that time I suddenly had the feeling that maybe there still exist a few islands of happy coincidence where something or someone above us reaches into our life and turns it in the right direction. That's what I believed. I became a believer. And now, I don't know whether I should stop believing or not. What do you think?

MIDGE: Why are you asking me of all people? Women cheated on me, they lied to me, and they threw things at me.

ALEX: But in the end you managed. In the beginning with Eve, I thought you had really lost it. No sane person would ever sleep with a mannequin, right? To say nothing of taking her out to parties ... I was convinced you'd end up in an institution.

MIDGE: I know. It must have looked pretty strange. Didn't it?

ALEX: You bet it did. But now I see how well it works. You two have a beautiful relationship. It was a tremendous experiment, but you succeeded. You triumphed.

MIDGE: Well ... thanks.

ALEX: That must mean that the islands of happy coincidence do exist, right?

MIDGE: Maybe for you that happy island wasn't the phone booth, but the break-up with Jeanette.

ALEX needs to think about it for a while.

ALEX: Aha. *(Pause.)* So, you think it would be OK if I borrowed that vacuum cleaner?

MIDGE: Take it. I won't need it any more.

ALEX: Thanks.

He leaves with the vacuum cleaner. EVE enters, and leaves immediately with MIDGE. Music. We are now in a psychiatric clinic. MOTHER appears sitting on a chair. MIDGE, EVE, PETER, and FATHER enter. Each has brought her something in a glass bottle or a jar: mineral water and canned fruit. FATHER has brought a beer for himself, since there is no beer to be had in a psychiatric clinic. PETER has brought blood.

MOTHER: I am sorry for what happened. But I couldn't hold it in any longer.

Father: We brought you some canned fruit.

Mother: Thank you. That is very nice of you.

Peter: I brought you that blood.

Mother: Why are you whispering?

Peter: Sorry. How are you doing here?

Mother: I'm good ... Nobody expects any advice from me here. Nobody even expects me to say anything reasonable. That's what makes it so lovely here. But it has its darker sides too. Sometimes I have horrible depressions. I feel like jumping out of the window or swallowing sleeping pills. Of course that's how I felt even when I was still normal. But mostly it is quite pleasant here.

Everybody is introduced.

Peter: This is Eve.

Eve: Good afternoon.

Mother: Good afternoon. I am Peter's mother. I used to be relatively normal, but I went mad, and now I am a madwoman. But I find you very nice.

Eve: Thank you.

Mother: So what do you do?

Eve: I used be a mannequin in a department store.

Mother: You don't say. In which one?

Eve: In the White Swan. Department of women's clothing.

Mother: Did they hang clothes on you?

Eve: Yes.

Mother: How was it?

Eve: Actually, I don't remember it very well. Then he bought me, *(She points to Midge.)* and we began living together. At that time I was still a mannequin. Then I came alive.

Midge: Eve saved me. She opened my eyes.

EVE: He believed that women are angels. He saw God's messengers in them.

MIDGE: But now it's clear that it was different.

PETER: How?

MIDGE: My women were not messengers from God.

PETER: So what were they?

MIDGE: They were just perfectly ordinary women.

PETER is genuinely taken aback.

PETER: No kidding? That never occurred to me.

MOTHER: And you have a nice relationship now?

MIDGE: Yes. It was a miracle. It started as a perversion but it turned into love. That is extremely rare.

MOTHER: That's an interesting thing you say. In our case it was the other way round. It started as love, and it ended as madness.

FATHER: I wanted to tell you that I think we have a nice relationship. What happened with you will not change anything.

MOTHER: Yes. We do have a nice relationship.

FATHER: I love you.

MOTHER: You don't need to say it if it is not true.

FATHER: It is true.

MOTHER: You seem nervous. Are you in hurry?

FATHER: I have a performance. At the National Library.

MOTHER: What performance?

FATHER: The newsreels, you know.

MOTHER: The original ones?

FATHER: The originals. Somehow it caught on, media-wise ... I have quite a lot of offers. I even need to decline here and there.

MOTHER: I wish I could be there.

FATHER: I don't think they will let you out.

MOTHER: So do it here for me.

FATHER: This is not the best place ...

MOTHER: A short one, please ...

FATHER thinks for a little while, he prepares, and starts reciting. As opposed to the previous recitation however, the music now is very different. The choice of the music is up to the director, but it should be something in the style of Jocelyn Pook, so that the words can assume a different meaning.

FATHER: *(Slowly reciting.)* The festively decorated Moravian town of Haná was witness to a tribute to the honest work of our citizens, which is held in the highest esteem not only by the Party and the Government, but by our entire socialist society. As they ascended the main platform, the precious guests were greeted by tumultuous applause from the participants in the May Day parade. The Chairman of the Federal Assembly of the Czechoslovak Socialist Republic, comrade Alois Indra, ascended the stairs, and was seated in the place of honor next to the Chairman of the Southern Moravian Regional Committee of the Czechoslovak Communist Party, comrade Milan Mamula ...

MOTHER: Careful. Mamula was the Chair in Northern Moravia ...

FATHER: Did I say Southern Moravia? This never happened to me before, I apologize. Thank you. *(He continues.)* ... next to the Chairman of the Northern Moravian Regional Committee of the Czechoslovak Communist Party, comrade Milan Mamula, and the Ambassador Extraordinary of the Union of Soviet Socialist Republics to the Czechoslovak Socialist Republic, the esteemed comrade, Vasili Vasilievich Mackevich.

MOTHER watches FATHER. She is full of love for him. She takes his hand. Music up. Lights down/Lights up.

PETER is alone. He writes poems on the wall of the psychiatric clinic. Enter JEANETTE with a small TV in her arms. She puts the TV on the floor and watches PETER.

JEANETTE: You remember how you called me during the night? You know, when that blanket thing happened and you wanted to hold my hand. Well, I am here now.

PETER stops writing for a while, but then he continues.

JEANETTE: If ever you should feel that something strange is happening around you, I will help you.

PETER: It's not happening around me. It's happening inside me.

JEANETTE: Don't worry. There's nothing strange inside you.

PETER: Don't you know what's happening in Chechnya?!

JEANETTE: Peter, I am really scared now.

PETER: I'm scared, too.

JEANETTE: But I am scared that you'll do something stupid.

PETER: So don't be scared, OK?!

JEANETTE: Well, I am scared.

PETER: And what should I do about it?

JEANETTE: You need to start behaving normally ... you need to throw away all the newspaper clippings ... buy new shoes ... watch TV when you feel like it, listen to music ... and I will be with you whenever you need me ... Come on, you don't want to end up in the loony bin.

PETER contemplates the possibility. He comes to JEANETTE.

PETER: Whoof!

He sits down next to JEANETTE. They are not touching.

PETER: Why don't I have a TV here, by the way?

JEANETTE: Because you tossed it out of the window.

PETER: No kidding? Why did I do that?

JEANETTE: Because you were afraid that you wouldn't watch it.

PETER: And now. Am I not afraid any more?

JEANETTE: No.

PETER: Am I scared?

JEANETTE: You are not scared. Everything will be fine ... Everything will turn out fine.

Suddenly we hear FATHER's voice coming from the TV.

VOICE: In the late night hours of yesterday, an unknown suspect committed an act of arson in the Hilton Hotel in Prague ... The fire, apparently set in the elevator shaft, quickly spread into several stories of the building ...

PETER: Wonderful!

VOICE: The fire did not claim any victims; the damages however may reach several million dollars ...

Music. Flames start burning around PETER and JEANETTE. All women from the play appear upstage They are dancing. JEANETTE gets up and leaves. We see GEORGE running across the stage. He is coughing and choking. Gradually, everything calms down, and PETER is left alone amid the smoldering remains of the "hotel." He is picking up half-burned pieces of paper ... Enter his BOSS.

BOSS: Mr. Hanek, do you have a minute? Are you happy with your work here?

PETER: Yes.

BOSS: Your work hours are suitable?

PETER: Yes.

BOSS: So why do you want to leave us. Did you get a better offer?

PETER: I want to try writing poetry.

BOSS seems to be skeptical; he doesn't know what to think about this.

BOSS: Really?

PETER: I tried to lead a normal life, but it wasn't possible. Until now I suffered under it all. But from now on, I want to try to use everything that's happening around me as inspiration. Everybody I meet will become a poem.

BOSS: I see.

PETER: I already have some ideas ..."An Aging Composer with a Soda-Siphon Filled With His Own Urine" ... "A Woman, Mad With Grief, Calling a Phone Booth in Front of Her House ... Expressly Wishing to Make Sexual Contact." ... "My Father, After Forty Years of Marriage, Wearing My Mother's Dress..." I even have one about you.

BOSS: About me?

PETER: It's called, "A Boss Who Liked Little Boys But Did Not Throw Himself At Them, He Only Liked Them, That's All" ... *(BOSS shakes his head and laughs.)* ... "And He Shook His Head and Laughed" ... "And Told Everybody About It Who'd Listen" ...

BOSS: I'm not sure that a poem can have such a long title.

PETER: It's not a problem.

BOSS: OK. Well, let me hear from you when it's finished.

They shake hands. BOSS leaves. PETER is alone onstage. He takes the cardboard box that used to serve as his bed, and empties MOTHER's clippings on the floor. Then he gathers all the objects that he accumulated during the play: MIDGE's toilet paper with the long "poem," a vial of MOTHER's blood, his childhood notebook with the list of "shot" politicians, and the notes for "How to Hold Onto a Woman." He writes an address on the cardboard box. Then he climbs into the box and closes the lid over himself. He pulls his hands through the openings on the sides, and with a box tape machine he tapes himself in the box. Then he pulls his hands back into the box, and closes the openings behind him.

Enter two MAILMEN.

MAILMAN #1: Good morning. *(Pause. He notices the box.)* This must be it, I guess.

MAILMAN #2: Jesus, this is heavy.

MAILMAN #1: What did they put in it? Coconuts, or something. It's gonna rot anyhow before it arrives.

MAILMAN #2: *(Looking at the address.)* Some sort of a strange address ... Chechnya ...

MAILMAN #1: Oh well ... Coconuts to Chechnya. Let's go.

They carry the strange heavy package with the peculiar address away. Fade to black.

Push Up 1–3

ROLAND SCHIMMELPFENNIG

Translated from German by Melanie Dreyer

Push Up 1–3 premiered at the Schaubühne in Berlin, Germany, in November 2001, directed by Thomas Ostermeier.

CHARACTERS

HEINRICH

ANGELICA

SABINE

ROBERT

PATRICIA

HANS

FRANK

MARIA

A.

Heinrich: I work for a pretty big corporation. I sit downstairs, behind a glass window in the lobby, and everyone who works in the building walks by me. Our building is big, really big, sixteen stories, and next to me are monitors displaying images from the security cameras. We work in the central office in shifts, usually in pairs. During the night shift, we walk the building. During our nightly rounds, we check every room; we unlock and re-lock every single room. It takes time. The building is extensive, we have everything you could imagine: executive suites, conference rooms that always smell of cigarette smoke at night, an area for each department and sub-department, management offices, development offices, the artists' department, laboratories, and a giant computer room in the basement that stores data from all over the world: data from our branches in the U.S., South Africa, India. Next to the security monitors, I have my own little television set. Of course, that's not officially allowed, but no one says anything. Not even Kramer, who's with the woman who more or less owns the company. Kramer basically runs the place. I don't really know what she does. But when she comes by, I shut the TV off. Sometimes I even see the commercial for our firm on television—in this ad a man carries a woman over a huge puddle. Then there's a slogan and our logo. *(Pause.)* Seems odd to me. Like it's been stolen from something. In any case, the ad's been running for over a year now and it's time for a new one: maybe something completely different—somewhat more to do with me—or our products. I mean, I just don't get the connection. We usually work two to a shift. I'm often with Maria. Maria sees the ad completely differently. She likes it, but I'd rather have something with more action. I like action films. Or thrillers. Maria and I talk about a lot of the things that we see on TV during our shift. About lovers in a film, for example. I mean, in real life it's not at all like that. People don't just get together: it rarely happens that two people see each other and then bang they're in love—that never happens. Or like in our ad, a man in a park carries a woman over a huge puddle. When does that happen? Right? Isn't that right, I ask Maria, I mean, look at us. I'm not going to carry you over a puddle. And she laughs.

1.1.

An executive office. Angelica and Sabine sit across from one another.

Angelica: It's great that you're here. *(Short pause.)* I'm so glad. I was so curious how you—I'm so sorry that you had to wait ten minutes. This is really great.

Sabine: You don't have to reassure me. I'm not nervous.

Angelica: There's no reason to be nervous.

Sabine: Sure there is. But I'm not.

Angelica: No? I am a little.

Sabine: You?

Angelica: Yes, of course.

Pause.

Sabine: You can save it.

Angelica: What?

Sabine: All the pleasantries. We don't need to make small talk here.

Angelica: Is that what I'm doing?

Sabine: We both know the conflict that's here in the room.

Angelica: Perhaps we see things differently.

Sabine: You say that you're glad that I'm here.

Angelica: Yes—

Sabine: You say that you're sorry that I had to wait outside in the lobby with your secretary. But that's not true. You're not sorry. To keep someone waiting longer than five minutes is clearly an act of passive aggression. And you know that.

Pause.

Angelica: Okay. I hope my secretary made it clear why you had to wait. I had to—

Sabine: You're trying to fabricate a specific conversational climate here. You want to manufacture an atmosphere of friendliness, collegiality, and sensitivity that's totally inappropriate. You say you're nervous, although that probably isn't the case at all. You just say that to defuse the situation. But the situation doesn't need to be defused. It doesn't matter how you "see things." We obviously have conflicting interests here.

Angelica: Wait a minute. Hold it.

SABINE: No—

ANGELICA: Yes—

SABINE: It's absolutely—

ANGELICA: Stop.

SABINE: The course of this entire conversation up to now—

ANGELICA: Stop.

SABINE: *(Stands up, if she's still sitting.)* No—

ANGELICA: Sabine! *(Short pause.)* Can we begin to talk now?

Short pause.

SABINE: If you like. Go ahead.

1.2.

ANGELICA: Throwing coffee in her face was a mistake. Loss of control. But she deserved it. That piece of shit really deserved it. She sat there and tried to distinguish herself with impertinence. Tried to simply outplay me. Wanted to show her strength. Self-confidence. A little forced, but not bad at all. In her stupid blue suit. She probably has four just like it in her closet. No taste, just pretension. And success. Sat there and didn't touch her coffee, all upset that she had to wait ten minutes. Basically, I already knew when she came through the door. I just wanted to see her again. She sat across from me and astonished me with her audacity. Her unbelievable audacity to even ask for this appointment. How does she do that? How did she win him over—the way she looks? With her pathetic aura of know-how and ambition?

1.3.

ANGELICA: You're twenty-eight. That makes you the youngest department head in the entire company.

SABINE: I know.

ANGELICA: You have my complete confidence. Even though you've only been working for us for a year and a half. With no oversight from above.

SABINE: That's not true.

Angelica: No?

Sabine: No. Kramer regularly reconciles the productivity of my department against the standards, expectations, and requirements of the board. That results automatically in constant quality control.

Angelica: Yes. Right. The standards and requirements of the board of directors. How could I forget that. He does that. Kramer. Are you happy with this arrangement? It doesn't sound like it.

Sabine: Of course.

Angelica: Are you happy with Kramer?

Sabine: Yes. I—

Angelica: You can be completely open. The fact that Kramer and I are a couple shouldn't inhibit you in any way.

Sabine: My working relationship with Kramer is absolutely trouble-free.

Angelica: Trouble-free. Good.

Sabine: I'd like to talk now about your rejection—

Angelica: Wait, wait. I just want to be sure that we're coming from the same place. That there are no misunderstandings. We don't know one another at all.

Sabine: I highly doubt that there's a—*(Stops herself.)* Alright.

Angelica: You got your degree in the U.S., and following that worked for two companies in Japan, Korea, and Taiwan. Now you work for us supervising your own team of twenty people, some of whom are twice your age, and you produce the best numbers. Correct me if I say something that isn't true.

Sabine: No, no.

Angelica: You're a top employee. Kramer says you're efficient, reliable, and innovative. Truly impressive. Truly.

Sabine: Yes. And that's why I don't understand why you—

Angelica: Yes, yes.

Sabine: What?

ANGELICA: Yes, I know—of course. Not so fast. Coffee?

SABINE: No, thanks.

ANGELICA: You don't want any coffee?

SABINE: No, thanks—

ANGELICA: Are you sure?

SABINE: No, thanks. *(Nevertheless, ANGELICA pours two cups. SABINE doesn't touch hers.)* Please—

Pause.

ANGELICA: You think I simply do whatever I like here.

SABINE: And that's true.

ANGELICA: No. Forget that.

SABINE: I wouldn't know how

ANGELICA: Stop.

SABINE: No—

ANGELICA: Forget about the power structure of the corporate system. Here we're flexible and unorthodox. Like you. Performance is what counts. Or is that not your sense of things? *(Short pause.)* That wouldn't be very fair.

SABINE: Why are you telling me this? How can you talk about the power structure of the corporate system and claim that it no longer exists? Of course it exists. When you offer me a cup of coffee. When you allege to have confidence in me, which is clearly not the case. I work for you. You determine what I do. So—let's not deceive ourselves.

ANGELICA: Exactly.

SABINE: What?

ANGELICA: I said: exactly. Let's not deceive ourselves. Good.

1.4.

Sabine: I haven't had sex for two years. And I'm twenty-eight. I get up every morning at six o'clock. I take a cold shower and then eat breakfast. Usually fruit. In my bathrobe. With the television on. That's what I do every morning, except Sunday. Every morning I watch television from six-thirty to seven o'clock. The programming isn't very good at that hour, but I sit in front of it and think about nothing. Then I get dressed. I never put on what I wore the day before. Never. Although many of my things look alike. I have a lot of things. Clothes. I chose my apartment with that in mind. Closet space. There are two clothes closets in my current apartment. I have difficulty deciding what I should wear. It's a problem. I often change my entire outfit several times before I decide what I should wear. Until I finally make up my mind. It's not easy. It's agony. When I'm finally dressed, I style my hair and put on my make-up. My haircut's ok, there's not much I can do with my hair. Make-up is difficult, especially in winter when it's dark outside. Not too much. Only expensive brands. From Japan, for example. *(Short pause.)* When I'm done with my face, I take the elevator down to the garage. Now it's eight o'clock. Halfway there I stop and turn around. I ride back up. Because I feel awful. I can't stand it. I can't stand it. I unlock the two safety locks on my apartment door and go to change my clothes. I no longer like what I have on. I usually wear blue. I don't really like blue, except for maybe jeans or a sweater, but I usually wear blue, regardless. I grew into it, somehow, only wearing blue. Only buying blue when it came down to it. Everything that I buy is blue. So—color-wise, everything goes with everything else. Nevertheless, halfway down I turn around and then I change my clothes again. I change everything. My pantyhose, my panties, my bra. I feel ugly. I have to hurry, the clock is ticking, and I stand in front of the mirror in the hallway and think I look ugly. Finally, it's a little after eight-thirty; it's high time, I really have to go. I take the elevator to the garage again. I get into the car. I can't turn around again. It would be absolutely impossible to turn around again. Look in the rearview mirror. My make-up is repulsive. I don't like my lipstick. I'm at least able to put on new lipstick during a traffic jam on the highway. I can do my eyes later at the office. Just don't want to look cheap. I arrive at work and I have the feeling that no one sees me. That's good. That's terrible.

At nine-fifteen, I meet with my team. None of the women at the table wear blue. Except for jeans or a sweater maybe, but we rarely see that here. In our meetings. Many of them are ordinary. Really ordinary. Most of them. No one wears blue. *(Short pause.)* I look into the faces around the table and ask myself who among them got laid last night, and how often. Or this morning. While I took my cold shower. While I was watching television thinking about nothing. All of them, I think. Everyone except me.

1.5.

Angelica: You've made quite a career here. And, of course, you'd like to continue pushing up. I understand perfectly. *(Short pause.)* That's how I was. You're like me. Right?

Sabine: Perhaps.

Angelica: Sure you are.

Sabine: If you think so.

Angelica: We could be friends. No. We couldn't.

Sabine: Aha.

Angelica: You could act like it at best. Because you'd have that power structure in your head the whole time, and how you want to reach the top.

Sabine: This isn't about whether or not we could be friends. This is about nothing more than my qualifications, which you refuse to recognize. This conversation is absurd.

Angelica: Qualifications. Yes. *(Short pause.)* Odd that we haven't run into one another more often in passing. Have you ever been up here on the sixteenth floor?

Sabine: A few times.

Angelica: That's it? *(Short pause.)* In Kramer's office, I would guess.

Sabine: Precisely.

Angelica: Do you like it up here?

Sabine: Sure. Are you making small talk again?

Angelica: Precisely. *(Pause.)* You applied for Delhi.

Sabine: And you've rejected my application.

Angelica: Yes.

Sabine: For no reason.

Angelica: For no written reason.

Sabine: For no reason. With no explanation. Conversation. Or phone call. Nothing. That's why I asked for this appointment.

Angelica: Of course you did. You are, after all, the one who wants something.

Sabine: Which means—

Angelica: I knew you'd come.

Sabine: But you haven't given me any answers.

Angelica: Yes, in a minute. First, I wanted to get better acquainted with you. *(Short pause.)* Our center in Delhi is the heart of our development department.

Sabine: I've provided some important initiatives for the development department. Decisive initiatives. You shouldn't do me any favors. You should put me where I can be most useful to the company. In Delhi.

Angelica: But I wouldn't dream of sending you to Delhi.

Sabine: Why not?

Angelica: This isn't about being useful to the firm. No one expects that. This is about personal advancement.

Sabine. That's understandable. *(Short pause.)* What I don't like are your methods.

Sabine: My methods are extremely efficient, as you yourself said. The advantages for the company are clear.

Angelica: If I give you this job, it will mean I'm promoting you, short or long term, to the top of the company, to the executive level, because with the know-how that you could gather in Delhi, you'd become as good as irreplaceable to us.

Sabine: That would be true for anyone who got this job. That doesn't have anything to do with me personally. The way I see it, there are only two possible factors for your not trusting me: first, my age, and second, my gender. Didn't you just say that the internal power structure no longer exists?

Angelica: Yes, yes, sure. *(Short pause.)* But what if your own employees use this power structure?

SABINE: I don't understand what you mean.

ANGELICA: I mean exactly what I said: But what if your own employees use this power structure?

SABINE: Whom do you mean?

ANGELICA: You.

SABINE: Me?

ANGELICA: Yes, you.

SABINE: I have no idea what you're talking about.

ANGELICA: No?

SABINE: No.

ANGELICA: Kramer recommended that I send you to Delhi.

SABINE: Yes?

ANGELICA: Yes.

SABINE: Then give me the job.

ANGELICA: No.

SABINE: I'm clearly qualified.

ANGELICA: Could be.

SABINE: But—

ANGELICA: But you're not going to get the job.

SABINE: Why not?

ANGELICA: Because Kramer recommended it.

SABINE: I see—

ANGELICA: Yes.

Pause.

SABINE: You're married to Kramer. What's wrong with a recommendation from Kramer?

ANGELICA: *(Hesitating.)* Kramer.

SABINE: I want the job. You don't have anyone who would be better.

ANGELICA: Who says so?

SABINE: I say so. Kramer says so. Take a look at my resumé.

ANGELICA: *(Laughs.)* I thought you said take a look at my lingerie.

SABINE: What?

ANGELICA: Nothing.

1.6.

ANGELICA: My husband doesn't sleep with me anymore. Kramer. I'm XX years old. I get up every morning at six o'clock. I take a cold shower and then eat breakfast. Usually fruit. At the kitchen counter. In my bathrobe. With a towel around my head and slippers on my feet. So that I won't freeze and catch a cold. The little television set that we put in the kitchen is on. That's what I do every morning, except Sunday, and sometimes Saturday. I watch TV from six-thirty to seven o'clock. The programming isn't very good at that hour, but I sit in front of it and think about nothing. It's great. Then I start to get dressed and put on my make-up. I never put on what I wore the day before. Never. It used to take a long time before I knew what I was going to wear. It was an agonizing process every morning, until I was dressed. It still takes a long time, but back then I had no idea what I should wear—I just go shopping more often these days. That doesn't fundamentally change the problem, but it helps. At least temporarily. If I no longer know what to wear, I go shopping. Or I order something. But usually I go shopping because I need someone to help me. A saleswoman. Advice. I ask the saleswoman what looks good on me or what she'd recommend. I let the saleswoman dress me, as it were, and sometimes it goes really well. But not often. The good thing about expensive stores is that the saleswomen often have better taste than in the cheap ones. But not always. It isn't that I fail to notice that the saleswoman has no taste. I don't know how I recognize it. Maybe the eyes. Or the hair. Or the teeth. Once I start shopping, I buy a lot. I never look for just one thing. When I shop, I look for an entire new wardrobe. Skirts. Blouses. Suits. Jeans, for which I'm usually too fat, or only feel too fat, as the saleswoman insists. Dresses, shoes. Scarves. Belts. Ridiculous stuff. This shopping spree gives me a sense of security. The security that I can buy things, that I can have things I really need. Every two months, I take two sacks to the Red Cross center. Or

I give the things to my neighbor's two daughters. But of course they don't fit. They only take them to be polite. These sacks often contain things I've never even worn. Things that I knew I'd never wear when I bought them. Sometimes. Things I'd hang in the closet in the evening, planning to wear them the next morning, and that I no longer liked the next day. Because nothing went together. Light-green sweater. Gold summer sandals, for which I suddenly couldn't find the right skirt. Double-breasted jackets with shoulder pads. Silver Lurex sweater for special occasions.

These are slip-ups. A loss of control. These are critical lapses. But one only realizes that after the fact. Someone once recommended that I buy everything in one color. Because it would be easier to combine items. But which color is right for me? I can't begin to decide that. So I put something on that I'll end up giving to the Red Cross in a maximum two months' time. And then I style my hair and begin to put on my make-up. It's about eight. Kramer gets up and disappears into the shower in his own bathroom. My haircut's ok; there's not much I can do with my hair. Make-up is difficult. Especially when it's dark outside. Don't apply too much. Just what's necessary. Only expensive brands. From Japan, for example. *(Short pause.)* I get to work around nine, Kramer next to me—that's a requirement. Everyone looks at me. No one looks me in the eye, but everyone looks at me. I used to think it was all in my head. Kramer said as much. But it isn't. It's awful. I have my first meeting at nine-thirty. In front of me sit a bunch of freshly shaved men. In suits that I've already seen. Very ordinary. Most of them. *(Short pause.)* I wonder if they ask themselves when I last got laid. I told that to Kramer. A while back. A few years ago, when things were different.

1.7.

ANGELICA: Do you think I'm attractive?

SABINE: Do you want an honest answer?

ANGELICA: *(Hesitates. Smiles.)* No.

SABINE: I think you're attractive.

ANGELICA: Do you think Kramer finds me attractive?

SABINE: I couldn't say.

ANGELICA: Do you find Kramer attractive?

SABINE: Kramer's good-looking.

Angelica: I think so, too. *(Short pause.)* Does Kramer find you attractive?

Sabine: You'll have to ask Kramer.

Angelica: I don't think you're particularly attractive.

Sabine: Aha.

Angelica: But I don't think I'm particularly attractive either. As I said, we're a lot alike. Exceptional in our professional life, but other than that, totally ordinary. All right, you're younger. If we were friends, Sabine, we'd only have to see each other in the mornings, and then we'd smile. Because each of us would know how long the other stood in front of the mirror every morning, desperately trying to make something out of her boring face with a little bit of eye shadow. Like billions of other women. Like all the supermarket cashiers and administrative assistants. Strange, isn't it? Think about how much money is spent worldwide—what a waste. If we were friends, we'd know these things. We could look into one another's made-up eyes and laugh. At ourselves. At our desperate efforts every morning in front of the mirror.

The two women look at each other for a long, long time in silence.

Sabine: I don't get what you're driving at.

Angelica: But you know why you're here.

Sabine: Yes. I asked for this appointment.

Short pause.

Angelica: And do you also know why you got this appointment?

Sabine: It's my right—

Angelica: Because Kramer recommended you.

Sabine: Yes, I know.

Angelica: He said the Indians are too fast for everyone else.

Sabine: I'm fast.

Angelica: I know. I know how fast you are. You have a keen, analytical mind. You recognize the gaps in the system.

SABINE: That's my job.

ANGELICA: Right. *(Short pause.)* And that's why you shouldn't fuck around with me.

SABINE: I'm not.

ANGELICA: Um hello, Sabine. And how. *(Pause.)* You got here a year-and-a-half ago. Kramer wants to give you Delhi. Do you know what that means?

SABINE: Tell me.

ANGELICA: That means Kramer fucked you, Sabine. *(Pause. Hatefully.)* He fucked you. And he's probably still fucking you. Is he still fucking you?

Silence.

SABINE: Yes. *(Pause.)*

ANGELICA: I thought you would deny it.

SABINE: Really?

ANGELICA: And that's why he's sending you to Delhi. As a little thank-you for the fucking.

SABINE: I doubt it.

ANGELICA: When was the last time?

SABINE: What?

ANGELICA: When was the last time he fucked you?

Short pause.

SABINE: About two hours ago. Downstairs in my office.

ANGELICA: Good. He fucked me yesterday evening. In our living room.

SABINE: *(Smiling.)* We seem to share a common fate. *(Short pause.)* Why don't you just throw me out?

ANGELICA: Actually, I was trying, indeed, to create a climate of friendly objectivity, collegiality, and professionalism. I tried. You didn't. I want you to understand something: the problem isn't that you're fucking my husband. The problem is that you had to. *(Suddenly.)* That you're not good enough. Who knows how you actually got this far, how many you blew in the elevator in—where was that? Japan, Korea, and Taiwan. Maybe that's where your talents lie. Maybe that's your true calling. It's a shame we can't use someone like that in Delhi—a woman who slowly and deliberately fucks her way to the top. *(She catches herself briefly.)* That a woman with your training, with your alleged qualifications, as you call them, believes she could move up like this, is just pathetic. But that you're doing it in my company, with my husband, is truly offensive. How stupid do you think I am? It's not going to work, Sabine. But why am I telling you that? You know that already. You have that keen, analytical mind. And that's why you'll ride the elevator to the fourth floor now and clean out your office. You stupid piece of shit. You stupid, stupid piece of shit. *(She throws the cup of coffee in her face.)*

1.8.

Sabine: Of course, I never was involved with her husband. Absolutely unthinkable. My relationship with Kramer was purely professional. He appreciated my work, but he wasn't interested in me or my tits. He never was. If he had been, I'd have gone to bed with him. Immediately. But it was great that she thought I'd fucked him. It was great how convinced she was. That she believed me. I went down the hall to the elevator with coffee in my face, in my hair, on the blue suit which is just like four others I have hanging in my closet. Petra, her secretary, looked at me stupidly. But she saw me. I left the office door open, which I never do. I waited for the elevator and felt the coffee run down my neck. I stared at the glowing button next to the elevator door and heard a sound coming from her office. I remembered things I'd heard on the television that morning. I could hear the announcer's voice. I could see her in front of me, in her suit. Kramer came out of his office and walked past me. No greeting. He probably didn't even see me. Surely not. Otherwise he would have asked—and then the elevator arrived.

Angelica: I stayed sitting behind my desk. She went out and left the door open. Cheap. I knew I'd never see her again. She'd go down to the fourth floor and clean out her things. And fuck off. I sat there and I couldn't concentrate. I remembered things I'd heard on the television that morning. I could hear the announcer's voice. I saw her in front of me, in her suit. Suddenly I felt like I had a hair in my throat. A long hair that went all the way down my esophagus. I tried to swallow it, but it wouldn't go away. It almost made me vomit. I tried to take it out with my fingers, but I couldn't reach it. I stuck almost my entire hand in my mouth, and I still couldn't reach it. During this I made a retching sound that I tried to suppress because the door was still open. I felt the sweat run down my neck. Outside I heard steps; an elevator opened. Kramer stuck his head in the door and asked, "Is everything alright, sweetheart?" "Yes," I said, "yes, yes, sure, everything's fine."

B.

Indian music. Early morning: it's five forty-five. HEINRICH sets his bag down and opens his locker. He takes his coat off and hangs it up. He takes off his shoes, his sweater, and his pants, and puts them away carefully. Then he takes out his uniform and puts it on. Lastly, he puts on his shoes again and takes a couple of things out of his bag that he'll need that day. He still has time. As always, he'll replace his colleague from the night shift at five minutes to six.

2.1.

ROBERT and PATRICIA. In ROBERT's office. Both are early thirties. He sits behind his desk. She sits in front. He has a stack of papers in his hands and reads. A charged and prickly silence. Pause. He turns a page and continues to read. Finally:

ROBERT: This is no good.

Short pause.

PATRICIA: What?

ROBERT: You heard me right: This is no good.

Short pause.

Patricia: This—

ROBERT: You can forget it.

PATRICIA: I don't understand—

ROBERT: It's simple—

PATRICIA: Wait a minute, why—

ROBERT: This—

PATRICIA: I can—

ROBERT: Yes—

Patricia: I cannot—

Robert: Yes you can—

Patricia: I certainly cannot—

Robert: Yes you can—

Patricia: No—

Robert: You can forget it. Forget it.

Short pause.

Patricia: What is that supposed to mean?

Short pause.

Robert: What is that supposed to mean?

Patricia: Yes—

Robert: What is that supposed to mean?

Patricia: That was the question; that was my question, yes—

Robert: It's completely clear: It means that you—

Patricia: Clear? Nothing is clear. It's not at all clear. Absolutely nothing, nothing here appears to be clear.

Robert: This proposal—

Patricia: This proposal is—

Robert: This proposal is not—

Patricia: This proposal is my—

Robert: This proposal is unacceptable.

Patricia: Unacceptable?

Robert: Un–ac–cept–a–ble. It's not any good. You can't submit this. Period.

Patricia: What?

Robert: Yes—

PATRICIA: You have got to be—

ROBERT: This proposal—

PATRICIA: This proposal—

ROBERT: This proposal is worthless. WORTHLESS.

Short pause.

PATRICIA: It's worthless.

Short pause.

ROBERT: Yes.

PATRICIA: It's unacceptable.

ROBERT: It is.

Short pause.

PATRICIA: Unacceptable.

ROBERT: Exactly.

Pause.

PATRICIA: You're sick, Robert. *(Short pause.)* You're really sick. *(Short pause.)* You're not serious.

ROBERT: Dead serious.

PATRICIA: Bullshit. This is just your own interests—

ROBERT: I'm dead serious. This proposal is worthless. This proposal is out of the question.

PATRICIA: This proposal is my concept, and I have no idea what there is to discuss with you under these circumstances.

ROBERT: I could care less. This thing isn't going beyond my desk, you can count on that one-hundred percent.

PATRICIA: This thing is my new concept, and if you don't give it to Kramer—

ROBERT: Excuse me, excuse me—

PATRICIA: No, if you don't pass it on to Kramer, then I'll—

ROBERT: Did you just say "new"? Your "new concept"?

PATRICIA: Yes, this is my new concept—

ROBERT: But this concept isn't new, Patricia.

Short pause.

PATRICIA: Pardon me?

ROBERT: This concept isn't new.

PATRICIA: What?

ROBERT: This concept is old, Patricia. Old. *(Short pause.)* This concept is old. Old, old, old.

2.2.

PATRICIA: It was the best sex I'd ever had. *(Short pause.)* Our eyes met, and we both knew that it would happen. I could sense that he felt it, and he could sense that I felt it. We looked at one another from across the room, and we knew. Bang. A party on the sixteenth floor, executive suite. The party was in full swing. Kramer had given a speech. Corks were popping. Laughter in the room, soft music, muted light. Like in a film. I wear a short dress. He clinks his glass with another woman, but I know he's watching me. He's in his early thirties. I've heard a lot about him, but I've never met him. He's successful. A whiz kid, works closely with Kramer. What comes to Kramer passes his desk first. Ambitious, dedicated, you can see that. He can have anything; as long as he doesn't disappoint Kramer, he's got a brilliant future in front of him. The sound of many voices, glasses clink, laughter; behind the windows, the city night lies under us. I get one more drink, and without turning around, go slowly to the door. I walk down the hallway. Noiselessly, because my stilettos don't make a sound on the thick carpet. I have a glass of champagne in my left hand, and I run my right index finger along the wall of the corridor. I try the door handles. Most of the offices are locked. Kramer's office is open.

2.3.

Robert and Patricia in Robert's office.

ROBERT: This concept is old.

Patricia: This concept is new.

Robert: That's absurd.

Patricia: Absurd?

Robert: Absurd, yes.

Patricia: That's not absurd—*(Short pause.)* This is the concept for my new ad.

Robert: Good, good, good. The concept is new. *(Pause.)* The concept is new, *(Short pause.)* but the ad is old. Right?

Patricia: Maybe you can't read.

Short pause.

Robert: This ad is the same as the last ad.

Patricia: Pardon me?

Short pause.

Robert: It's just as old as the last ad—

Patricia: I don't think I'm hearing correctly.

Robert: —and you know that better than anyone.

Patricia: I don't know what you mean.

Robert: *(He throws the proposal on the desk.)* Sure you do.

Patricia: Oh yeah?

Robert: You certainly know that. Of course you know that, Patricia.

Patricia: You're talking shit. I don't have the vaguest idea what you're talking about. *(Short pause.)* And you apparently don't either.

Short pause.

Robert: The concept is neither here nor there; your new ad and your old ad are identical.

Patricia: That's bordering on lunacy.

Robert: The only difference is in the cost.

PATRICIA: First of all, it's clearly senseless to discuss this with you. Pure waste of time.

ROBERT: A twenty-fold cost increase for the same product—you must have missed that. In fact, we don't need to discuss it further. This is moronic. This is sick. Or just stupid. *(Pause.)* It's not good enough, and I'm not passing it on to Kramer. Not with me, Patsy, forget it.

PATRICIA: Fuck you. Fuck you, Robert. *(Short pause.)* And don't call me Patsy.

2.4.

ROBERT: It was the best sex I'd ever had. *(Short pause.)* Kramer gave a party on the sixteenth floor. Everyone was there. Champagne corks popped. Boisterous mood. View through the windows of the city lights at night. Almost like in the movies. Everything went well. Light music in the background. Kramer was in a good mood. Despite that thing with India. *(Short pause.)* She looked absolutely enchanting, gorgeous. She wore a short, dark dress. Our eyes met when she entered the room. We looked at one another, and we knew. She knew. I knew. It was clear. Of course, I'd already heard a lot about her. But we'd never been introduced. *(Short pause.)* The ad with the puddle was her idea. Her concept. And her victory. That puddle brought her to the top of the department within twelve months. *(Short pause.)* The puddle ad was a real breakthrough. It was a common term: the puddle. Patricia's ad with the puddle. Or: Patsy's ad with the puddle. Everyone calls her Patsy. *(Short pause.)* The puddle was almost legendary. *(Short pause.)* Kramer's wife is clinking her glass on mine, but I never let Patricia out of my sight for more than a few seconds. She stands at the other end of the room. I watch how she moves, how the light falls on her shoulders. I know she knows that I'm watching her while I talk to Kramer's wife—even though she doesn't look over at me. She gets herself another drink and goes to the door. Where is she going? She holds the glass in her left hand. *(Short pause.)* I give her a precise twenty-second head start, then I excuse myself from Kramer's wife and follow her. I just see her as she disappears into Kramer's office. I walk down the corridor. My feet don't make a sound on the carpet. Kramer's office door is slightly ajar.

2.5.

In ROBERT's office. PATRICIA and ROBERT.

PATRICIA: Fuck you. Fuck you, Robert. *(Short pause.)* And don't call me Patsy.

ROBERT: What?

PATRICIA: Patsy. You just said Patsy. Instead of Patricia.

ROBERT: I see, could be.

PATRICIA: Changing a person's name demonstrates a more or less conscious intent to dominate them—

ROBERT: *(Disinterested.)* Aha—

PATRICIA: If you don't call me by my name, it means that you don't accept me as I am. But that you'd like me to be different: perhaps a little easier to handle, for example. *(Pause.)* But that won't get you anywhere, Robert. *(Pause.)*

The problem isn't that the old and new ads are too similar. The problem is that you're too simple-minded to recognize the difference.

ROBERT: Right. Because there isn't any.

Pause.

PATRICIA: The new ad takes place in Central Park

Short pause.

ROBERT: And?

PATRICIA: And what? That's what it's about.

Short pause.

ROBERT: The new ad takes place in Central Park. The last ad took place in some park. What's different about Central Park?

Pause.

PATRICIA: The light.

ROBERT: Oh.

PATRICIA: Central Park is in New York. In the United States of America.

ROBERT: I know that. America, New York, yes. Central Park is in New York.

PATRICIA: Well then—

ROBERT: Other than that? Park, grass, path. Puddle, man, woman. *(Short pause.)* Everything's identical. Identical.

PATRICIA: Park, grass, path. Puddle, man, woman. *(Short pause.)* Did I hear you right?

ROBERT: Absolutely right.

Pause.

PATRICIA: You've forgotten something.

ROBERT: Park, grass, path. Puddle, man, woman. *(He thinks for a moment.)* Squirrel. The squirrel is new.

Short pause.

PATRICIA: Wrong.

ROBERT: *(Laughs.)* Wrong? Aha. Good. Maybe I have actually overlooked a definitive detail.

PATRICIA: Fall. September. The trees. The skyline. You forgot the skyline.

ROBERT: The skyline—right, the skyline. That's also in your—*(Short pause.)*—concept.

PATRICIA: The New York skyline.

ROBERT: The skyline—interesting. Man, woman, puddle, skyline. Respect. *(Short pause.)* Don't forget the squirrel, excuse me. The squirrel in autumn in front of the skyline. For that we're going to need—*(Short pause.)*—a New York animal trainer.

PATRICIA: The New York skyline is definitive.

ROBERT: I don't give a damn about the New York skyline.

2.6.

PATRICIA: I glide into Kramer's office and leave the door ajar. In the darkness, I stand at the window of the strange office and look at the lights of the city. If Kramer comes in now, I'll probably be fired. Immediately. There's nothing in Kramer's office that I've lost or that I need. Behind me the door opens—I see the yellow stripe of light on the carpet—and it closes again, but I don't turn around. He doesn't turn the light on. He stands right behind me. I can feel his breath. I know it's him. I know it. He puts his hand on my waist. He turns me to him and we kiss. He presses me against the window and pushes my dress up. We have sex. Unbelievably violent sex. *(Short pause.)* And afterwards, we went back to the party—we didn't speak to one another again—we mingled with the other people. As though we'd planned it. But we hadn't planned it. *(Short pause.)* We hadn't planned it. I wanted to call him in his office the next day, but—*(Short pause.)*—I didn't call. Not because I didn't want to call, of course; I wanted to call, but I thought it's better if he calls. I don't have a problem making the first move on principle—but—*(Short pause.)*—not with work or with men. But—but this was about something different. This was about more. This was—*(Short pause.)*—this was too important. *(Short pause.)* And that's why I couldn't call. It wouldn't have been right. It would have been a crucial mistake, I'm absolutely convinced of that now. I didn't want to give him the impression that I needed it. That now I needed it, basically—there was absolutely no reason to let him know he could have me. That's what it was about, to make it clear to him that I'm just like him. Just like him, the same status, just in another field. Creative, efficient. Tough when I have to be. In my early thirties, I've reached a position that others won't achieve in their entire career. We're so similar—we simply belong together. And that's why I didn't call him. *(Short pause.)* But I tried to run into him more or less by chance. I was on the lookout for him—in the parking lot, in the lobby, near the elevators, in the cafeteria, or after work in one of the little Italian restaurants nearby. Where everyone goes. *(Short pause.)* I tried to find out when he arrived at work and when he left, but I never ran into him. And he never called. *(Short pause.)* I was probably just a one-night stand to him. Maybe he does it all the time. It probably meant nothing to him. He probably never even gave it a second thought. *(Short pause.)* I became angry. *(Short pause.)* I became angry because he didn't realize who he was dealing with. He didn't call. I wasn't worth it to him. And that's why I wanted to punish him. No not just punish—ruin. I wanted to destroy him. Destroy. *(Short pause.)* And so I looked for him: in the lobby, in the parking garage, in the cafeteria, in the little Italian restaurants around the corner. But he wasn't there. *(Short pause.)* And then Kramer came up to me and said it was time for a new advertising spot, and asked if I'd met his top man: Robert—Kramer said I should get in touch with Robert regarding the new ad. It would be interesting for both of us.

2.7.

ROBERT: Kramer's office is dark. She stands at the window with her back to me. I stand right behind her. She smells just like I'd imagined. If Kramer comes into his office now and finds us here, we'll both be fired. Immediately. I lay my hand on her waist and turn her to me. We kiss. I press her against the window and push her dress up. We have sex. Passionate, violent sex. *(Pause.)* Afterwards, we mingle with the other party guests and Kramer says, "Robert, I've been looking for you"—*(Short pause.)*—of course I thought about calling her the next day. But—*(Short pause.)*—but then I didn't. I wanted to—but I didn't. In my professional position, one usually makes the first move, that's alright, I don't have a problem with that—on principle. Not in business nor—*(Short pause.)*—in my personal life. But—but this was, this was something different. This was about something big. This wasn't just a fling. This was about something more. This was big. This woman was important. This woman was sensational—*(Short pause.)*—you can't just call a woman like that. It would be a mistake, I'm sure of that. I didn't want to leave the impression that I somehow needed to see her again. We were in the same league, we just worked in different fields. We both were competent, flexible, innovative, and as hard on ourselves as we were on others. In our early thirties, we'd now reached a position that others would never achieve in their entire career. I wasn't inferior to her, nor she to me. She was like me, I was like her, and I wanted her to know that. We—she and I—we belonged together. And that's why I couldn't call her. *(Short pause.)* But I tried to run into her. By chance. In the parking garage, or in the lobby by the elevators. Or in the cafeteria, or in one of the little Italian restaurants in the neighborhood. But I never saw her. I was on the lookout for her. I tried to find out when she came into the building in the morning and when she left, but it didn't work. *(Short pause.)* And she didn't call. She never got in touch. No phone call, no note. Maybe to her I was just a one-night stand in the boss's office. She wasn't interested in me. She never got in touch. Maybe she thought I wasn't worth it. I didn't matter to her. *(Short pause.)* Eventually I became angry. I became angry because she didn't call me. *(Short pause.)* I became angry because she didn't recognize who I was, what we could be together. I meant nothing to her, and she would have to pay for that. One day I'd make her really pay for that. *(Short pause.)* And so I kept looking for her: in the parking garage, in the lobby by the elevators and the cafeteria, and in the evenings after work in the little restaurants and bars nearby. And then Kramer came to me and said it was time for a new advertising spot. He asked if I'd met Patricia—and said that I should get in touch with her. It would be interesting for both of us.

2.8.

In Robert's office.

Patricia: The repetition of the puddle in front of a different international background simultaneously connotes continuity and growth.

Robert: The repetition of the puddle connotes standstill and stagnation, regardless of the background. But the market is booming, Patricia. The market is booming. He who stands still will be left behind. The repetition of the puddle is lethal.

PATRICIA: We're not standing still. We're going to New York.

ROBERT: The New York version doesn't make the puddle better.

Pause.

PATRICIA: Why didn't you call?

ROBERT: What?

Short pause.

PATRICIA. Why didn't you call?

Pause.

ROBERT: You can't be serious—why would I do that?

Pause

PATRICIA: The success of the first puddle ad alone proves I'm right—the public wanted it. The public loved the first ad.

Pause.

ROBERT: It's not about that. *(Short pause.)* Why didn't you call?

PATRICIA: It—*(Short pause.)*—It—

ROBERT: I—*(Short pause.)*—The public wants development. The public wants the future, and not a copy of yesterday's idea.

PATRICIA: The puddle is not a copy.

ROBERT: This is about progress. Nothing else matters to the public.

Short pause.

PATRICIA: Let's go somewhere—

ROBERT: What?

Short pause.

PATRICIA: Let's go somewhere and have a drink—

Robert: Why—

Patricia: Let's go and get something to drink, and I'll explain to you the difference between a copy and a quote. *Short pause.*

Robert: Aha.

Patricia: And you can explain to me what you have against New York.

Short pause.

Robert: We don't have to go anywhere for that. We can do that here.

Short pause.

Patricia: That's right.

Robert: What?

Patricia: We can do that here. *(Pause.)* We should probably just fuck each other here and now. *(Short pause.)* That might solve the biggest part of our problem.

Pause. They look at one another. Finally:

Robert: Could be. *(Pause.)* But it won't make your ad better.

Pause.

Patricia: Whatever you want.

Robert: That's how it is.

Patricia: Absolutely whatever you want.

Pause.

Robert: You want to explain to me the difference between a copy and a quote? In some bar over a glass of wine? That's not necessary. You're quoting yourself, I already got that. *(Short pause.)* You're formulating a statement with your concept. You're formulating a statement for the firm. When you do the same thing as last year, you're implying a standstill. Apathy. And no one's interested in that. *(Short pause.)* It's not enough. I mean—don't forget: it doesn't matter where you hope to take your career; you won't make it if you can't perform. This puddle thing is probably the only idea you've ever had—

Short pause.

PATRICIA: That's enough, careful—

ROBERT: Although—you know what wouldn't surprise me at all—you probably stole the entire puddle idea from somewhere—can that be? *(Short pause.)* Is that true? Right? Did I guess right?

Short pause. They look at one another.

PATRICIA: That was it. *(Short pause. She stands up.)* That was definitely it.

ROBERT: This proposal is old, and it's trash. *(He throws it in the wastebasket.)*

PATRICIA: We'll see about that.

2.9.

ROBERT: She left. *(Short pause.)* I gave myself some time. I didn't care whether she spoke with Kramer before I did—because I knew that was her plan. I was certain about my position; she didn't have a chance. I took the proposal out of the trash can and read it through again. I sat back and waited. I looked out the window and counted slowly to one hundred. Maybe I hoped something would happen. Maybe she was right—maybe Central Park was a good idea. *(Short pause.)* Then I took the proposal and went to the elevator to ride up to Kramer, but I decided to take the stairs instead. *(Short pause.)* I stood still for a moment in front of Kramer's door on the sixteenth floor. I stood there in the corridor and heard the light click of a keyboard in the anteroom, and muted voices on the telephone. I love the sounds of the sixteenth floor; everything sounds different there—even the daylight there seems different. I felt nervous, but confident, at the same time. Whenever I'm on the sixteenth floor I get this feeling in my stomach—like this is where I want to be. *(Short pause.)* I stood in front of Kramer's office, and I thought of all the people that never made it. That wanted to be here, just like I do, in the executive suite, and who one day simply stopped moving up. Who had made some mistake, and for that reason were out of the running, while I moved by and continued on my way. *(Short pause.)* Maybe Kramer wasn't even there—maybe he was busy. *(Short pause.)* Kramer was a little surprised to see me. I thought she would have already been there, but she wasn't there yet. He read through the proposal, sitting on the edge of his desk where we—*(Short pause.)* I told him I didn't believe in the ad. That I thought it was a mistake to produce the puddle a second time. On financial, but more importantly, on conceptual grounds. The first puddle spot was a big success, yes, but the New York copy of the puddle would be a fiasco. The New York puddle would be an unmistakable sign of stagnation, and thus clearly a foreseeable disaster. I told him Patricia apparently doesn't understand how things work here. What's at issue. And that I wasn't interested in collaborating with her further. *(Short pause.)* And I told him that she probably stole the entire puddle idea from somewhere. *(Short pause.)* While I spoke, Kramer spent most of the time looking out the window, as he always did when he had to make a hard decision; but as I finished, he looked at me. He looked at me as though he'd never seen me before; he looked into my eyes, and although he didn't say anything—just nodded—I had the feeling that at that moment, something within him shattered. *(Short pause.)* As I left Kramer's office, she was walking down the corridor toward me. That was the last time I ever saw her.

Patricia: I left the office. I gave myself some time. I didn't care if he spoke with Kramer before I did; I knew that was his plan. But I was certain of my position—he didn't have a chance. I rode down to my office and printed the proposal again. I read it through once more. I sat behind my desk and waited. I looked out the window and counted slowly to one hundred. Maybe I hoped something would happen. Maybe he was right: maybe Central Park wasn't a good idea. And then I picked up the phone and made an appointment with Kramer so that I could introduce him to my new concept. Come on up, he said—in about ten minutes. I felt nervous, but confident, at the same time. Whenever I'm on the sixteenth floor I get this feeling in my stomach—like this is where I want to be. It's probably a cliché, but I want to have my own desk in one of those offices some day. I want a big apartment—preferably in New York—and I want to meet a good-looking man who will carry me over a big puddle in Central Park on a totally rainy day, because sometimes there are simply moments in which one can't continue alone. I want a child, and I want to sleep in pajamas, and the next morning, after a chaotic taxi ride, I want to climb into the elevator in a perfect suit with seemingly improvised, but nevertheless terrific hair, and ride up here. I want to walk to my office across the quiet carpet and through the open doors of the anteroom, hear the soft sound of keyboards. *(Short pause.)* Robert was just coming out of Kramer's office. That was the last time I ever saw him. *(Short pause.)* Kramer wasn't as surprised by the proposal as I'd expected—Robert had just shown it to him. But he found the idea of filming the puddle ad in New York terrific. Central Park. The light. The skyline. He was totally enthusiastic—he was delighted. He spoke of "expanding continuity." He found the idea charming. "Let's go to New York," he said. "Patsy, let's go to New York."

C.

Indian music. MARIA in front of her locker. She unlocks it. Early morning: It's five-fifty. She sets her purse down. She takes off her winter boots, hangs her coat, blouse, and skirt in the locker. She hurries—like she does every morning. She takes her uniform and comfortable shoes out of the locker, and puts them on.

3.

HANS and FRANK across from one another. HANS sits behind a desk. HANS is around sixty, FRANK around thirty.

HANS: Delhi—*(Short pause.)* I mean: Delhi. That word alone. The name. And how palpable suddenly everything becomes. Doesn't it? *(Short pause.)* No? It's right there. Fantastic. Don't you think?

FRANK: Yes, yes.

HANS: Seriously, what—*(Short pause.)*—what do you think about when you hear that name? Delhi. *(Short pause.)* You—you don't have to tell me if you don't want to. *(Short pause.)* You don't have to.

FRANK: What should I think about? *(Short pause.)* About India. About the city. *(Short pause.)* About our office.

HANS: Stop.

FRANK: Hmm?

HANS: Stop. *(Short pause.)* Be honest. And precise.

FRANK: Why?

HANS: You don't think about our office. You think about the management of our office.

Short pause.

FRANK: Well, yes.

HANS: I just wanted to clarify. *(Pause.)* I just wanted to clarify.

Pause.

FRANK: Well what do you think about?

Hans: When?

Frank: When you hear Delhi.

Hans: About Kramer. First, of course, I think about Kramer.

Pause.

Frank: Ok. And then?

Hans: And then—*(Short pause.)*—then I think about an airplane.

Frank: Aha—

Short pause.

Hans: It's my experience that it's better to visualize things if you want them to come true. One must visualize it. *(Short pause.)* That's why I think about an airplane.

Frank: Sure. *(Short pause.)* About an airplane. What kind of airplane?

Hans: I think about a big airplane. Because it's taking me there. About a Boeing.

Frank: I surf a lot. I surf almost every night.

Short pause.

Hans: Because an airplane is going to take me to Delhi. Far away from here. A big bird takes me to Delhi. Carries me over the Indian subcontinent.

Frank: And I keep getting heavier. I've gained twenty-two pounds in the last ten years. Especially since I've been working here, I keep getting fatter.

Hans: Eleven hours nonstop, landing in New Delhi, Indira Gandhi International Airport.

Frank: Twenty-two pounds in ten years. That's forty-four pounds in twenty years, and so on. Maybe it will increase exponentially—that would mean that when I'm forty, I'd weigh one-hundred-and-ten pounds more than I do now. And that I'll gain forty-four pounds between forty and fifty. And so on. I'll weigh two-hundred-and-sixty-four pounds when I'm sixty. Two-hundred-and-sixty-four pounds. That's almost three-hundred pounds. *(Pause.)*

Hans: Do you work out?

Short pause.

FRANK: Why do you ask?

HANS: No, you don't work out. *(Short pause.)* Do you? *(Short pause.)* No answer. No. You should, though. It keeps your head clear. It's good for your power of visualization. Independent of the body. Of your body.

FRANK: I surf every night. I get a take-out pizza and a couple of beers on the way home from work; I get home and I turn on the computer. *(Short pause.)* I play a couple of rounds on the flight simulator and eat the pizza with one hand as it slowly gets cold. I had my last girlfriend when I was twenty-seven. Since she left, I've been more or less alone. About ten o'clock, I open the second beer and log onto the net.

HANS: At times, Delhi has ninety-eight percent humidity. It gets hot there. Up to one-hundred-and-twenty degrees. The heat shimmers on the street. Let's say that you're there—let's say you're working there: you've got to be in shape. You've got to have your body in top condition. Otherwise, you won't last. Otherwise, you'll be flown back after four weeks. It wouldn't be the first time.

FRANK: And you? Do you work out?

HANS: Every day.

Short pause.

FRANK: On the net, one's sense of time changes, continues to change. Even now. *(Short pause.)* I'd never pay for pictures off the Internet. There are plenty of sites with free pictures. Thousands of free pictures. *(Pause.)* Whenever I'm on the net, I get hungry.

HANS: I keep getting thinner. I continue to lose weight. I'm in my early sixties. A few years ago I was really big. Heavy. Too much yellow fat on my hips. I never watched my weight. I just ate too much—all the time, early in the morning, then another breakfast in the cafeteria. Two big meals a day, lunch and dinner. And snacks in between while at work. Chocolate. Nuts. Chips. Beer and wine in the evening. No exercise. Every ten years, twenty or so pounds heavier. At thirty, one-hundred-fifty pounds, at forty, one-hundred-and-seventy-five, at fifty, two hundred. More and more. But now—I get regular checkups. I'm ok. My doctor's happy with me. My daughter isn't. If this keeps up, Papa, she says, I'll take that thing away from you. She gave me "that thing" herself—a year-and-a-half ago. Because I wasn't getting enough exercise—before my heart gave out. "That thing" is a home trainer. One of these bicycles that you can put in a room and ride in place.

Frank: Whenever I'm on the net, I get hungry. That's the problem.

Hans: The home trainer sits in the living room, right about where the loveseat used to sit. While I work out, I either look through the big windows into the garden, or at the television and stereo. My wife used to take care of the garden—it's slowly going to seed. Slowly becoming overgrown. Doesn't matter. Bugs the neighbors—yeah and so what?

Frank: Chocolate. Nuts. Chips.

Hans: My daughter and I took the loveseat down to the basement. I don't get many visitors any more. When I come home, I've already eaten. I eat somewhere along the way, in the city. A salad. Not much. Something with tofu. It rarely happens that I'll go shopping and cook at home. Or that I go out to eat. I wouldn't know with whom. I come home and change my clothes. I make a cup of tea. And then I climb onto the home trainer and start my workout. During the week my daily workout lasts about four hours. I couldn't always do so much. I've gotten better. I start relatively slowly and then gradually increase the tempo. I had trouble with my knees at first, but that went away. I cover between fifty and sixty miles in one evening. Next to the home trainer is a road map with mileage information, so that I can see what I've ridden. *(Short pause.)* Or I put tapes in the VCR of different stages of the Tour de France. I've ridden the bike through an entire stage—of course, not in the evening, you couldn't do it—but on the weekend. Of course I can't keep up—but I'm in good form nevertheless—for my age. There are a lot of young guys that I would outdistance. I just turned sixty—I could still have twenty or thirty more years in front of me. Twenty or thirty years: a lot of time. A whole lot of time. *(Pause.)* The only question is, what comes next? *(Short pause.)* That's why I work out. That's really why I do it. *(Short pause.)*

Frank: I'm only interested in the hard stuff. Teenagers don't interest me. I especially like the Italian, Hungarian, and French Free-Pix sites. Megasalope alone has hundreds of pictures. Hundreds of women. The photos are real, they're genuine, the women in those photos really do it, but they don't have names, they only have numbers. But I give them names anyway. And while I look at the photos of Natasha, Suzie, or Julia, I forget the code, the numbers, the program architecture. I stop thinking about it. *(Short pause.)* I sit in front of the computer and ask myself where Susie on Megasalope is from. Where these pictures originated: France, or Hungary, or America? Or Germany, Italy, or Russia? Where did they undress for the camera? Maybe she lives here around the corner. Who's the man who made the photos with her? Who's the photographer? Does she always do this? Or did she do it just this once? How much did she get, if she got anything for it? How old is the photo? Where is she now? Where is she now while I'm here? What is she doing right now as I look at her photograph? Is she thinking about it? Is she thinking about how someone might be looking at her right now? Or Natasha, for example—one evening her photos just simply disappeared, the entire page suddenly has another face. An update. Natasha is gone. Maybe there are more pictures of her somewhere else on the net—but where? I search the server for her at night, but I don't find her. I've never found the same woman on two different sites. The photos are interchangeable, but none of them is Natasha. Maybe she doesn't exist anymore. I search the entire net and don't find her, and all of this takes a really long time. *(Pause.)* Finally, around one, I turn the computer off. I sit there with an open mouth, and feel the air dropping into my lungs. There's nothing in my head for a moment. *(Music.)* And then the numbers return, the code, the programming steps, and I consider how one could make all of that—the information highways, the servers, the processors, the programs—faster, more complex, and better. *(Short pause.)* And that's why I'm the right man for Delhi. *(Pause.)*

HANS: I know that you've applied for Delhi.

FRANK: I see. *(Pause.)*

HANS: And you of course know that I've applied. Of course you know that. I mean—you work for me after all

FRANK: Is that right?

HANS: For me, yes. Or for my team. Or for my department. Or for the firm. For Kramer. Doesn't matter. At least you do that for now. *(Short pause.)* Now what does that mean? I mean—suppose you get the job in Delhi—and I don't. You'll board a plane for India while I stay here? So that I can be laid off with the next wave of reorganization in the fall—after twenty-five years? *(Short pause.)* Because I don't believe you intend to take me with you to Delhi. Am I right? You're not stupid. But can you really see that? Me in early retirement? *(Short pause.)* I can't. I mean, I can't see it—except that it would improve your chances. *(Short pause.)* But it's great that you're going to try anyway. Very sportsmanlike. Doesn't fit you at all. *(Short pause.)* Nevertheless, I think we should clarify some fundamental things here.

FRANK: Aha.

Hans: Yes. *(Short pause.)* I believe you haven't yet understood a crucial point.

Frank: Yes?

Hans: The power of visualization.

Frank: Right. The power of visualization. Your theme.

Hans: Right. Pictorial and spatial power of visualization.

Frank: And?

Hans: And what?

Frank: You said I hadn't understood a crucial point. I'd be interested to know what that point might be. *(Short pause.)* Honestly.

Hans: Oh, yes, right: You—*(Short pause.)* How far away from you is the wall behind me, would you say?

Short pause.

Frank: The wall—

Hans: Yes, the wall. How far from you is it? *(Pause. Frank shrugs his shoulders.)* Actually, a very simple question, isn't it? You see the desk, me, behind me the bookcase and the wall. The wall interrupts your view after how many feet would you say?

Frank: No idea.

Hans: *(Hotly.)* Why doesn't that interest you—why are you so imprecise?

Frank: Okay, after ten feet.

Hans: Ten feet? Eight-and-a-half. Tops.

Frank: Good, eight-and-a-half—so?

Hans: Eight-and-a-half feet to the wall. That's your field of vision. *(Short pause.)* And now try to imagine what I see. *(Short pause.)* My perspective is quite different. *(Short pause.)* I don't see the wall at all. I see the front edge of my desk, behind that you, behind that, maybe thirteen feet away, the door to my office.

Frank: And?

Hans: You see: they're completely different—I mean—we're in the same room, but we see things completely differently. We don't share the same picture.

FRANK: I don't care. Maybe eventually you'll get to the point.

HANS: Maybe you'd like to see it for yourself? Come over here. We'll change places for a minute.

FRANK: Thanks, that's not necessary.

HANS: Not necessary. Then you mean that you can imagine it. *(Short pause.)* How—this here—appears from my perspective. *(Short pause.)* Possible. Maybe. *(Short pause.)* I doubt it. I don't think you have the necessary imagination. The vision.

FRANK: I get by, don't worry.

HANS: And that's why you don't have the necessary drive.

Short pause.

FRANK: Depends on what for, I'd say.

HANS: What for? *(Short pause.)* For Delhi. I mean the necessary drive for Delhi. What did you think? *(Short pause.)* I mean, what if I get the job? And you don't? Could happen. What'll you do then? I can hardly take you with me when you wouldn't have taken me.

FRANK: I assumed that when I applied, I'd get the job. That simple.

Pause.

HANS: Yes, yes. How long have you been with us?

FRANK: You know that better than I do.

HANS: Aha. Good. *(Short pause.)* I thought we were having a conversation.

FRANK: I wouldn't know what about.

HANS: It's very simple: I ask a question, you give an answer. I ask how long you've been here, and you say, for example: six years. And then I say: the time goes so fast. I brought you here six years ago—you've been my protégé for six years and now you want to take my job away from me. But that's not going to happen.

Short pause.

FRANK: Yes it will—

HANS: Are you sure? Six years, and you keep getting fatter. *(Short pause.)* Don't you?

Frank: You—

Hans: Could it be? Could it be that year after year you'll just keep getting fatter? I mean, if things keep progressing as they are—not a pretty picture. *(Short pause.)* And that's why we're going to go and get something to eat now. *(Short pause.)* Do you know that little Italian restaurant around the corner? Or would you rather go somewhere else? Doesn't matter to me as long as the wine is good. For our farewell.

Frank: What farewell?

Hans: I knew that would make you curious. Our farewell dinner. Finally something that interests you.

Frank: What farewell are you talking about?

Short pause.

Hans: I have reliable information that I'm at the top of Kramer's list.

Frank: What list?

Hans: The list—*(Short pause.)* Oh come on, Frank, you can figure it out.

Frank: No, I have no idea, what list do you mean?

Pause.

Hans: The list. The list for Delhi. I'm supposed to take over the supervision of Delhi.

Pause.

Frank: Ah—

Hans: Yes—and I think we should celebrate, don't you?

Short pause.

Frank: Where did you get that?

Hans: What?

Frank: That you're at the top of the list—where did you get that? You certainly didn't get it from Kramer—

Hans: Why—no, I got it from someone close to Kramer.

Short pause.

Frank: Aha.

Hans: The information is one-hundred percent correct, absolutely reliable, don't worry about that. I expect Kramer's phone call any minute. *(Pause.)* I can clearly picture it: the two of us in the restaurant. Despite everything. I don't carry a grudge. After a conversation in the elevator, down to the lobby, it's been a long day, and then straight to Maurizio, a great little Italian restaurant nearby. I reserved the table for eight-thirty. Not a table up front, but in back, where it's more quiet. No mineral water today, just champagne—Maurizio already knows—oysters, and then a very simple minestrone, antipasto, spaghetti with eggplant, tomatoes and pine nuts, and an ostrich filet for the final course, then flan for dessert. And to go with it, a marvelous Barolo—how long has it been since I've had a good bottle of wine? How long has it been since I've eaten that well? No one will mention that we're not really properly dressed—they're very discreet, and I'm a good customer—or at least I was at one time—when my wife was still here. When we were celebrating something. Like today. And so the evening flies by—we both laugh at the stories we tell each other: about our weight, our workout techniques. About the Tour de France

Frank: Sometimes I wish I could talk to Natasha. I mean really, really talk to her.

Short pause.

Hans: A little after twelve, it's getting time to leave, one more espresso, today's exceptional, and Grappa on the house. What a wonderful evening.

Pause.

Frank: The problem is, Hans, your information is wrong. What you were told isn't correct.

Hans: Is that right?

Frank: Yes. *(Short pause.)* You're not taking over Delhi. *(Pause.)* I'm taking over Delhi. *(Pause.)* I'm going to smell like saffron as I leave the research center and stroll down the sunny streets to my house. Everything blooming violet and white. Colorful birds and little monkeys live in the trees. An elephant grazes in the yard. I sit at my desk on the first floor of my house and look out. I don't surf as much as I used to, but I've found Natasha again—on a Czech site. Of course I'm not absolutely certain. One never is.

Hans: Who said that?

FRANK: Kramer said that.

HANS: Kramer—

Short pause.

FRANK: Kramer's given the supervision of Delhi to me.

HANS: That can't be.

FRANK: Yes.

Pause.

HANS: How long have you known this?

Short pause.

FRANK: For three days.

Short pause.

HANS: For three days—*(Short pause.)* Why didn't you say something before? Why didn't Kramer share that with me? *(Pause.)* Why didn't Kramer tell me? *(Short pause.)* I just saw him yesterday.

Pause. Frank is particularly quiet.

FRANK: Of course we'll go eat. I don't know who else I would go with. We'll celebrate. But it's my treat. We'll go to that Thai restaurant, Benjarong. Sometimes I get take-out from Benjarong, I like the service at the counter. We'll sit at the window and look at the street. He eats a vegetable soup, I get wonton soup, with a side of spring rolls to share that he won't touch. Afterwards, beef with peanuts and rice for me, and fried tofu for him.

HANS: The Indians burn their dead on the side of the road. When a man dies, supposedly the widow also meets her death. But it doesn't happen the other way around. The men remain.

FRANK: And we'll talk. About the net. About our weight. About working out. About Indians.

HANS: My daughter thinks I should make more of my evenings and weekends. Get out and see people. She says, otherwise, she's going to take my trainer away. *(Laughs a little. Short pause.)* When I've finished my workout, I peek into the kitchen to see if I've turned off the stove, then I turn out the lights in the kitchen and the living room. I check to see if I locked the front door, turn out the light in the downstairs hallway, go up the stairs to the second floor, shut off the stairway light, take a short shower, brush my teeth, and lie down in bed in what used to be our bedroom. The house is too big for me alone, but I'm not ready to give everything up yet. I lie in bed. It's one in the morning. I feel the air drop into my lungs. I think about my home trainer. If I should have someone check it. *(Short pause.)* And then I wonder if I turned the stove off—downstairs in the kitchen. *(Pause.)* I get up again. I turn on the stairway light and go down. And I check the stove. It was off. I check the front door again. I go back into the kitchen to see if I turned the light out again after I checked the stove—and then I take another quick look at the burner. Off. Then I go back up the stairs, but turn around again halfway up, go down and check the front door knob once again. Locked. The outside light is off. The hallway light is off. The living room light is off. The stove is off. *(Short pause.)* Isn't it? *(Short pause.)* And what about the basement light? Wasn't I in the basement a little while ago? Was that today? The light in the basement is off. The basement door is locked. I go back up and lie down in bed. Light off. Is the stairway light off? I get up again and look to see whether I turned off the stairway light. It's off.—Everything's locked. Everything's off.

FRANK: Are you ok?

Short pause.

HANS: Do you have a girlfriend? How nice for you. What's her name? *(Short pause.)* That's nice. Sounds Russian. What a pretty and unusual name.

FRANK:

A big bird takes me to Delhi:
Takes me to Madras, to Bangalore,
Carries me east, to the morning, in the night,
Carries me to the Indian subcontinent.

D.

MARIA: I work for a big corporation. In the so-called mother building, the headquarters of the firm—it's a high-rise building. I work downstairs, off of the lobby, in the central office. Everyone who comes in or out of the building walks by us. The people look funny as they hurry by us in the morning. Especially the women when they come in a little after nine and are really in a hurry. My shift starts three hours earlier, at six. I'm one of the people who sit in the train at five-forty in the morning. In spite of that, I like the early shift best. The night shift is the worst. During the night shift, we have to walk the building, and it scares me. We have to look in all of the rooms and offices, and I always think that one night, we might find someone who has hung himself after work. It could happen. Some old guy. A couple years away from retirement. It's happened before. When I arrive for the morning shift, my colleague Heinrich is usually already there. He's already put on his uniform, unpacked his breakfast. And he's already turned on his little TV that he secretly sets next to the other monitors. There's not much going on between six and seven, just the cleaning staff slowly leaving the building—and that's why Heinrich and I usually watch TV together then. Our firm even has its own advertising spot. Heinrich doesn't like the ad very much, but I do. I don't understand what it has to do with our company, but I don't care. Now there's a new ad, although it's basically like the old one—but the new ad takes place in New York, in Central Park. You can see the skyline. A woman stands in front of a big puddle in Central Park. She can't go any further in her heels, and then a good-looking guy helps her. He just carries her—he takes her and carries her over the puddle—like a bride over the threshold. Heinrich doesn't like it. Heinrich wants more action—but I think it's great. I think it's romantic. Sure—the whole thing was stolen from that film with Michelle Pfeiffer and George Clooney, but—who cares? I mean, it doesn't really matter. Heinrich always says, "But that's not how it is, that would never happen in real life." And then he looks at me and says, "Isn't that right, isn't that right, Maria? Look at the two of us. I'm not going to carry you over a puddle." And then I imagine how it would look for Heinrich to carry me over a puddle and I laugh. Always. Almost every morning.

Hamlyn

JUAN MAYORGA

Translated from Spanish by David Johnston

Hamlyn premiered at Teatro de la Abadía in Madrid, Spain, in May 2005, directed by Andrés Lima.

CHARACTERS

Commentator

Montero

Julia

Rivas

Paco

Raquel

Josemari

Girl

Feli

Gonzalo

COMMENTATOR: Lights. *Hamlyn.* Scene One.

MONTERO: This is *not* a press conference. Is that clear? This is off the record. And confidential. I called you all personally because I wanted to talk to you here, now, while the city's still sleeping. Because that's the reason you're here: to find out what goes on while the city sleeps. Come over here for a moment.

COMMENTATOR: Montero invites the journalists to look through a large window.

MONTERO: Every evening, just before I leave the office, I take one last look through this window. You can see the whole city from here. All the new developments. The Museum of Contemporary Art, the stadium, the auditorium ... our new spectacular city. Like dazzling jewels. That blind us to the other city. There *is* another city.

COMMENTATOR: Pause.

MONTERO: Each night, just before I leave the office, I lean into this window, I light a cigarette. I said it's not a press conference. Yes, I smoke. In private. And I think about the people of this city. I think about the children.

COMMENTATOR: He points to a lighted window in another building.

MONTERO: That child for example. Late for a child to be still up. He probably can't sleep and his father's trying to get him to sleep by telling him a story. He probably can't sleep because he's afraid and his father doesn't understand what it is that's frightening him. I wonder what it is ...

COMMENTATOR: He goes over to a table. On it, a closed box.

MONTERO: I have just signed the warrant. Over the next few hours the police will make a series of arrests. Some of them will be of well-known citizens, people that are highly thought of, and this will have an inevitable effect on public morale. That's why I've called you here. You are the media. It is up to you to make sure that whatever it is people find out, they find it out in the most positive way. You will all take your own line on this, but the common denominator must be that it is a responsible line.

COMMENTATOR: Pause.

MONTERO: Tomorrow, along with other colleagues, you will be called to a press conference. You will be shown material that we have just seized. This. Take a look at it now, if you have the stomach.

Commentator: He opens the box. The journalists hesitate. One of them finally steps forward. The box contains slides, grouped into five piles. The journalist lifts a slide and holds it against the light. Then the others do the same.

Montero: This is just the tip of the iceberg, I'm afraid. The city's facing difficult times. There will be a public outcry. But we must act responsibly. All of us, we all work to the same purpose: the public interest. And we will be transparent with you, as we always are, and you will exercise your responsibility towards the city, as you always do. That is my belief, and I have called you here to express that belief to you.

Commentator: The journalists put the slides back in the box, they shake their heads as though they can't believe what they have just seen, their expressions are of disgust, they leave in silence. And when he's finally alone, Montero lights a cigarette and leans into the window. He gazes over towards that other window where the sleepless child is still with his father. A sudden memory floods into Montero's mind. He remembers his father telling him about the Pied Piper.

Montero: Once upon a time there was a lovely city called Hamlyn. But one day the people of Hamlyn woke up to find that their city was overrun with rats.

Commentator: *Hamlyn.* Scene Two. Montero goes into Jaime's bedroom. He leaves his shoes outside the door so as not to disturb him. He watches him sleep. He goes to his own bedroom, carrying his shoes. He gets ready for bed, trying not to wake Julia. But Julia is already awake.

Julia: What time is it?

Montero: It's late. Go back to sleep.

Commentator: He gives her a kiss.

Julia: What is it? Is there something wrong?

Montero: You'll read about it in the papers in the morning.

Julia: Do you want to talk about it?

Commentator: Montero gets into bed and puts his arms around her.

Montero: No.

Commentator: Pause.

Montero: How's Jaime? Is he okay?

Julia: Why?

Montero: No reason.

Commentator: Silence.

Julia: He wouldn't eat his dinner. He was too tired.

Commentator: Pause.

Julia: Can you not sleep?

Montero: No.

Commentator: *Hamlyn.* Scene Three. Montero has dark rings under his eyes. He finally got up at five o'clock, knowing he wasn't going to be able to sleep, had a shower and walked down to the Courthouse. He paces round his office until he's informed that Rivas has arrived. Rivas offers his hand. Montero doesn't notice or appears not to notice, and asks Rivas to sit down.

Montero: Coffee?

Rivas: Please.

Montero: Milk, sugar?

Rivas: Just milk.

Commentator: Montero pours him a cup. He takes a cup too, black with no sugar. The two men sit opposite each other, across the table. The box with the slides is still there. A third person is present, an official who transcribes every word.

Montero: You're a highly respected man. You orchestrated a campaign against a power station.

Rivas: A waste incinerator. We got it closed.

Montero: You've started adult literacy schemes, campaigned against drug abuse …

Rivas: We pick up where the authorities leave off. In an area like ours, as poor as ours, you can never say there's nothing left to be done.

Montero: You live there?

Rivas: No.

Montero: Born there?

Rivas: I'm one of the lucky ones. I was born … well off. I went to good schools, I had everything I needed. When I first went there it was like being on a different planet. If only my youngsters had half the advantages that I had. Even a small percentage of that half.

Montero: "My youngsters."

Rivas: I've started a remedial project. For kids who've lost their way. They need a chance.

Montero: You seem to devote a lot of time to them, to your youngsters. How do you earn a living?

Rivas: I studied medicine. But I never finished. It didn't … inspire me. We have shops. Electrical goods. I have very little to do with the business. That's how I manage to devote so much time to them.

Commentator: Pause.

Montero: You go to church on Sundays?

Rivas: I'm old-fashioned. About that, and a lot of other things.

Montero: "Anyone want a lift to church?"

Rivas: Sorry?

Montero: Do you know why I asked you here?

Rivas: The police sometimes ask my advice. I know the whole area well.

Commentator: Pause. Judge Montero tips the contents of the box onto the table. It's covered with slides.

Montero: Take a look. Whichever one you want.

Commentator: Rivas picks up a slide. He looks at it. He puts it back in the box.

Rivas: Downloaded from the Internet. It's not against the law. I'm not defending it, but it's not against the law.

Commentator: He finishes his coffee.

Rivas: If it's for private use, not for sale, it's not against the law. Not in this country.

Montero: Who are those children?

Rivas: I told you. They're images from the Internet.

Montero: They're not your youngsters?

Rivas: No. They're not.

Commentator: Pause.

Montero: "Anyone want a lift to church?" "Local people associate you with that question: 'Anyone want a lift to church?'"

Rivas: I drive through on my way to church. If anybody wants one, I give them a lift.

Montero: Some youngster, you mean.

Rivas: No. Anyone. Young or old.

Montero: Nothing else. Once church is over, it's "see you next week."

Rivas: I get them lunch sometimes. We go for a burger or a pizza and they love it. Those kids get nothing but bread and a scraping of margarine for days on end. A burger's a real treat for them.

Montero: So you get them something to eat. And some weekends, you go somewhere else.

Rivas: We go up to the funfair, sometimes.

Montero: And then.

Rivas: And then everyone goes their own separate ways.

Montero: You never take them out of the city.

Rivas: No. Well, we organize the occasional camping trip.

Montero: The occasional camping trip. Apart from that, you never take them out of the city.

Rivas: No.

Montero: You've never taken them to your chalet.

COMMENTATOR: Pause.

RIVAS: I don't have a chalet. My mother does.

MONTERO: You know you have the right to legal representation.

RIVAS: I don't need any. I've done nothing wrong.

MONTERO: These slides were found in the garage at the chalet. Along with magazines, videos ... and toys.

RIVAS: I know my rights. Possession of images is not illegal if there is no intent to distribute them.

MONTERO: You've never photographed any children.

RIVAS: I've taken photographs. Artistic photographs.

MONTERO: You have a lot of visitors to the chalet. Have you ever organized any sort of ... showing there?

RIVAS: No.

COMMENTATOR: Montero shows him eight photographs of adult males.

MONTERO: These gentlemen have one thing in common. They have all visited your chalet. Your mother's chalet.

RIVAS: So, my friends visit me ...

MONTERO: Good friends to have. Important people. Are they the ones in the pictures, with the children? They're careful to keep their faces turned from the camera.

RIVAS: I don't know who they are. They're from the Internet.

MONTERO: As well as your friends, there have been minors seen at your chalet. Children.

RIVAS: Yes, there have been children. So?

MONTERO: You didn't produce that material and you don't distribute it?

RIVAS: No.

COMMENTATOR: Pause. Montero takes out a piece of paper.

MONTERO: I'm going to read you an e-mail. It's signed by "Unicorn."

Commentator: Pause.

Montero: "Dear Friends: I have had the most wonderful time this weekend with my angel. But each day I think time passes, and he is less and less of a little boy…"

Rivas: There's no need to continue. I wrote that and other e-mails. What does it prove? And what right do you have to intercept other people's e-mail? Is that legal? It proves nothing. There are hundreds of groups like that on the Internet. It's nothing more than a self-help group.

Montero: You organize trips, exchange materials …

Rivas: We exchange advice, experiences, that's all. It's a way of unburdening yourself. You think you're a freak until you find out that there are hundreds of people, thousands, who feel the same way. It's a place you can communicate what you feel to people who understand …

Montero: Your angel, who is he? The one you had the most wonderful time with.

Rivas: It's a figure of speech.

Montero: "I have had the most wonderful time this weekend with my angel."

Rivas: I'm saying I was happy. Metaphorically.

Montero: You're not talking about anyone in particular.

Rivas: No.

Montero: You're not talking about Gonzalo.

Rivas: Gonzalo's eighteen.

Montero: Then maybe Josemari. How old is Josemari?

Commentator: Pause.

Rivas: I have a special relationship with Josemari.

Montero: What sort of relationship? You play hide and seek with him?

Rivas: He's different. There's something special about him.

Montero: How long have you known Josemari?

Rivas: About four years.

MONTERO: How did you get to know him? Did you give him a lift to church?

RIVAS: It was through his father. His family was in ... difficulties. His family's constantly in difficulties. Six kids, his mother always pregnant, and his father always on benefits. I do what I can for them.

COMMENTATOR: Silence.

MONTERO: Somebody reported ... several days ago ... that an adult was abusing a child. The child was spending weekends in the company of an adult, in a chalet.

RIVAS: Who? Who told you that?

MONTERO: Someone who's got Josemari's best interests at heart.

RIVAS: Someone who's got Josemari's best interests at heart? Nobody's got his interests more at heart than I have. I would never abuse him, that's the last thing I would ever do. I'd die rather than harm that child.

MONTERO: Do you want legal representation?

RIVAS: There has to be some mistake. Nobody who knows me could imagine I'd ever hurt Josemari. Who told you I did?

MONTERO: Would you agree to meet him? The person who brought the complaint.

RIVAS: Yes. There has to be some mistake.

MONTERO: Now?

RIVAS: Yes, now. I want this cleared up now.

COMMENTATOR: Montero makes a call. For several minutes Montero and Rivas wait in silence. They do not look at each other. Finally, two policemen and an eighteen-year-old come in. Montero gestures to the young man to sit opposite Rivas. Just a few feet apart. Rivas and the young man. Long silence.

RIVAS: How could you do this? Stab me in the back. You're making this up, Gonzalo, aren't you? You know I'd never do anything to hurt Josemari.

COMMENTATOR: Silence.

RIVAS: Is that what you said? A child's being abused by an adult. Is that what you said?

COMMENTATOR: Silence.

RIVAS: Tell the judge you were lying. Tell him it's a lie.

COMMENTATOR: Silence. Rivas turns towards Montero.

RIVAS: Get him out of my sight, please.

COMMENTATOR: The judge gestures to the policemen, who take the young man out.

RIVAS: I can see what's going on here. What sort of credibility does he have? This is a grudge. We had a fantastic relationship, but one day he stopped being fun to be with. I still wanted to go on being his friend. "I still want to go on being your friend." He didn't understand. He thought I was replacing him. I couldn't get him to understand. How do you tell an eighteen year old that time passes? You look him in the eye and you say: "You're growing up." I couldn't find a way. And now this knife in the back. Those photos are revolting, I know they are, but they've nothing to do with Josemari. I've never laid a finger on Josemari.

COMMENTATOR: Silence.

RIVAS: Can I ask you one favor: I don't want my mother to find out. Tell her I'm here for any reason you like. Anything but this.

COMMENTATOR: *Hamlyn.* Scene Four. It's past eleven at night when Montero finally leaves his office. He's about to hail a taxi, but changes his mind, he decides he'd rather walk. He goes past places he sees every day from his window: the stadium, the Museum of Contemporary Art. In the little square just outside the auditorium he comes across a group of boys who seem to be waiting. A Mercedes stops beside them, with its window rolled down. One of the boys gets into the Mercedes. Montero walks on, it's after one before he gets home. He takes off his shoes and checks that Jaime is sleeping. He carries his shoes into his bedroom. Julia has fallen asleep in front of the television. Montero switches it off and pulls the bedclothes over his wife. He doesn't want to wake her up, but she speaks to him. Without opening her eyes.

JULIA: He had a fight at school.

MONTERO: A fight?

JULIA: Boys' stuff. Are you okay?

Montero: Tough day. You?

Julia: I called by the travel agents. We have to make up our minds. Paris or Vienna.

Montero: I can't picture Jaime fighting.

Julia: Kids. They start shoving each other and they end up rolling around on the ground.

Commentator: Silence. Montero gets ready for bed. They talk about having another child. They don't put it like that: "Give him a brother," they say. Montero gets into bed with Julia. They lie apart.

Commentator: *Hamlyn.* Scene Five. The office, just after three o'clock in the afternoon. Montero has only been out once in the whole day, just for half an hour to grab a bite to eat. He's spent the rest of the time reading the press dossier. It's the first thing he does every morning: read the press dossier. He's disappointed in the way the press is covering the case. "The one man who's being held in custody is only the tip of the iceberg." "Isolated case or extensive network?" "Network." "Iceberg." Do they not understand the difference between journalism and literature? The evening before, when Rivas finally left his office, Montero ordered him into solitary confinement. Montero didn't want to talk to the press, but gave instructions as to what the press could be told and what it couldn't. The press knows that someone is in custody, but they don't know his name. When they go into Montero's office, Josemari's parents have no idea what they're doing there. Montero realizes they find these surroundings intimidating. Or perhaps it's the silent presence of the other man, the official, poised to write down every single word that comes out of their mouths. Montero tries to think of questions that will relax them, "How was it getting here?" "The area you live in, is there a good bus service?"

Paco: It's not a bad area. It's getting better. You used to have to go to the city center for everything. Isn't that right, Feli?

Commentator: Feli is looking at a framed photograph on the judge's table. Montero five years younger, with Julia and Jaime. The photo was taken by Amparo, the girl who used to look after Jaime.

Montero: Have you always lived there?

Paco: She's from there. I got work, so I stayed.

Montero: How did you meet Pablo Rivas?

Paco: Young Pablo? Is he all right?

Montero: Mr. Rivas is fine. How long have you known him?

Paco: How long would it be, Feli? When did he start coming up to the house? Wasn't it with the support group? Young Pablo and some of his friends from university, they set up a group. A sort of meeting, you might say. We used to meet in somebody's house, like mine, to talk about problems we were having. He was in charge, you might say.

Montero: You talk about him with … affection.

Paco: We wouldn't have a bad word to say about him.

Montero: Does he call in often?

Paco: He's always welcome in our house.

Montero: He helps out with the children?

Paco: Yes, he does. School books, jotters, trainers … He's always coming round with stuff for them.

Montero: For all of them?

Paco: For all of them. Although you can tell he's got his favorites. At the start he used to get on best with Gonzalo. Now it's Josemari. Isn't that right, Feli? He bought him a bike as a reward, for doing well at school.

Commentator: The phone rings. Montero knows it's important because he's asked them to hold his calls. It's Julia, from Jaime's school. Montero watches Paco and Feli out of the corner of his eye. Paco is looking around as though he's in a museum. Feli still looks intimidated. She's never been anywhere like this. Perhaps some of you in the audience might have felt like that too at some time. It's up to you to create that sensation. *Hamlyn* is a play without lights, without set, without costumes. A play in which it's the spectator who imagines the lights and the set and the costumes. Montero says "I'm on my way" or "I'll be there in half an hour" and hangs up.

Montero: So Josemari spends a fair amount of time with him. With Mr. Rivas.

Paco: And we're glad of it. Where we live, there isn't much good company to be had. Young Pablo's from a different sort of background, you can tell a mile off that he's not from the area. He goes to church and then the cinema or the swimming baths. As long as Josemari's with Pablo, you're okay, because you know he's not going about getting into trouble with the other boys in the area.

Commentator: *Hamlyn.* Scene Six. Jaime's school.

Montero: Where is he?

Raquel: In the classroom, with your wife. Sleeping. He's fine, really. After the fight, we were talking and he just fell asleep. I didn't give him anything to calm him down, nothing. Accumulated tiredness. Tension.

Commentator: She offers her hand to Montero. An unexpectedly strong hand.

Raquel: Raquel Gálvez. I'm the school's child psychologist.

Montero: It's not like him, fighting. He's never been a violent child, quite the opposite. We don't understand what's happening.

Raquel: Don't try and understand too quickly. Just watch him. Watch each other.

Commentator: Silence.

Raquel: Take him home, he'll rest more easily there. If you need anything, don't hesitate to call. Whenever.

Commentator: She hands him a card. "Raquel Gálvez. Pediatric psychologist." Jaime is still asleep when they put him to bed in his own room. Then Montero and Julia go to their bedroom. They get ready for bed.

Julia: The other boy was bigger. Three years older.

Montero: We'll have to talk to the headmaster. It's disgraceful …

Julia: Jaime started it.

Commentator: Silence.

Julia: You'll have to talk to him.

Montero: I'll talk to him.

Julia: When?

Montero: Tomorrow. I'll pick him up from school. And when this is over I'm going to take him fishing. Two or three days, just the two of us.

Commentator: *Hamlyn.* Scene Seven. The scene with the child. Children are a problem in theatre. Children can hardly ever act. And if they can, the audience focuses on that, on how well the child can act. In this play *Hamlyn* Josemari is played by a grown-up. A grown-up actor who doesn't try to act like a child.

Montero: How old are you?

Josemari: Ten.

Commentator: He looks twelve. There's a key round his neck. He's not in the judge's office, but in a room with some toys that Montero ordered in. Montero lets him play for a while before asking his first question.

Montero: How long have you known Mr. Rivas?

Josemari: Who?

Montero: Your parents call him young Pablo.

Josemari: Pablo?

Montero: How long have you known him?

Josemari: All my life.

Montero: Is he your friend?

Josemari: He was my brother's friend first.

Montero: Gonzalo's?

Josemari: Yes, Gonzalo's.

Montero: He takes you to church, doesn't he? Do you like going to church with him?

Josemari: He has a beamer.

Montero: And after church?

Commentator: Montero has to repeat the question. Josemari is distracted as he notices the official.

MONTERO: He's writing down what we say. So that if we forget what we said, we can always go back and read it. Look.

COMMENTATOR: Josemari struggles to read: "How old are you?" "Ten." "How long have you known Mr. Rivas?"

MONTERO: And after church?

JOSEMARI: We head out. Bowling, ice-skating. If there's anything on, we go and take a look. Picnics, bumper cars …

MONTERO: And the chalet … have you ever gone to Pablo's chalet?

JOSEMARI: It's not his. It's his mother's.

COMMENTATOR: Silence.

MONTERO: Have you been there?

JOSEMARI: It's got a pool.

MONTERO: Just with him, or with other people?

JOSEMARI: Sometimes on our own and sometimes with Pablo's friends.

COMMENTATOR: Montero places eight photographs of adult males in front of Josemari. He asks him to point to the ones he remembers having seen in the chalet. Josemari points to three photographs.

MONTERO: What about boys? Did you see other boys there?

JOSEMARI: Sometimes.

MONTERO: Boys you know?

JOSEMARI: Sometimes I did. Sometimes I didn't.

MONTERO: What were their names?

COMMENTATOR: Silence.

JOSEMARI: Javi, Christian, Manolo, Rubén … the other Christian, Quique … Iván, Luis, Sebastián … Goyo …

MONTERO: Did you ever sleep over at the chalet?

JOSEMARI: Sometimes we went to church on Saturday night and Pablo brought me back home on Sunday evening. It gave us more time to do things.

COMMENTATOR: Silence.

MONTERO: So you both go to church, really?

JOSEMARI: Yes.

COMMENTATOR: Silence.

MONTERO: And those times when you sleep over with him, where do you sleep?

JOSEMARI: In bed, where do you think?

MONTERO: And him?

JOSEMARI: Pablo?

MONTERO: Pablo.

COMMENTATOR: Pause.

JOSEMARI: Are you going to take me away?

MONTERO: Have you done anything wrong?

JOSEMARI: No.

MONTERO: Then nobody's going to punish you. The people who do bad things, they're the ones who have to be punished. If anyone's done anything bad to you, he'd have to be punished.

COMMENTATOR: Pause.

JOSEMARI: I don't like it when he takes photos.

MONTERO: He takes photos?

JOSEMARI: I don't like it.

MONTERO: What sort of photos?

JOSEMARI: We pretend we're fighting, but we're not really, and he takes photos.

MONTERO: With no clothes on?

Josemari: Sometimes.

Commentator: Pause.

Montero: Did you ever sleep in the same bed?

Josemari: Sometimes there aren't enough beds to go round.

Montero: Did he sleep in your bed?

Josemari: Are you going to take me away?

Montero: No.

Commentator: Pause. Josemari nods his head.

Montero: And the others. Pablo's friends who go to the chalet as well. Did they ever sleep in your bed?

Josemari: Not with them. They go with other boys.

Commentator: Pause.

Montero: Did he touch you?

Josemari: Like when he was giving me a bath?

Montero: He gives you baths?

Josemari: At night.

Montero: Apart from the bath, has he ever touched you?

Josemari: No.

Montero: He touches you when he bathes you. When he sleeps with you? Does he touch you then?

Commentator: He asks the same question three more times, until Josemari nods his head.

Montero: Your willy.

Commentator: He asks him three times. Josemari nods his head.

Montero: Did he ask you to touch him?

Commentator: Josemari nods his head again.

Montero: To touch his willy?

Josemari: Yes.

Montero: Has he only asked you to touch it? Did he try and do anything to you with his willy?

Commentator: Pause. Josemari nods his head.

Josemari: But I don't like it. I told him I didn't like it.

Commentator: Josemari speaks very quickly as if he wanted to get it all out in one go.

Josemari: He knew I didn't like it and he stopped doing it.

Commentator: Pause.

Montero: Would you like a coke?

Josemari: Okay.

Montero: Are you hungry?

Josemari: Can I have a burger?

Commentator: Montero looks at his watch. It's only half an hour before Jaime gets out of school. Montero calls his secretary. He asks her to phone Julia to say he won't be able to pick Jaime up and would she please do it. He also asks her to get a burger and Coca-Cola.

Montero: Your parents told me he bought you a bike because you did well at school. Was that why, because you did well at school?

Commentator: Montero continues asking him questions until Josemari tells him he's tired. Then Montero sends him to a doctor, to be examined. Montero waits in his office, smoking, until the medical report arrives by fax. He reads it several times before ordering a car to take him to Rivas's mother's chalet. That night he checks through the same places that he first saw when he was searching them. There is nothing new, but everything—the pool, the car in the garage, Rivas's bedroom—everything seems smaller, impoverished. Meanwhile, the policemen who took Josemari to the hospital have brought him back to where he lives. Josemari opens his front door at half-past midnight, using the key that's hanging round his neck. At that same moment Rivas is smoking in his cell, Paco has gone out for a walk, and Feli gets out of bed as she hears the key turning in the lock.

COMMENTATOR: *Hamlyn.* Scene Eight. Over the next few days Montero orders the minors whose names were given by Josemari to be found.

JOSEMARI: Javi, Christian, Manolo, Rubén ... the other Christian, Quique ... Iván, Luis, Sebastián ... Goyo ...

COMMENTATOR: They all come to the room with the toys. Montero asks them all the same questions.

MONTERO: Were you ever in that chalet? Did anyone give you presents? Did they take photos of you? Did they bathe you? Did you sleep there? Did anyone touch you?

COMMENTATOR: *Hamlyn.* Scene Nine. Time has passed. Time's the most difficult thing of all in theatre. It's not enough to say: "Ten days later." Or "The card has been lying on the table for an hour." Only the spectator can create time in theatre. If that's what the spectator wants, then the card has been lying on the table for an hour, beside the phone. The card says: "Raquel Gálvez: Pediatric Psychologist."

RAQUEL: If you need anything, don't hesitate to call me. Whenever.

COMMENTATOR: It's mid-afternoon by the time Montero decides to call. Raquel shows no surprise. He wants to talk to her, but perhaps not at the school, why don't they have lunch together? They meet in a café, far from the Court buildings and the school. Raquel asks about Julia. Montero replies that Julia's fine.

MONTERO: She's fine.

COMMENTATOR: The truth is he's not sure, he doesn't know if she is fine. They haven't spoken much recently. They don't speak. It's just a bad patch, they've been through others, they've been married ten years. They had intended to celebrate their tenth anniversary with a weekend away: Vienna or Paris. But it didn't happen. Raquel's wearing a red dress that reminds him of Julia ten years younger.

MONTERO: It won't be long before there'll be no way to keep him in. And we'll spend the whole day wondering where he is, who he's with ... What sort of world are we leaving to our children, it worries me. Children today, anything can happen. When I'm at work, I convince myself I can actually make a difference, but I go to bed every night with the feeling that I'm just flailing around in the dark.

RAQUEL: Don't be hard on yourself. I'm sure you're doing what you can.

MONTERO: Flailing around in the dark. I don't even know how to talk to my own son. I go to him and I don't know what to say.

RAQUEL: Talking to your own child is the most difficult thing in the world.

COMMENTATOR: Silence. Montero fills Raquel's glass.

MONTERO: Do you know what I'm working on?

COMMENTATOR: He opens his briefcase and brings out the press dossier. He shows her a headline: "Child Abuse Ring Uncovered."

RAQUEL: I've read about it. It's horrible.

MONTERO: It's irresponsible. I can imagine the journalist rubbing his hands: "the story of the year." He's got the story of the year and he writes literature instead of sticking to the facts.

RAQUEL: So, it's not true?

MONTERO: It is true. But we've got no proof. When I began the case I felt that for the first time I could do something for people. All my career I've had to take tough decisions, I've thought a thousand times over this isn't for me. And suddenly here was something that made sense of my life as a judge.

COMMENTATOR: Silence.

MONTERO: That newspaper's ten days old. Each day that passes, they lose interest. From the front page to page twenty, from three columns to fifty words.

COMMENTATOR: Silence.

MONTERO: All I've got is the boy's statement. The others have refused. Some of them say they've never been to the chalet. Others that they didn't see anything out of the ordinary. I've only got one boy, and the doctors found no sign of any abuse. Not that that means anything. But sometimes I wonder: maybe it is all a story. Maybe the boy just made it up.

RAQUEL: There are criteria for determining the coherence of a statement. To distinguish between the truth and a story, as you put it. We call it: discourse credibility evaluation.

COMMENTATOR: Silence.

RAQUEL: It makes my blood run cold to think about those children.

MONTERO: I imagine you're particularly sensitive to news like that.

RAQUEL: My family wants me to change my job. They say I get too involved. Things like this leave me in shreds. And for them to get away with it.

MONTERO: I've only got the word of a little boy. Not enough. I need proof. What I wouldn't give for some proof.

RAQUEL: I look at the parents.

COMMENTATOR: Silence.

RAQUEL: I look at the parents and I understand everything. I understand why those children have that look of fear in their eyes. The people who should give them security, all they do is teach them to be afraid. That's the worst crime of all.

COMMENTATOR: Silence.

MONTERO: I'd have to be a hundred years older to judge something like this. And I'd need another thousand years to find the right words for my son.

RAQUEL: How did your father begin? That is if your father ever talked to you.

MONTERO: He told me "The Pied Piper of Hamlyn," and he drew conclusions from it.

RAQUEL: Really?

MONTERO: It was my favorite story. I don't know how he managed, but my father was able to relate it to anything he wanted to say to me.

RAQUEL: Tell it to me.

MONTERO: "The Pied Piper?" Here?

RAQUEL: Are you embarrassed in case someone overhears?

MONTERO: Once upon a time there was a lovely city called Hamlyn. But one day the people of Hamlyn woke up to find that their city was overrun with rats. They looked at each other helplessly, in despair, because the rats had already got inside their houses.

Commentator: He tells her the whole story. Then they talk about different things, but they keep coming back to the story of the man who punished the city by taking away all its children with his flute. They're still talking about it when they leave the café. Montero helps her to get a taxi. He's about to catch one too, but then decides to walk. He doesn't walk homewards, but towards the south. As he leaves the center behind him, the streets become wider and longer. He walks for an hour, until he comes to a square. Although this is the first time he's been there, he recognizes the square where Rivas stopped his car. "Anyone want a lift to church?" Montero wanders round the local streets. He recognizes places, or has the impression he recognizes them: the church, Josemari's school, Paco and Feli's house. There are no lights on on the second floor, but he thinks he catches a glimpse of Feli behind a curtain. It's already dark when Montero leaves the area. It's cold, but he decides to walk. He doesn't walk in the direction of his home, but towards the Court. He phones twelve journalists, summoning them for two hours later. He makes clear: "This isn't a press conference."

Montero: This isn't a press conference. It's an opportunity for us to speak in a way we couldn't do in a press conference.

Commentator: But they ask the sort of questions they would in a press conference. Of the twelve summoned, only three appear. They ask rapid questions, as if they wanted to get it over and done with, they'd like to be in their beds. "Can we publish the name of the man in custody?" "Is the Church implicated?" "Any politicians?"

Montero: Now I have a question for all of you: how do we prepare the city to learn the worst? Because we still don't know what the worst is. I know I can't frighten any of you, you've had to report horrors. All I ask is that you are more careful than ever—I know you're always careful, but this time more than ever—with the words you choose. For Josemari's sake, make sure you make no mistakes. Hopefully Pablo Rivas will be an end of it, hopefully when we give the bastard thirty years. Some of you are parents. How would you tell Josemari's story to your children? No, I know it's not easy. Talking to your own child is the most difficult thing in the world.

Commentator: *Hamlyn.* Scene Ten.

Montero: Would you prefer the window closed?

Commentator: Rivas doesn't reply. It's the same Rivas of two weeks ago, but seven pounds lighter. Montero closes the window. He's spent the night in his office. At nine they brought him a jug of coffee and the press dossier; at ten he sent for Rivas. He sets a cup of coffee in front of him. Rivas doesn't drink it. Montero has his black, no sugar.

Montero: In our first interview, when I asked you how you had met …

Rivas: I only asked you for one thing. I asked you to keep it from my mother. Journalists went to ask her what I was like as a child. Had I been abused as a child, they asked my mother.

Commentator: Silence.

Montero: Do you think I gave your name to the press? I didn't give it. But it's hard to rein them in when they have the bit between their teeth. They flock to the doors of the Court every morning and they go crazy for a good story. And there's no better story than one involving children.

Commentator: He sets the press dossier in front of Rivas.

Montero: If only they would stop at writing bad literature. But literature isn't enough for them. They want to pass sentence too. Without hearing what the accused has to say. They've passed sentence already.

Commentator: He opens the dossier in front of Rivas.

Montero: I haven't passed sentence. I want to hear what you have to say. It's not a good story I'm looking for. I want the truth. The origin of the evil, that's what I'm looking for.

Commentator: Silence.

Montero: In our first interview, I asked you how you had met Josemari. You replied as follows:

Commentator: "It was through his father. His family was in … difficulties. His family's constantly in difficulties. Six kids, his mother always pregnant, and his father never off benefits. I do what I can for them."

Montero: "I do what I can for them." What does that mean?

Commentator: Silence.

Rivas: Paco, the father, I helped him to stop drinking. Well, I tried. I tried to boost his confidence, his self-esteem was at rock bottom. We used to talk, I helped him look for work … Until I lost patience with him and I thought it would be better to focus on the boys. Josemari and I hit it off from the start. I used to go and pick him up from school and we would go to a café and he'd do his homework. Before that if he didn't go to school, his parents never even noticed. He's clever. He started making progress straight away. That's why it's so hard to accept that … I can understand what Gonzalo said as jealousy, jealousy between kids, but Josemari … He knows that I'd never do anything to hurt him. Someone has put that filth into his head.

Commentator: Silence.

Montero: So you, if we can put it like this, gave moral support to his family. What about support of a more material kind?

Rivas: Whenever I could, I gave them a hand. Books, clothes …

Montero: Money?

Rivas: Occasionally, when they were absolutely broke.

Montero: Could you be more specific? About the payments?

Rivas: They weren't payments. Paco's a disaster, he can't hold a job for more than a week. You go into that house and your spirit collapses.

Montero: You gave them money regularly? A fixed amount.

Rivas: No, only when they were absolutely broke.

Montero: More or less, how much would you calculate you've given them?

Rivas: Impossible to say.

Montero: More or less.

Rivas: Really, I have no idea. Ask them.

Montero: Try and remember. It's important. When did the payments start?

Rivas: I told you they weren't payments. I told you …

Commentator: Silence.

Rivas: Was that how it was with Josemari? You kept on repeating the question until he told you what you wanted to hear?

Montero: Are you interrogating me?

Rivas: Is that how you do it? You ask the same thing a hundred times, a thousand times, as often as you have to, until you get the answer you were looking for. I imagine it's pretty easy with a youngster, especially when he's frightened. With a frightened youngster, you'd only have to ask him the same question ten times.

Montero: Sit down, please.

Rivas: Easier than looking for proof, isn't it? That's tedious, looking for proof can spoil such a nice theory. Especially in a case like this. A chance to shine. How many run-of-the-mill cases have passed over your desk, before this one came along. Suddenly, something worthy of your talent: A network of pederasts! I can imagine your excitement. Just what the city was waiting for: a monster and a savior. We all want to feel innocent. They show us a monster and we feel like little lambs. You give the people a monster and the press tells them what the monster was like as a child. "The origin of the evil, that's what I'm looking for." The origin of the evil is inside your mind. Don't look at me like that, the monster only exists in your mind. It was you who put that shit into Josemari's mouth. You'll never understand what there is between that boy and me. You'd understand if you listened to Josemari. Nobody listens to children. Do you want the truth? Let him speak, with no questions. The only truth is that I love that child. I love him like nobody else will ever love him.

Commentator: Silence. Montero gestures to the official to stop writing.

Montero: You must feel very sure of yourself to talk to me like that. Very sure or very desperate. You have powerful friends, who you're protecting and who are protecting you. We'll see when it comes to the trial. We'll see if you're as arrogant then. And we'll see how many friends you have left then. Who wants to be the friend of somebody like you?

Commentator: He makes Rivas look through the press dossier.

Montero: They've passed sentence already. If we let them, they'd tear you apart with their bare hands. This is about children. The whole city feels sullied. The punishment has to be huge. The whole city against one man. A rich man who wins the trust of a poor family so he can get into bed with their children. No, I can see it's not a story you want to boast about in front of mummy.

RIVAS: I haven't got into bed with any child.

MONTERO: Do you not like children?

RIVAS: If I like them, I put up with it.

MONTERO: Is that what you're going to say to the prosecutor? "I like children, but I practice self-control."

COMMENTATOR: Silence. Montero gestures to the official to start writing again.

MONTERO: Mr. Rivas, I'm asking you to be more precise about those payments.

COMMENTATOR: Silence.

RIVAS: The wife, Feli, she insisted on writing everything down. A pair of tights, and she writes it down. It'll all be there in her notebook, amounts and dates.

COMMENTATOR: *Hamlyn.* Scene Eleven. Montero has Rivas taken away and he paces from one side of his office to the other, from one side of his brain to the other. He makes a call from the chair Rivas was in and sits there in silence, until he realizes that it's night. It's a moonless night and Montero walks towards the south, along streets that become wider and longer, until he reaches the square. "Anyone want a lift to church?" Paco and Feli's house is only three blocks away. The street door smells of urine. Somebody's smoking in the dark.

GIRL'S VOICE: Got a cigarette?

COMMENTATOR: Yes, a girl. Very thin.

GIRL: Journalist? Or one of Pablo's friends? Josemari's? Have you got a cigarette?

COMMENTATOR: Montero can't remember if Paco and Feli live in 2A or 2B. 2B is open. Montero moves around in semi-darkness in a small flat, although it's hard to see just how small in the darkness. It smells of urine in here too. Montero is about to leave when he spots something moving on the settee. It's a small child, about three or four years old. Montero tells him to go back to sleep and covers him with what appears to be a blanket. The child asks for a drink of water. As he looks for the kitchen, Montero bumps into something that may be a cradle. He finds a switch. It's not working.

FELI: The electricity's off. They've cut us off again.

Commentator: Feli doesn't ask: "What are you doing here?" Feli doesn't usually ask anything.

Feli: I never leave them on their own. I popped out for some milk, at the Chinese. It's always open.

Commentator: Feli moves around with a little flashlight She heats a baby's bottle on a camping stove in the kitchen.

Feli: I've got some instant coffee.

Commentator: Montero accepts, though he finds it undrinkable. In spite of everything, the kitchen looks clean and tidy. Montero had imagined it would be chaotic and dirty. He had imagined dirty clothes scattered all over the place, mattresses on the floor, a dog. It smells of urine, but it's children's pee. Feli gives the little boy water and a bottle to the baby in the cradle.

Montero: Where are the others? If I'm not mistaken, you have six children.

Feli: The baby's my eldest daughter's. Robert and Dani are out collecting cardboard. Gonzalo, since all this began, I'm never sure where he is. And Josemari, well you'll know where he is.

Montero: Josemari's fine.

Feli: The policemen said it was you gave the order.

Montero: That's right.

Feli: They came for him about six hours ago. Will he not come back to sleep?

Montero: A few days away from all the fuss will do him good.

Feli: A few days?

Commentator: Montero points at a bicycle.

Montero: Is that the one Rivas gave him?

Feli: The chain's broken. Paco wanted to go with Josemari, but they wouldn't let him. Did they have to come with the siren on? The whole neighborhood knew what was going on.

Montero: You're right. There was no need to have the siren on. And your husband? Where's your husband?

Feli: He said he was going out on the cardboard run with the boys. Or he might be with his friends, I don't know.

Montero: They pick up cardboard that's been dumped and sell it by weight. Is that how it works?

Feli: You can get a good price for cardboard lately.

Montero: How long has it been since your husband had steady work?

Feli: He's had better times. He never got the chance to study, but he's good with his hands.

Commentator: She shines the flashlight onto a wall. There are papers fixed there with tacks. Drawings begun by an adult and finished by a child. Horses.

Feli: When he was young, he did caricatures in the street to earn a bit of money. Josemari likes drawing too. The two of them go off with their pencils and they lose all track of time.

Montero: How long has the electricity been off?

Feli: A week.

Montero: When this sort of thing happened in the past, you'd go to Rivas, wouldn't you?

Feli: We thought he was our friend.

Montero: How much did he give you? Twenty? Fifty? A hundred?

Feli: He gave us a hundred once. They were going to evict us.

Commentator: Feli walks away with her flashlight. That must be Josemari's bed, thinks Montero. He thinks about his son Jaime's room at home, about the posters on the walls. Feli comes back with a lined jotter. She opens it in front of Montero.

Feli: Everything's in here. Electricity. Gas. Twenty-five, fifteen … And in this column what we owe. Young Pablo, twenty, young Pablo, twenty-five.

Montero: Always Rivas.

Feli: You could always count on him.

Montero: The first entry is from four years ago. Was that the first time Rivas gave you money?

FELI: It's what friends do, help each other.

MONTERO: Was that the first time?

FELI: I don't know. I've no head for dates.

MONTERO: It's getting late. You've had a difficult day, I'm sorry. But it's my responsibility to make sure Josemari's safe. The only thing I want is for our children to be safe.

FELI: Are you going to take the others?

MONTERO: The important thing is that the children are safe.

COMMENTATOR: Silence.

FELI: He heard Paco had got the sack from the supermarket and he came to see if we needed anything. It was the first time. Before that it was other sorts of things. Gonzalo always came back with something from Pablo. Not money though.

MONTERO: What sort of something?

FELI: Cigarettes, a bottle of something ... Then Paco and Gonzalo fell out and it stopped.

MONTERO: Your husband and Gonzalo don't get on well ... is that what you mean?

FELI: They certainly don't get on well.

COMMENTATOR: Silence.

MONTERO: He says he doesn't know where Gonzalo is.

COMMENTATOR: Silence.

FELI: His friends told me they've seen him in a bar in town. They said it was the "Brando," like the actor.

COMMENTATOR: Silence. Montero points to the drawings on the wall.

MONTERO: Can I have one?

COMMENTATOR: Feli agrees. Montero chooses a red horse.

MONTERO: How many months has it been?

FELI: Six.

Commentator: Silence.

Montero: You'll have Josemari home before you know it. As soon as we're sure he'll be safe here.

Commentator: Silence. Montero goes to leave.

Montero: Don't worry about the electricity. I'll look after that. Thanks for the coffee.

Commentator: The thin girl is still smoking in the darkened doorway. Montero thinks about the baby in the cradle. The girl asks for another cigarette: Montero gives it to her. There's something in her eyes that reminds him of Josemari.

Commentator: *Hamlyn.* Scene Twelve. Julia is in the sitting room, waiting for him. He has no idea how long it is since they actually spoke to each other. She has.

Julia: They've expelled him. When I went to pick him up, he was in the headmaster's study. This afternoon, in the playground, he started a huge fight. Him against the rest.

Montero: That's what the headmaster says. What does he say?

Julia: Why don't you ask him?

Commentator: Silence.

Montero: I don't want to wake him up. I'll talk to him tomorrow.

Commentator: They walk to the bedroom in silence. Jaime hears them going down the corridor. He's sitting on his bed. He's overheard: "They've expelled him. When I went to pick him up, he was in the headmaster's study. This afternoon, in the playground, he started a huge fight. Him against the rest. That's what the headmaster says. What does he say? Why don't you ask him? I don't want to wake him up. I'll talk to him tomorrow."

Commentator: *Hamlyn.* Scene Thirteen. Montero greets her with a kiss on the cheek.

Raquel: Well, I'm here, but if it's about Jaime . . .

Montero: What can I get you?

RAQUEL: If it's about Jaime, I can't do any more than I've already done. I've asked the headmaster to give him another chance. He won't even discuss it. Perhaps when things have calmed down a bit ... The real problem is the parents. The parents of the other children.

MONTERO: I didn't call you to talk about Jaime. It's about Josemari. I want you to meet him. To help him.

COMMENTATOR: An hour later they're in the Care Home. The Care Home is where Josemari lives. Two policemen went to get him from his parents' house and put him in the car. Josemari had no idea where the car was taking him. When they got there, they washed him, gave him new clothes, and took him to the refectory where he met his new schoolmates. As they walk towards Josemari's room, Montero and Raquel look at the photographs hanging on the walls: photos of animals. Like the other twenty-nine children who live in the Care Home, Josemari has his own room. A white room. In all of the rooms and corridors and the refectory of the Care Home, the dominant color is white. The room has a window that looks out onto the playground. There's a group of children playing soccer there. Josemari isn't joining in. The superintendent signals to him and Josemari follows him down a white corridor to room number seven.

MONTERO: Hello, Josemari, how are you?

COMMENTATOR: Josemari doesn't notice Montero's outstretched hand or seems not to notice.

MONTERO: We've come to see how you're getting on. How they're looking after you. This lady's Raquel.

COMMENTATOR: Josemari doesn't look at her. On the second visit, Raquel brings him some drawing paper and a box of coloring pencils and as he draws he occasionally seems to listen to her, and at the end she writes her phone number down on a bit of paper.

RAQUEL: In case you feel sad or you feel like talking. Any time you want.

COMMENTATOR: On the third visit, Raquel asks him what sort of cake he wants for his birthday. On the fourth visit she asks him about his parents: "Have they got a car?" "Do they take you swimming?" "Do they help you with your homework?"

MONTERO: Why's he not talking?

RAQUEL: It's natural he should feel confused. All of this is too much for him. Children like this have no way of understanding what's happening to them, they don't know what's normal and what isn't, they start thinking that they've caused this whole problem for their families. That's what we have to avoid at all costs: them feeling guilty. They haven't been allowed to be children. All they've been taught is to be afraid. They don't need to hear threats. When he told you what happened to him, Josemari knew he was crossing a boundary. He can't go back, but he's too frightened to go forward. He needs help to continue. That little boy is asking for help, but he can't do it in any clearer way. His silence is all he has.

COMMENTATOR: They usually have a drink in this bar before they go their separate ways. On the evening of the fifth visit, Montero shows Raquel a letter. Raquel reads it in silence.

RAQUEL: It's textbook. On one hand he's ashamed. On the other … Textbook. The typical attitude of a man who thinks being a father is more about rights than responsibilities. "Whenever you come home, I'm going to show you how to paint with watercolors. That's what I love best of all, to pass the little knowledge I have on to you." How could a man who didn't even know whether his son had gone to school write that? He didn't write that for Josemari. He wrote it for us. "Be a good boy. Do what the teachers tell you." He wants to suggest a sense of responsibility.

MONTERO: What about the other letter? What do you think of that?

COMMENTATOR: From Paco's lawyer to Judge Montero.

MONTERO: It's a formal petition, to which I'll have to reply. He's given it to lawyers, God only knows who's paying for them.

RAQUEL: The lawyer will have probably written both of them.

MONTERO: What do you think?

RAQUEL: It's not a good idea. At this stage of the patient's development, it could be disastrous.

MONTERO: When do you think that meeting could take place without risk? I have to fix a date. I can't stop him from seeing his son forever.

RAQUEL: What does the mother say?

MONTERO: He's the one who's requesting it. So, when would be reasonable?

RAQUEL: When the patient's had sufficient time to reconstruct his life project.

COMMENTATOR: "Life project." She's talking about a ten-year-old boy. "Life project." The words should ring in the theatre. Words: "Care Home." "Child Protection Agency," "Human Rights." This is a play about language. About how language is formed and how it is deformed. Raquel is still talking at the other side of the table. She doesn't say "family," she says "family unit." She doesn't say "Josemari," she says "patient." Raquel talks away and Montero looks through the window. Some boys are playing football on the pavement. Montero watches one who isn't taking part in the game. Montero would love to break the window to see better or to breathe.

MONTERO: It's not going to be easy. It's clear he wants a fight.

RAQUEL: Wanting to fight proves nothing. It's logical. Let him fight.

MONTERO: He's right. It's his son, after all.

RAQUEL: He's not fighting for his son, but for his standing in the community. He's fighting to preserve his social status. Give him back the boy and he'll show him off throughout the whole area.

COMMENTATOR: Silence. Montero shows Raquel a drawing. The horse that was hanging on the wall beside Josemari's bed. Standing on the horse, balancing like in the circus, a man and a boy.

MONTERO: He did drawings in the street. Five-minute caricatures.

COMMENTATOR: Pause.

MONTERO: I thought that Feli, his mother, would turn against him, but it hasn't worked out like that. I haven't got a single shred of evidence against him. I can't keep him away from Josemari for much longer.

COMMENTATOR: Raquel points to the boy standing on the horse's back.

RAQUEL: That's how that man sees his son. Looks at the boy's face. At his eyes.

COMMENTATOR: *Hamlyn.* Scene Fourteen.

MONTERO: Why could we not find you? Were you hiding?

GONZALO: I'm here, aren't I?

COMMENTATOR: He's here, in a bar called Brando. To find it, Montero has only had to open a city guide. The rest was more difficult: to get in, choose a table, buy a drink, put up with the stares until Gonzalo came in. There are only men in Brando, some of them younger than Gonzalo. That's the place we're in. Here.

MONTERO: Far from home. I heard you don't show your face much around there any more. Why would that be?

GONZALO: Change of scenery.

MONTERO: So sudden? You didn't feel threatened?

COMMENTATOR: Silence.

MONTERO: Who's threatening you?

COMMENTATOR: Silence.

MONTERO: Pablo Rivas? His friends?

COMMENTATOR: Silence.

MONTERO: If it's not Rivas, who?

COMMENTATOR: Silence.

MONTERO: It's our job to protect you. If you want, you can have a policeman at your side. Wherever you go.

GONZALO: I can look after myself. I just want you to stop pestering me. You've caused me problems with far too many people.

MONTERO: We won't pester you any more. We'll talk a while and then I'll leave you in peace.

GONZALO: We've nothing to talk about.

MONTERO: A month ago, you had plenty to talk about. You told me a whole lot of things. But you didn't tell me everything.

COMMENTATOR: He's referring to their first conversation, a month ago. Gonzalo called the Court; Montero was on duty. That's when it all began.

MONTERO: You didn't tell me your parents got money from Rivas.

COMMENTATOR: Silence.

Montero: I've seen the notebook your mother keeps, where she writes things down. Did you know your parents got money?

Commentator: Silence.

Gonzalo: My father, not my mother. Pablo gives it to my father and my father gives it to her to buy stuff.

Montero: Did Rivas give him money in front of any of you?

Did you ever see anything?

Gonzalo: Pablo always carries money. My father tells him what he needs and he gives it to him.

Commentator: Silence.

Montero: Your father got money from Rivas. Because you or Josemari went with him?

Commentator: Silence.

Montero: You say you can look after yourself. Maybe. What about your little brothers? Can Josemari defend himself on his own?

Commentator: Silence.

Montero: For the time he spent with you or with Josemari, was that why Rivas paid your father?

Gonzalo: I suppose it was. Nobody gives something for nothing.

Commentator: Silence.

Montero: Shall we go down to the Court and you can say all that again? Everything you've said about your father.

Commentator: Pause. Gonzalo walks over to the bar. He sits down on a stool and he makes a gesture at Montero. A brutal gesture that Montero had never seen before, but which he understands immediately.

Commentator: *Hamlyn.* Scene Fifteen. Josemari's birthday, in a reception room in the Care Home. Josemari comes in holding Raquel's hand. His mother and brothers and sisters are waiting for him. Feli kisses him first, then everyone else does. The last person to kiss him is the thin girl from the doorway. Josemari won't look Feli in the eye.

Feli: Sit down here, beside me. Sit up straight.

Commentator: Montero and Raquel stand apart from the gathering, observing. Before coming into the room, Raquel has told Josemari there's no need to be frightened.

Raquel: Don't be frightened. If at any moment you feel bad, give me a signal and we'll go back to your room.

Feli: So tell us what you do with yourself. What do you do in the mornings?

Commentator: Josemari tells them what he does: classes, football.

Feli: And in the afternoons?

Commentator: Josemari tells them what he does in the afternoons.

Feli: Is the food nice?

Josemari: It's okay.

Feli: Tell us more things. It's been so long since we've seen you. Did you know Gonzalo's got a job? Tell him, Gonzalo.

Commentator: Gonzalo says it's not sure yet, that he's got a week's trial, in a bar in the city center.

Feli: Do you want us to bring you anything from home?

Josemari: Where's Daddy?

Commentator: Paco's outside, in the van. A borrowed van.

Feli: He's got a job too. That's why he couldn't come. So is there anything you need? Clothes? Money?

Josemari: They give me pocket money, for when I go out.

Feli: You can go out?

Josemari: With my career.

Commentator: He looks at Raquel. She points to her watch as though saying ...

Raquel: We need to press on.

Commentator: Raquel goes out and comes back with the cake.

Raquel: He chose it himself.

Commentator: Josemari blows the candles out. They produce their presents. Feli gives him a shirt. Gonzalo, *Around the World in Eighty Days.*

Feli: And this is from Daddy, with a big big hug.

Commentator: It's a box of paints and drawing paper. Montero and Raquel see them to the door. Then they return to the reception room to help Josemari gather up the presents.

Josemari: Why did my father not come?

Commentator: Two days earlier the psychologist had written the following report for the judge.

Raquel: At our first interview, the patient strove to present an autonomous personality, but on a deeper level we have detected a negative self-image rooted in a profound sense of abandonment. Our intervention was oriented towards enabling the patient to develop his autonomy through a series of self-selected objectives that mark stages of his life project. Nevertheless, our strategy has been impeded by the patient's distrust of the adult world, manifesting itself in aggressive displays towards conventional signs of affection. Such aggression is characteristic of minors from unstructured family groupings, as is the case here, where the patient adopts a markedly ambiguous attitude towards this grouping, especially in matters relating to the biological father. On one hand, he wishes to present a normal bond with him. On the other, he fears paternal punishment arising from his sense of guilt over the events that rendered his sectioning advisable. In other words, a belief has been induced in the patient to the effect that he has damaged the person who has not been able to protect him. This is in turn a source of anguish for the patient, which he projects against adults in general, impeding treatment. It is for that reason that we recommend that the patient should not enter into any contact with the biological father until we have a reasonable guarantee that the unlikely benefits are not outweighed by any possible damage. Furthermore, we recommend that the patient should not be exposed to telephone or written contact that could impact upon his emotional stability.

JOSEMARI: Why did my father not come?

COMMENTATOR: Silence. Montero asks Josemari to sit down again, where he was before. But it's not Feli who's beside him now, but Raquel. The judge asks the questions. You could say she acts as his translator. She knows how to talk to a child.

RAQUEL: Do you remember what you told the judge about what you did with Mr. Rivas . . . with young Pablo, you used to call him in your family, didn't you?

COMMENTATOR: Silence.

RAQUEL: But you didn't tell him what your father thought about that.

COMMENTATOR: Silence. It's a hard silence to listen to. To listen to a child is the hardest thing in the world. It'd hard to get close to a child and them not to be afraid

RAQUEL: Does your father like you going with Pablo?

COMMENTATOR: Silence. Raquel goes close to Josemari. She speaks very close to his ear.

RAQUEL: Don't be afraid.

COMMENTATOR: Silence.

JOSEMARI: If I don't see him for a couple of days, he says to me: "Go on, phone him."

RAQUEL: Does he make you go with Pablo?

JOSEMARI: I don't want to sometimes, but he says to me: "Go and see him, he's very good to us."

RAQUEL: And do you feel you have to go with Pablo?

JOSEMARI: If I don't call, he dials.

RAQUEL: Do you know whether Pablo gives money to your father?

JOSEMARI: He's stingy. He promised me a really good bike, but he bought me a cheap one.

RAQUEL: Does he give him the money in front of you?

JOSEMARI: I don't know.

RAQUEL: You go out with Pablo and Pablo gives money to your father. Is that right?

Josemari: I don't know.

Raquel: He gives him money for the time you're with Pablo?

Josemari: He doesn't know what Pablo wants. If he did, he wouldn't let me go with him.

Commentator: Silence.

Raquel: Josemari, don't be frightened of telling us the truth. You're not on your own. The judge and I aren't going to leave you.

Josemari: My father doesn't know what Pablo wants. If he finds out he'll kill him.

Commentator: Silence.

Montero: Go on, off you go and play with your friends. Score lots of goals.

Commentator: Silence.

Raquel: Either he's protecting his father or he's frightened of him or he's deceiving himself. Or perhaps a bit of everything. Have you seen his drawings?

Commentator: She's referring to the drawings he did with the coloring pencils and paper she gave him.

Raquel: It's all there. The father who doesn't know how to be a father. And that woman. How can you still think she's telling the truth? You still believe she didn't know? Is there any way she couldn't know? She knew, but she turned a blind eye. They all knew, but all of them deny it. The law of silence, the shame that won't let them speak. Just think about the children left in that house, with those people. And look how Josemari depicts them.

Commentator: Meanwhile Josemari goes back to his room. He lies down on the bed and starts reading *Around the World in Eighty Days.* It's the first time Gonzalo's ever given him anything. On page seven, Josemari will find a letter stuck there with scotch tape. The letter's written in capitals.

Rivas: Dear Josemari: Do you like the book? The birthday fairy didn't want to give you anything this time because you've been very bad to me. The fairy said: "Forget him." But I said I can't just forget him. But I was very cross with you. More than cross, hurt. I still am. I don't know why you said all those things to the judge. You know how things were between you and me. It was you who came to me. And when

I tried to stop you, or when I went back to Gonzalo, you called me: "Pablo, you haven't been for ages. Are you cross with me?" And you said you missed me. That's why I can't believe you said those things. If you did, they're not your words, you've let yourself be tricked. Don't let them trick you. We've nothing to be ashamed of. But don't try and tell them that. They're sick people. I don't know when we'll see each other again. Are you doing your homework? Do your studies so I can be proud of you. When I can I'll send you some more books. If you need anything, tell Gonzalo. Do you know what I'd really like? You to send me one of your drawings.

COMMENTATOR: Josemari turns the letter over and starts drawing. A horse or a rat. It looks like a rat. Then another and another, a million rats.

COMMENTATOR. *Hamlyn.* Scene Sixteen. That same night. He's just about to go through his front door when Montero hears a voice behind him.

VOICE: Mr. Montero.

COMMENTATOR: Montero recognizes the voice, but doesn't turn round.

PACO: It's a month since they took him away. I go down to the Court every day, but nobody tells me anything. Be patient, they say. And today, when at last we're allowed to visit him, I can't even go in and wish him happy birthday. The lawyer doesn't know what to do.

COMMENTATOR: Silence. Montero turns round to face Paco.

MONTERO: Is this what your lawyer advised? To accost me at night in the street, outside my house. Why don't you and your lawyer come and see me in the morning in my office? We could talk more comfortably.

PACO: I did it on my own. I couldn't stand it. I had to talk to you. A conversation between you and me, man-to-man. I don't need a lawyer to talk man-to-man.

COMMENTATOR: Silence. Montero gestures towards a nearby bar.

MONTERO: Let's go for a drink.

COMMENTATOR: They sit at the table farthest from the television. At another table an old man's eating a sandwich. The barman's watching the television, even while he serves them. There's nobody else in the bar.

Montero: They'll have told you that Josemari's doing well. He has a lot of friends in the Care Home.

Paco: They told me he's got a psychologist.

Montero: They're helping him.

Paco: No, it's okay. Psychologists aren't what people think. Going to see a psychologist doesn't mean you're crazy. It's to understand what's happening to you and get your life back in shape.

Montero: Josemari is your fourth child, isn't he? The fourth of six.

Paco: And one on the way.

Montero: There's not many people as brave as you nowadays.

Paco: People only care about themselves.

Montero: But it's got to be hard, providing for a family like that.

Paco: The house isn't so small. There's room for all of us.

Montero: To feed eight mouths …

Paco: I'm not saying it's easy. But I've always said that where there's a will.

Montero: How do you manage?

Paco: By working here, there, and everywhere. People have got picky. I work everywhere.

Montero: Like where?

Paco: Unloading in the market …

Montero: And the cardboard run?

Paco: Yes, the cardboard run too.

Montero: You've no fixed work. No fixed contract.

Paco: It's just that I haven't found the right thing. What I'd really like is to earn my living in something to do with drawing. Can I borrow your pen?

Commentator: He takes a paper napkin. With rapid strokes, he produces a caricature of Montero.

Paco: The truth is I'm going through a bad patch. But I know someone who's going to sort me out. It goes through patches. Good times, not so good times.

Montero: And times when you've got nothing at all. No?

Paco: Yes, I suppose so.

Montero: And how do you get by in the bad times?

Paco: We try and put a bit aside when things are going well.

Montero: You manage to save, with six youngsters. I'm impressed. Because your wife wouldn't have time to work. I mean outside.

Paco: That's right.

Montero: Do you get any help from your older children? Your son, Gonzalo, does he contribute at all?

Paco: Ah well, things aren't that easy with Gonzalo. We don't get on. You know what kids are like today, they think they know it all. You try and give them a bit of advice and it's as if you'd spat at them.

Montero: It was Gonzalo who introduced you to Pablo Rivas, wasn't it?

Paco: That bastard ... No, I met young Pablo in the support group. At that time I was drinking a bit and he got people together ... with the same problem. There's a lot of people in our area like that.

Montero: Did Rivas give you any other sort of help? Financial help, for example.

Paco: You can't always plan. Sometimes two bills come in together at the worst moment. They threaten to cut off the electric ... Electric, water ... You've no choice but to pay these things.

Montero: So if that happens, what do you do?

Paco: You go to whoever you can for help.

Montero: To Mr. Rivas, for example?

Paco: Bastard!

Montero: Did he ask for anything in exchange?

PACO: In exchange? We were friends, at least I thought we were. Maybe he'd ask me to give him a hand with something—moving or changing the oil in his car.

MONTERO: What's the most he ever gave you?

PACO: I'm not sure. Fifty. They were about to cut off the gas.

MONTERO: He gives you money without asking for anything in return.

PACO: As a loan. We're going to pay it back. Feli has it all written down, right to the last penny. That's what I said to her: "We're going to pay it back, right to the last penny."

MONTERO: I've seen the notebook.

PACO: You have?

MONTERO: There's a recorded payment of a hundred and fifty.

PACO: There could be. I'm not sure.

MONTERO: I'm struck by the fact that you write it all down.

PACO: To pay it back. Not to forget.

MONTERO: I still don't have any clear sense of what your relationship with Rivas is like.

PACO: My relationship? If I set eyes on him, I'll kill him. I welcomed him into my home, and look how he pays me.

MONTERO: And you never suspected anything? Be honest, we're talking man-to-man. There's nobody taking notes, no tape recorders. Tell me: nothing ever crossed your mind?

PACO: People said some things about his friends. Big cars driving about the district, you can imagine. But if anyone had said to me that young Pablo was up to that sort of thing, I'd have gone for them.

MONTERO: And he never offered you money in return for...?

PACO: I'd have killed him. And that bastard's walking the streets, as free as you please, as if butter wouldn't melt in his mouth.

MONTERO: Ask your lawyer. He'll explain it.

PACO: You know, the little shit is back about the place, in his fancy car. His mother's got enough money to make sure he's got the best lawyers on his side.

MONTERO: Has he tried to contact you?

PACO: He'd better not show his face to me.

MONTERO: Has he phoned?

PACO: No.

MONTERO: He hasn't tried to offer you money?

PACO: He'd better not.

MONTERO: He hasn't tried to help you in any way? Getting you a lawyer, for example.

PACO: I pay for my own lawyer. I pay it myself.

MONTERO: How do you know Rivas is back about the place? Have you seen him?

PACO: Friends have. I hardly go out. I can't go out. Neighbors turn their back on me The press has been hounding me for a month, dragging my name through the dirt. At school my kids have to put up with all sort of things being said about me.

MONTERO: If you think the press is misrepresenting you, you have the right to defend your reputation.

PACO: My lawyer tells me not to say anything, or I'll make things worse. He's trying to get me to agree to a deal. With you. He told me it's what happens. He wants me to say I knew in exchange for being allowed to see the boy on weekends. Why the fuck does he want me to say I knew? That my son was being ...

MONTERO: Are you proposing a deal? Is that what you wanted to discuss?

PACO: All I want is to see my boy.

MONTERO: Our psychologists think you shouldn't see him just yet. You'll have to be patient.

PACO: The lawyer says that you can keep this going for months. That you're able to give him the runaround.

MONTERO: The runaround? I find that offensive.

Paco: First you order a report from the psychologist, then another report from so and so …

Montero: I think this has been a mistake. This conversation has been a bad idea.

Paco: They won't even let me talk to him on the phone.

Montero: We have to make sure the child isn't intimidated in any way.

Paco: Intimidated? All I want … I don't understand what he's doing there.

Montero: What do you not understand? It's very simple: when the family fails to protect, the State has to intervene.

Paco: I'm more than able to protect my children.

Commentator: Pause.

Montero: I'm not sure Gonzalo would agree with you. I asked him about the money. "For the time he spent with you or with Josemari, was that why Rivas paid your father?" Do you know what Gonzalo said?

Commentator: "Nobody gives something for nothing."

Paco: You've no idea. What the fuck would you know about living in an area like that? It was Josemari's chance. The chance to get out of there. Young Pablo and I talked about it a whole lot of times. That he was going to take him to study. To a university abroad.

Commentator: Silence.

Paco: I thought he'd be better of with Pablo than with me.

Commentator: Silence.

Paco: Has Josemari seen the papers? What the papers are saying about me?

Montero: No.

Commentator: Silence.

Paco: Put me in prison, do what you want with me, but let me see my son. You've a son too.

Commentator: Silence.

Montero: Make a new application. But I can't promise you anything. We have to be sure that the unlikely benefits are not outweighed by any possible damage. At this stage in the process, a meeting like that could harm Josemari. And it's him, Josemari, we have to think about. About his life project.

Commentator: Pause. Montero thinks that Paco wants to hit him. But Montero knows Paco won't. Paco pays for his Coca-Cola and walks towards the door. Before leaving, he turns round towards Montero.

Paco: You've got a son. Imagine somebody tried to separate you. Imagine somebody tried to take him away from you.

Commentator: Paco leaves. Montero puts the caricature in his pocket and orders another drink.

Commentator: *Hamlyn.* Scene Seventeen.

Julia: He hit me.

Montero: What?

Julia: He hit me.

Commentator: Pause.

Montero: I have to talk to him.

Julia: Now. You have to talk to him now.

Montero: You don't want me to wake him up.

Julia: You have to talk to him now.

Commentator: Pause. Montero goes into Jaime's bedroom. Jaime is sitting on the bed. He's heard: "He hit me. What? He hit me. I have to talk to him. Now. You have to talk to him now. You don't want me to wake him up. You have to talk to him now." The bedroom door opens and Jaime sees his father's silhouette against the landing light. Montero goes in.

Montero: Do you mind if I turn on the light?

Jaime: I'd prefer you didn't.

COMMENTATOR: Montero wonders if he should turn on the light or not. If he isn't giving in by leaving it off. He decides to turn it on, dazzling Jaime. Montero wonders how long his son has been sitting on the bed in the dark. He wonders if Jaime often spends his time sitting on the bed in the dark. The judge sits at the foot of the bed and looks around the room. The books, the posters, nothing seems out of the ordinary. He doesn't want to say the first thing that comes into his head. He knows how important it is to choose his first words carefully. He can't find them: those first words. As he's leaving Jaime's bedroom, he sees Julia on the landing, sitting on the floor, her head between her hands. He leaves the apartment and calls the elevator, but then changes his mind and calls the other one, the one that goes down to the garage. He's never liked driving, but tonight that's exactly what he does. Tonight, the night of the day that Josemari celebrated his eleventh birthday, none of them can sleep: Gonzalo, Rivas, Paco, Feli, Julia, Jaime, Josemari, nobody can sleep as Montero drives. He only stops twice, both times for an elevator in the same garage. From that garage he can see the whole city, the Museum of Contemporary Art, the auditorium, the new stadium ... Dawn breaks and Montero feels like the light passes him by. He buys a newspaper at the garage: he opens it at the news page. Nothing, not a word. Montero goes back to the car, but now he wants to go somewhere. He arrives at the Care Home before nine o'clock. The superintendent is surprised to see him because he usually visits Josemari in the afternoon. "The boys are at breakfast," he says and gets Josemari called. But Josemari isn't in the refectory, or in his room. Josemari isn't in the Care Home. Montero calls Raquel.

MONTERO: Is he with you? Has he called you? Where do you think he might be?

COMMENTATOR: Then he issues three detention orders: Josemari, Paco, and Rivas. Paco is arrested half an hour later, in his home, in front of Feli and their smallest children. They handcuff him. The handcuffs hurt his wrists. Rivas is arrested an hour later, in his mother's house. By midday, when Raquel arrives at the Care Home, Josemari still hasn't shown up. At six o'clock Montero receives a call.

MONTERO: They've got him. Twenty miles east from here.

RAQUEL: How could he have got there?

MONTERO: But it's ... It's the opposite direction.

RAQUEL: He must have been disorientated.

COMMENTATOR: At seven o'clock Josemari is going back into his room. He's limping.

He hurt himself jumping over the fence. In bed, he picks up *Around the World in Eighty Days*, and the paper and paints his father gave him.

MONTERO: You can paint if you like, while we're talking.

COMMENTATOR: Josemari starts painting, sitting on the floor.

RAQUEL: We'll talk about what happened today later on. It was wrong. Something could have happened to you. We won't ask where you were going. If someone helped you, we're not going to ask who. Whose idea it was, or if you were going to meet someone, you can tell us in your own time. We just want you to understand that we're going to make sure it doesn't happen again.

MONTERO: You're very good.

JOSEMARI: My father taught me.

COMMENTATOR: For the first time, Josemari looks up from his painting: a red horse.

JOSEMARI: You told me they weren't going to take me away

RAQUEL: You're safe here. Everyone here loves you.

JOSEMARI: I want to go home.

RAQUEL: Why do you say that? Nobody takes advantage of you here. Nobody tries to use you. Nobody . . .

MONTERO: Leave us on our own, please.

RAQUEL: Sorry?

MONTERO: Please, leave us on our own.

RAQUEL: Do you want me to wait outside?

MONTERO: There's no need. I'll call.

COMMENTATOR: Before she goes out, Raquel turns towards Josemari.

RAQUEL: I don't know what you're playing at, but you're not going to fool me.

COMMENTATOR: She goes over to the boy. She gives him a kiss.

RAQUEL: Don't be afraid. I'll always be at your side.

COMMENTATOR: She goes out. Silence. Montero and Josemari are alone for the first time. Perhaps we should highlight the moment with some music. Flute, of course. But what music did the Pied Piper play? Has anyone ever heard it?

MONTERO: You and I have never talked on our own. Man-to-man.

COMMENTATOR: Montero puts his hand on Josemari's head, he caresses it. He holds the boy's head against his chest. Montero feels his own heart beating very fast.

MONTERO: Once upon a time there was a lovely city called Hamlyn. But one day the people of Hamlyn woke up to find that their city was overrun with rats. They looked at each other helplessly, in despair, because the rats had already got inside their houses. And then there came to Hamlyn a man who played the most beautiful music on his flute.

COMMENTATOR: Curtain.

Sa ka la

Jon Fosse

Translated from Norwegian by Sarah Cameron Sunde

Sa ka la premiered at the Aarhus Teater in Aarhus, Denmark, in April 2004, directed by Johan Huldt.

Note on the Translation

In translating plays there are always things that are "untranslatable." Since plays are meant to be experienced live, one cannot simply translate words; one must translate the action that lies underneath the words. Actions and subtleties are cultural, and it is imperative to translate specifically for the culture that one is working in. When I began translating Fosse's work, I was very taken with the idea that I was translating contemporary Norwegian theatre into the American idiom. I realized I was wrong. It is not about taking the language into modern-day America and making it colloquial but making Fosse's unique voice come through in the American English language. His is a voice like we've never heard in Norwegian either. I want *that* part to work for an American audience.

Yah = Norwegian "ja" = yes

Yah = American "yeah," only not so nasal, please.

Also, Yah = yep, hmm, ok, so, well, fine, oh, sure, yeah, uh-huh, tsk, ugh ...

These other words have not been inserted in place of the "yah" because repetition is vital. My goal is to provide an affirmative in American English that lives somewhere between "ja" and "yeah" and carries a great deal of flexibility with it. It should be simple and not sound foreign. It can be used for emphasis in certain cases, but it should primarily be used as a "filler" where the breath or thought holds for just a second. The "yah" serves to link the characters, while also allowing room for one word to be character-specific. I encourage the creative team to find ways into the sound that allows the repetition to help tell the story without putting too much emphasis on the "yah." In all cases, the "yah" should help, not hinder, telling the story of this theatrical world. Some "yahs" may be most helpful if they are silent. When the "yah" appears at the beginning of a line, please do not make the mistake of thinking that there is a comma after the yah, before the rest of the phrase. Instead, try to think about it as if the yah simply leads to the rest of what is being said.

Since Jon Fosse uses no punctuation except for the line-breaks, whether a line starts with a capital letter or a lower-case letter is important. This holds true both for the spoken text and the stage directions, which are imbedded in the text. For example, *Pause* relates to the preceding text differently than *pause* would. And since repetition and slight variation on the repetitions is key to his technique, *somewhat short pause* is different from *Short little pause*.

This translation is dedicated to John and Meredith Warren. It would not have been possible without the support of Jon Fosse, The Royal Norwegian Consulate General, Oda Radoor (dramaturg), Anna Gutto (co-artistic director, Oslo Elsewhere), Einar and Cammy Sunde, and all the theatre artists, producers, and technicians who brought it to life.

SARAH CAMERON SUNDE

CHARACTERS

Henning

Johannes

Mom

The Nurse

The Youngest Daughter (Nora)

The Oldest Daughter (Hilde)

The Friend (Trine)

Karsten

The Brother (Ola)

To the left: a window, a sofa

To the right: a window

Henning
comes in
We married sisters
you and I
that's what happened
Henning turns around

Johannes
comes in
Yah
yah that's what
happened

Henning
I
Henning
took Hilde

Johannes
And I
Johannes
took Nora

HENNING
And when you marry the daughter
yah well Mom comes too

JOHANNES
So both of us are married
to Mom

HENNING
And clearly
yah clearly you attend the party
when Mom turns sixty

JOHANNES
And the big day
yah today's
the day

HENNING
Because today she
the great
the grand
the incomparable
turns sixty

JOHANNES
And that should be celebrated

HENNING
It must be celebrated

JOHANNES
Of course it will be celebrated

Short pause

HENNING
At the very least

Short little pause

JOHANNES
But there'll just
be a few of us

Henning
There isn't really enough space
somewhat short pause
obviously

Johannes
No obviously not
Short pause
It'll be the immediate family
as they say

Henning
Yah
somewhat short pause
and then of course
she
is coming
yah you know

Johannes
Yah

Henning
She's coming yah
Trine
somewhat short pause
but unfortunately
apparently she's bringing her husband

Johannes
She has a husband

Henning
Yah
and he's coming
with her

Johannes
Trine
yah

Henning
She and Mom are such good friends

JOHANNES
And they are so alike

HENNING
Maybe that's why
they get
along so well

JOHANNES
Definitely

HENNING
Apparently his name is Karsten

JOHANNES
asking
Trine's husband
Short pause

HENNING
Yah

JOHANNES
Quite a lady that Trine
yah

HENNING
In oh so many ways
Trine
yah
yah I've been there

JOHANNES
You have

HENNING
Yah

JOHANNES
Sure

HENNING
Pretty damn sure
And it wasn't half bad

Johannes
You've been there

Henning
Yah
Short pause

Johannes
Long time ago

Henning
Not too long

Johannes
Me too

Henning
You too
Henning and Johannes begin to laugh
Me
I've been there many times

Johannes
But a long time ago

Henning
I wouldn't say that
Somewhat short pause

Johannes
I wonder what Trine's husband is like

Henning
Me too

Johannes
You've never met him

Henning
No
somewhat short pause
no obviously not
Pause

JOHANNES
By the way
yah it's nice that you and Hilde are throwing the party

HENNING
Hilde felt like
yah like we should do it

JOHANNES
We could have done it
instead

HENNING
It's ok that we're doing it
right

JOHANNES
Yah sure

HENNING
Yah
short pause
Mom didn't really seem to want
to throw her own party

JOHANNES
But she probably would have
yah if no one else had done it
I mean
it's not like she's the type to not throw
any party at all
to celebrate her life quietly
or whatever you'd say

HENNING
Quiet isn't her forte

JOHANNES
That's one way of putting it
Pause

HENNING
She is nice

though
Kind

Johannes
Sure she is
Pause

Henning
Very nice
She only wants what's best
it's like she
wants everything to be ok
and she is
kind
yah as the day is long
she is kind

Johannes
She is
Short pause

Henning
Well she did welcome me into the family

Johannes
Me too
Short pause

Henning
She is generous
in her own way

Johannes
Generous and kind

Henning
She is
Short pause
And you
yah you're doing ok

Johannes
Oh yah thanks

Somewhat short pause

And you

HENNING

Oh yah thanks
pretty much the same
yah

Pause. HENNING goes over to the window, looks out, then looks at JOHANNES

Yah that's how we met
yah
we married sisters
you the youngest
and I the oldest

JOHANNES

That's what happened
yah

JOHANNES walks over to the window, stands next to HENNING and looks out

What a beautiful day

somewhat short pause

it was a beautiful day
the day she turned sixty

somewhat short pause

that's good

somewhat short pause

because we do love her
don't we

HENNING

We do

somewhat short pause

of course

Short pause

JOHANNES

And they'll be here soon

Short pause

HENNING

I'm sure they will

Pause. HENNING goes and sits on the sofa and THE NURSE and THE YOUNGEST DAUGHTER roll a hospital bed onstage, place it to their right

THE NURSE
Yah this is the room
yah

THE YOUNGEST DAUGHTER
Yah
Short pause
And
you know
I don't think I told you
yah that it's her sixtieth birthday today

THE NURSE
No
no you didn't tell me that
Asking
She turns sixty today

THE YOUNGEST DAUGHTER
Yah
somewhat short pause
yah she
and I
yah I was supposed to pick her up
we
the immediate family
were supposed to celebrate her birthday
and when
yah when I got there
yah I found her on the floor
in the bathroom
she lay there
cuts herself off

THE NURSE
Yah you told me that

THE YOUNGEST DAUGHTER
And I'm thinking
yah how long could she have been lying there

THE NURSE
Well the doctor thought
yah that she hadn't been lying there all that long

THE YOUNGEST DAUGHTER
That is what he said

THE NURSE
I'm sure she hadn't

THE YOUNGEST DAUGHTER
But that nothing can be done

THE NURSE
Sometimes that's how it is
somewhat short pause
yah
yah there's too much damage
and
yah like the doctor said
yah it's a severe stroke

THE YOUNGEST DAUGHTER
But it's so awful
yah that nothing can be done

THE NURSE
Yah
Pause. THE YOUNGEST DAUGHTER sits down on the edge of the bed, strokes MOM'S hair. THE NURSE also goes over to the bed. Pause

HENNING
stands up
Yah I'm sure they'll be here any minute
yah
HENNING walks towards JOHANNES

JOHANNES
walks away from the window
Yah

Henning
It might be fun

Johannes
You think so

Henning
Maybe
somewhat short pause
So maybe it's not exactly the kind of party one looks forward to
Somewhat short pause
But anyway
somewhat short pause
yah you fall in love
how stupid right
and then there you are
with your wife and your mother-in-law
and whatever else comes with it

Johannes
Yah

Henning
Including your sister-in-law's childhood friend and
cuts himself off

Johannes
asking
Trine
Henning nods
She was Hilde's friend

Henning
Was

Johannes
Yah
Short pause
But it could be worse for us

Henning
Or it could be better

JOHANNES
Sure it could

HENNING
But I'm fine
I am
yah I'm a happy man

JOHANNES
Me too
Short pause

HENNING
But you two haven't had kids either

JOHANNES
We're thinking about it

HENNING
Yah
Pause

JOHANNES
Yah
of course
short pause
yah I'm fine
too
it's not that
Pause

HENNING
We are I think
yah as good as one can expect
somewhat long pause

JOHANNES
But they really should be here soon

HENNING
Yah
yah imagine that
Mom turns sixty today

JOHANNES
Yah
yah she is
like
a Mom
to all of us
isn't she

HENNING
She is generous

JOHANNES
Caring
as they say

HENNING
And today
she turns sixty

JOHANNES
She'll be here soon

HENNING
Yah
yah I'm sure they'll be here soon
and Mom
she
I bet she'll be the first
you'll see
this is her day
y'know
her big day
and when she gets here
yah

JOHANNES
Stand up straight
Stick out your chest

HENNING
And when she walks through the door
she'll hold one arm out

HENNING sticks out his chest, lifts his head up to look important, walks swaying his hips, holding his little finger out, he imitates

No is that really you
It's so great to see you
This is so great
So nice
So cozy
So good
So fantastic
So fucking fantastic
and so outstanding
and so grand

JOHANNES
Because everything is so fantastic

HENNING
Everything is so incredible

JOHANNES
And so extremely outstanding

HENNING
imitates
And I am most outstanding of all

JOHANNES
Because I have the biggest boobs

HENNING
imitates, shaking his chest
I have the biggest boobs

JOHANNES
And today is my sixtieth birthday

HENNING
imitates
Imagine me
one so grand
so young
so youthful

so
yah to put it bluntly
yah so attractive
with bite
and I am sixty years old
imagine that

JOHANNES
And that Trine
she's just as divine

HENNING
Don't go there

JOHANNES
One is young and divine
the other is old and divine

HENNING
Don't say that to Mom
yah about her being old
that stuff about being divine on the other hand

JOHANNES
No of course not
Pause
No
cuts himself off
yah I guess it's not
somewhat short pause
that easy for Mom
either
she really just wants to be grand
and
yah
cuts himself off. Short pause
And she is alone a lot of the time

HENNING
Yah that's how it is
Short pause

I think she sometimes gets together with
yah with that Trine
they go out to cafés and stuff
HENNING starts to cross the floor, wiggles his hips, stands there with his head turned
Imitates
Hey you

JOHANNES
imitates
Yah you
HENNING and JOHANNES start to laugh. Pause. HENNING walks over to the window, looks out, and JOHANNES walks over and stands next to him. Pause. THE NURSE steps out a bit into the room

THE NURSE
Yah
somewhat short pause
I actually have to
go
you know
yah there's a lot to do
somewhat short pause
but I'll come back
I'll check back in
yah in a bit

THE YOUNGEST DAUGHTER
What should I do

THE NURSE
You should just stay here with her

THE YOUNGEST DAUGHTER
Isn't there anything I can do

THE NURSE
Just stay here
somewhat short pause
and
yah
yah you've
already

called your sister
and your brother

The Youngest Daughter
Yah I called my sister
yah
and
yah she's supposed to call our brother

The Nurse
And they're coming

The Youngest Daughter
Yah
somewhat short pause
yah my sister is coming at least

The Nurse
That's good
somewhat short pause
Yah I'll check back in again in a bit
then
somewhat short pause
and if you need anything
yah don't hesitate to call for me
yah
The Nurse goes out. The Youngest Daughter strokes Mom's hair again

The Youngest Daughter
Mom
can't you say something to me
don't just lie there
Pause
say something to me
my love
Short pause
don't just lie there
The Youngest Daughter takes Mom's hands
Mom
don't just lie there
can't you say something

how you're doing
say something
HENNING starts walking around
please
Pause
Mom
somewhat short pause
Mom
Say something
please
Mom
can't you
Mom
Don't just lie there Mom
sweet Mom
sweetie
Pause

MOM
a
a
somewhat short pause
a
Pause

THE YOUNGEST DAUGHTER
Mom
is there anything I can do for you
my kind lovely Mom
Long pause

HENNING
Yah they'll be here soon
don't you think

JOHANNES
Oh yah

HENNING
Nora was supposed to pick up

yah the birthday girl
right

Johannes
also starts to walk around
Yah

Henning
And Hilde's supposed to come
as soon as she's done at work
Short pause
And then of course
he's coming
yah him
the brother
Ola

Johannes
Right he's coming
of course he's coming
Pause

Henning
And we have to spend time with him too
there's no escaping it

Johannes
That might be the worst part

Henning
Spending time with him the hopeless brother
yah

Johannes
Yah the brother
yah

Henning
Don't go there

Johannes
He doesn't exactly make himself useful

HENNING
No can't argue with that
Pause

JOHANNES
But we have to live with him too
somewhat short pause
You marry the daughter
somewhat short pause
and the mother

HENNING
The Mom
yah

JOHANNES
goes on
and the brother
Short pause
Yah that's what happened
Short pause
But now they have to get here
so we can get the party over with
be done with all this
Short pause
With the brother
somewhat short pause
Ola
And with the Mom
Short pause

HENNING
Yah yah
somewhat short pause
but she is nice
Mom
kind
yah
Pause

I think
yah that Hilde feels bad
that she doesn't visit her often enough
yah you know

Johannes
But she's got a lot to do
work
everything
somewhat short pause
and if they don't get along
yah well then they just don't

Henning
Maybe that's how
it was
yah maybe my Hilde stuck with the father
and your Nora stuck with Mom
growing up
maybe that's how it was

Johannes
It's often like that
Pause

Henning
looks at the clock
But now they should be here
Pause

Johannes
also looks at the clock
Yah the time has come

Henning
Yah
Short pause

Johannes
You're sure he's coming
yah the brother

HENNING
Apparently he said
he was coming
yah

JOHANNES
Yah

HENNING
Yah he's a character

JOHANNES
Character is one way of putting it

MOM
a
a
a
a
a
somewhat short pause
sa
somewhat short pause
a
somewhat short pause
a

JOHANNES
I'm sure they'll be here any minute
yah

HENNING
They should've been here by now
yah

MOM
a
a
a
a
somewhat short pause

la
somewhat short pause
a

Johannes
But why aren't they here

Henning
Good question

Johannes
Yah Nora's supposed to pick up Mom
somewhat short pause
and then come straight here

Henning
And Hilde was supposed to come when she was done at work
yah she should've been here by now
she's never this late

Johannes
Neither is Nora
somewhat short pause
yah according to what she said
Pause
It's strange that no one's here

Henning
Yah
Short pause

Johannes
But we can't really do anything
but wait
Short pause

Henning
We could go outside
maybe
the weather is nice

Johannes
We could

HENNING
Get some air
yah

JOHANNES
Yah let's go outside

HENNING
Let's do that

MOM
a
somewhat short pause
sa
la
somewhat short pause
a
a
in pain
a
slowly
a
Short pause
a
Short pause
a

HENNING
Yah
let's go
HENNING and JOHANNES start to leave

MOM
a
sa
la
a
a
somewhat short pause
o

somewhat short pause

sa

la

l

a

o

a

Short pause

a

Pause. HENNING *and* JOHANNES *walk out*

a

somewhat short pause

sa

la

a

ma

Short pause

ma

a

a

whining

a

ma

ma ma

a

somewhat short pause

a

ma

a

ma

ma

a

Short pause, a little louder

ma

ma

mama

mam ma

a

somewhat short pause

a

somewhat short pause

a

THE YOUNGEST DAUGHTER

Mom
Mom
Are you getting worse
How are you Mom
Mom

THE YOUNGEST DAUGHTER puts her hands on MOM's forehead

Mom

MOM twists a bit

Don't be afraid Mom
I am here
I'll take care of you
I will
And soon
yah they're coming soon
Hilde's coming
And Ola
right

MOM

a
a
la
a
m
ma
a

in pain

a
a
a

THE YOUNGEST DAUGHTER

Mom
I don't want you to be in pain

is there anything I can do for you

MOM
a
a
o
s
a
s
a
somewhat short pause
a
Short pause

THE YOUNGEST DAUGHTER
Don't be scared
sweet Mom
I'm here
I'll take care of you
THE YOUNGEST DAUGHTER strokes MOM's hair, strokes and strokes, and MOM closes her eyes. Pause. THE YOUNGEST DAUGHTER stands up, goes over to the window, stands there and looks out. Pause. THE NURSE comes in, she has a bowl with water and a sponge

THE NURSE
How's it going

THE YOUNGEST DAUGHTER
I don't know
it's the same

THE NURSE
Is she sleeping

THE YOUNGEST DAUGHTER
I don't know
she's making some noises
sometimes
but
yah
yah she's not saying anything

THE NURSE
No
Short pause

THE YOUNGEST DAUGHTER
What should I do

THE NURSE
Just stay here

THE YOUNGEST DAUGHTER
Is she in pain

THE NURSE
I don't think she's aware
somewhat short pause
she probably can't feel anything
somewhat short pause
but
yah if her mouth gets too dry
yah well she can't really drink
but here you go
yah I've brought some cold water
and a sponge
yah it'd be good if you could moisten her lips

THE YOUNGEST DAUGHTER
With the sponge

THE NURSE
Yah
THE NURSE and THE YOUNGEST DAUGHTER go over to the bed, and THE NURSE hands the bowl and sponge to THE YOUNGEST DAUGHTER
Her lips seem dry
yah
THE YOUNGEST DAUGHTER wets the sponge, puts them to MOM'S lips, moistens her lips
And she turns sixty today

THE YOUNGEST DAUGHTER
Yah
Pause

Yah we were supposed to celebrate her sixtieth birthday
I was supposed to pick her up
yah
yah I guess I told you that
Short pause. The Youngest Daughter moistens Mom's lips again
To The Nurse
Do you think that's enough

The Nurse
Sure

The Youngest Daughter
You don't think
yah that she was lying there for a long time

The Nurse
No
No I don't
don't think about it
somewhat short pause
and the doctor didn't think so either
right

The Youngest Daughter
And what if I hadn't
cuts herself off

The Nurse
Don't think about it
Pause
I'm sure your sister will be here soon

The Youngest Daughter
Yah
yah she's coming

The Nurse
That's good
Short pause

The Youngest Daughter
There's nothing they can do

THE NURSE

No
it was a severe stroke
there's so much damage
that it wouldn't be much of a life
yah the doctor said
yah that it will have to take it's course
he thought that
cúts herself off. Pause
I actually have to move on
THE NURSE goes out, and THE YOUNGEST DAUGHTER again wets the sponge and puts it to MOM'S lips, moistens them. MOM opens her eyes suddenly

MOM

a
a
a

THE YOUNGEST DAUGHTER

What is it
somewhat short pause
What is it Mom
Long pause

MOM

a
e
a
Pause
s
a
Pause
a

THE YOUNGEST DAUGHTER

Don't be scared
hey Mom
I'm here
and Hilde's coming soon
and Ola

we'll be here
with you
we will
so don't be scared
my sweet Mom

Mom
sa
sa
Mom tries, without opening her eyes, to sit up in the bed, but she lies down again
sa
a
somewhat short pause
a
somewhat short pause

The Youngest Daughter
Mom
what is it
do you need
what do you need to
Pause
Mom
Mom
Just say it
Short pause

Mom
sa
a
in pain
a

The Youngest Daughter
But Mom

Mom
a

The Youngest Daughter
What is it Mom

Mom
a
sa
a
a

The Youngest Daughter
Mom
it's me
right
Nora

Mom
a
a

The Youngest Daughter
Mom
you do recognize me
Nora
Mom
It's Nora
And
cuts herself off
You recognize me
right
sweet Mom
you
sweet sweet Mom

Mom
in pain
a
a
a
pause

The Youngest Daughter
But Mom
pressing
Mom

THE YOUNGEST DAUGHTER sits down on the edge of the bed

Mom
you and I
you know
always
you and I

THE YOUNGEST DAUGHTER suddenly becomes very sad, almost starts to cry

you and I
you and I Mom
always that
you and I
you Mom
sweetie

pause

always you and I
you and I
always you and I

Pause

MOM

e
o
ol
sa
o

somewhat short pause

o
o

somewhat short pause

sa
a

softly

aa
men
sa

somewhat short pause

sa

Pause

THE YOUNGEST DAUGHTER
Mom
Pause. THE OLDEST DAUGHTER comes in

THE OLDEST DAUGHTER
Nora
THE YOUNGEST DAUGHTER looks up, slowly looks at THE OLDEST DAUGHTER, who stops. Pause. THE OLDEST DAUGHTER then goes toward THE YOUNGEST DAUGHTER, who doesn't look at her
This is so awful
And today
exactly today
on her sixtieth birthday
Today of all days
Short pause
And so suddenly
so completely unexpected
yah
Pause

THE YOUNGEST DAUGHTER
It's
cuts herself off

THE OLDEST DAUGHTER
It made me feel sick
actually

THE YOUNGEST DAUGHTER
Yah

THE OLDEST DAUGHTER
And I came as fast as I could
somewhat short pause
yah get out of there

THE YOUNGEST DAUGHTER
Yah
And you called Ola
Yah

THE OLDEST DAUGHTER
Yah yah of course

THE OLDEST DAUGHTER goes over to the bed

THE YOUNGEST DAUGHTER
And he's coming

THE OLDEST DAUGHTER
Yah yah
Short pause
No
no it's just so awful
Poor Mom
poor poor Mom

THE YOUNGEST DAUGHTER
She lay on the floor

THE OLDEST DAUGHTER
Yah

THE YOUNGEST DAUGHTER
In the bathroom

THE OLDEST DAUGHTER
Y'know I
cuts herself off
We really haven't always gotten along
not always
well actually
but
and you
yah you actually spoke to her
on the phone every day
right

THE YOUNGEST DAUGHTER
I did
Pause

THE OLDEST DAUGHTER
And so

THE YOUNGEST DAUGHTER
Yah she lay there

just lay there on the floor

THE OLDEST DAUGHTER
Yah

THE YOUNGEST DAUGHTER
In the bathroom
there on the floor
Pause. THE YOUNGEST DAUGHTER stands up, crosses the floor

THE OLDEST DAUGHTER
She didn't answer the door

THE YOUNGEST DAUGHTER
No
and I got scared
of course
so I let myself in
and then I knew
as soon as I came inside
I knew it

THE OLDEST DAUGHTER
Yah
Short pause
And then you called the
cuts herself off

THE YOUNGEST DAUGHTER
Yah and then
yah they came pretty fast
the doctor
the ambulance

THE OLDEST DAUGHTER
Yah

THE YOUNGEST DAUGHTER
Yah we were supposed to drive to your place
yah
somewhat short pause
and then

somewhat short pause

yah
yah instead we drove here
yah in an ambulance
somewhat short pause
It's awful
yah so awful
Pause

THE OLDEST DAUGHTER
And I've planned a party for her
and now
cuts herself off

THE YOUNGEST DAUGHTER
This can't be happening

THE OLDEST DAUGHTER
No
And they
yah Henning and Johannes

THE YOUNGEST DAUGHTER
Yah did you call Johannes

THE OLDEST DAUGHTER
I couldn't find his number
but yah
yah I called Henning
but he didn't pick up
there was no answer

THE YOUNGEST DAUGHTER
No answer

THE OLDEST DAUGHTER
Henning didn't answer
but I left a message
and told him to call Johannes

THE YOUNGEST DAUGHTER
Yah

somewhat short pause
but Johannes

THE OLDEST DAUGHTER
I told Henning to call him

THE YOUNGEST DAUGHTER
So Johannes doesn't know
Short pause

THE OLDEST DAUGHTER
I don't know
yah if Henning got the message
I had to come here y'know
Short pause
but
yah yah well I told Henning to call him

THE YOUNGEST DAUGHTER
Yah
Short pause
They
cuts herself off
Johannes was supposed to go to your place
yah after work
Pause
And there's nothing they can do
they're saying
it will just take it's course

THE OLDEST DAUGHTER
Nothing
somewhat short pause
But when you found her
yah

THE YOUNGEST DAUGHTER
Yah she just lay there

THE OLDEST DAUGHTER
She didn't say anything

THE YOUNGEST DAUGHTER
No
yah it's really awful
she just lay there
Short pause

THE OLDEST DAUGHTER
Maybe she
cuts herself off

THE YOUNGEST DAUGHTER
And I don't know how long she was lying there
I don't
no of course not
the doctor couldn't say
but not that long
for awhile
for a little while anyway
yah of course
somewhat short pause
it's so awful

THE OLDEST DAUGHTER
But not that long

THE YOUNGEST DAUGHTER
No

THE OLDEST DAUGHTER
I'm sure it wasn't that long
an hour
maybe

THE YOUNGEST DAUGHTER
No
no I don't
don't think so
Pause
And Johannes doesn't know yet

THE OLDEST DAUGHTER
I don't know

I cannot really
cuts herself off

THE YOUNGEST DAUGHTER
But Johannes has to come

THE OLDEST DAUGHTER
Y'know I did
cuts herself off

THE YOUNGEST DAUGHTER
Johannes has to come

THE OLDEST DAUGHTER
I'm sure he's coming
yah if only he
cuts herself off

THE YOUNGEST DAUGHTER
Yah
THE OLDEST DAUGHTER hugs THE YOUNGEST DAUGHTER. She stays standing there, holding her tight. KARSTEN and THE FRIEND come in, a little hesitant

KARSTEN
Yah this is nice

THE FRIEND
This place is ready for a party
that's clear
Short pause

KARSTEN
But I
somewhat short pause
yah I don't really belong here
it's like
I don't really know anyone
at all
yah well the Mom
I met her that one time
in passing
that's all

THE FRIEND
But you know me

KARSTEN
Yah yah
somewhat short pause
but still
I've never even met
cuts himself off

THE FRIEND
Who do you mean

KARSTEN
Yah her the one you were friends with
yah growing up

THE FRIEND
Hilde

KARSTEN
Hilde yah
Short pause

THE FRIEND
Of course
you have to be here

KARSTEN
When you were little
you were always together
but not so much later on

THE FRIEND
No
Short pause

KARSTEN
Did you have a falling out

THE FRIEND
No not exactly
maybe

Short pause

KARSTEN
But you and the mother
Mom
as you call her
you two became even better friends

THE FRIEND
Yah
kinda strange
I guess

KARSTEN
And today
as she celebrates her sixtieth birthday
you are the only one who comes
yah besides family
that is

THE FRIEND
I guess

KARSTEN
And then there's
me
of course
someone who doesn't belong here
somewhat short pause
and they made it pretty clear
yah the sons-in-law
what the hell is he doing here
they said
without saying a word

THE FRIEND
Now you've met them
at least

KARSTEN
Yah
Pause

THE FRIEND
And they sent us in here

KARSTEN
So they could get out of being with us

THE FRIEND
It does seem like that

KARSTEN
No what am I doing here really

THE FRIEND
You can't go

KARSTEN
Why not

THE FRIEND
No don't go
Pause

KARSTEN
Why did you become such good friends
yah you and that Mom

THE FRIEND
I don't know

KARSTEN
You are kinda alike

THE FRIEND
You think so

KARSTEN
Yah
KARSTEN goes over to the window, looks out
The way Mom
as you call her
is as an older person
or whatever you'd say
that's what you'll be like

THE FRIEND
Thank you very much
or
cuts herself off. Short pause. THE FRIEND also goes over to the window

KARSTEN
Anyway it's a nice day

THE FRIEND
Very nice
Pause. THE OLDEST DAUGHTER lets go of THE YOUNGEST DAUGHTER, and walks over to the bed

THE OLDEST DAUGHTER
turns to THE YOUNGEST DAUGHTER
I don't understand it
And so suddenly
totally unexpected
she was y'know
cuts herself off
yah I talked to her yesterday
and she was really looking forward to today
to the party

THE YOUNGEST DAUGHTER
Yah
she was really looking forward to it

THE OLDEST DAUGHTER
She said she'd have to come to terms with turning sixty
it would be ok
she could accept it
if she got this party in exchange
she said
Short pause
She was like a kid
Short pause
There wasn't anything
yah nothing was the matter
was there
yah except
yah well there was always something

The Youngest Daughter
There was

The Oldest Daughter
Something or other
Pause

The Youngest Daughter
Yah

The Oldest Daughter
But nothing specific
yah just
yah the usual things
I think

The Youngest Daughter
Nothing specific
that I know of
Pause

The Oldest Daughter
No it's so awful
Pause
I don't understand it
Short pause
And there's nothing they can do
but
yah
yah should we just accept that
there must be something they can do
yah the doctors
we can't just
cuts herself off
But is she speaking
I mean
yah is she saying anything
yah
The Youngest Daughter shakes her head

No

THE YOUNGEST DAUGHTER goes and takes THE OLDEST DAUGHTER by the hand, they walk away from the bed, as far as possible. THE FRIEND goes and sits down on the sofa

THE YOUNGEST DAUGHTER
softly, towards THE OLDEST DAUGHTER
Maybe
yah I think
yah maybe she can hear
The Nurse said that she couldn't
but

THE OLDEST DAUGHTER
She's not speaking

THE YOUNGEST DAUGHTER
She is speaking
or
yah some sounds
but
yah
yah it's
incoherent
meaningless
she's just saying
yah things

THE OLDEST DAUGHTER
Just saying things
But she can hear
maybe she can hear

THE YOUNGEST DAUGHTER
Yah
yah she's making sounds
kinda
but they don't mean anything
they're just sounds
Pause

THE OLDEST DAUGHTER
She can't speak

The Youngest Daughter
She just says
ahh
e
like that

The Oldest Daughter
And they can't do anything

The Youngest Daughter
The doctor said
yah
yah that she's so severely
yah damaged
that nothing could be done
he thought it was best
to just let it take its course
that's what he said

The Oldest Daughter
He said that
take its course

The Youngest Daughter
Yah

The Oldest Daughter
But
yah
yah should we just accept that
we can't
can we

The Youngest Daughter
What else can we do

The Oldest Daughter
Well that's true

The Youngest Daughter
Yah
Pause

THE OLDEST DAUGHTER
She's sleeping

THE YOUNGEST DAUGHTER
Yah it looks like it

THE OLDEST DAUGHTER
She must be sleeping
Short pause
And yah
yah it's good
that she's sleeping
because if
yah I'm thinking
I don't know how much she's taking in
yah if she can hear
yah you said she could
yah but
yah if she can understand
yah y'know what I mean
Short pause
yah if she's scared
if she's aware
yah

THE YOUNGEST DAUGHTER
We
yah she and I
yah
yah we
we are together
yah
yah I'm sure of that much
I can see it in her eyes
somewhat short pause
yah when her eyes are open

THE OLDEST DAUGHTER
Yah

The Youngest Daughter
Yah sometimes
anyway
somewhat short pause
we speak
yah
yah in a way
I know that
yah
Short pause
But I guess she's sleeping now

The Oldest Daughter
Yah
Pause. The Youngest Daughter goes over to the window, stands there and looks out. The Oldest Daughter sits down on the edge of the bed

The Youngest Daughter
But hey
what took you so long
yah to get here

The Oldest Daughter
So long

The Youngest Daughter
Yah
Short pause

The Oldest Daughter
I came as fast as I could

The Youngest Daughter
But it took so long

The Oldest Daughter
Yah
Pause

The Youngest Daughter
And you haven't gotten the message
yah to Johannes

THE OLDEST DAUGHTER
I tried to call Henning
yah like I said
but he didn't answer
I left a message
asking him to call Johannes

THE YOUNGEST DAUGHTER
But you got hold of Ola

THE OLDEST DAUGHTER
Yah
And he's supposed to come
yah right away
yah
Short pause
yah
towards Mom
yah sweet Mom
don't be scared
yah you
yah sweetie
HENNING comes in
sweetie
sweet Mom
don't be scared
you just
rest
now you'll get to rest
don't be scared
now you'll get to rest
THE OLDEST DAUGHTER takes MOM's hands, stays sitting and holds them in her lap

HENNING
Yah here you are
waiting

KARSTEN
I guess we are

Henning
They should have been here a long time ago

The Friend
Yah

Henning
I don't understand why they're so late

Karsten
No

The Friend
They'll be here soon
Henning sits down on the sofa

Karsten
Yah

Henning
I don't understand
Henning puts his arm on the back of the sofa and The Friend looks down. Johannes comes in
But there's nothing we can do
yah but wait

Karsten
No
Short pause

The Friend
Yah just think that Mom is sixty years old
It's unbelievable

Henning
No
Short pause

The Friend
She takes care of herself
she doesn't look
like she's sixty
no way

HENNING
No

THE FRIEND
She seems so young
Mom
Pause

HENNING
towards THE FRIEND
Good that you two are here
at least
and I just don't understand it
What are they up to
maybe it's the brother
Ola
yah you
yah you know him
The Friend nods
like maybe he's planned a surprise for Mom
with some sort of
trip or something

JOHANNES
Yah it's strange
that might be it
yah
yah that he's planned something or other

HENNING
Another one of his plans
Short pause
They could've at least called
Short pause
but that must be the point that we're supposed to call them
call and ask where they are
I'm sure that's part of the plan
too

JOHANNES
And then they'll be hiding behind a fence
or something

Henning
Or in the closet in the attic
Short pause
No I just don't understand
Short pause
if they'd been
yah coming in the same car
I'd be scared there'd been an accident or something

Johannes
Yah it's strange

The Friend
They'll be here soon

Henning
But they could have called

Johannes
It must be a plan
to do something or other

Karsten
Yah
yah something or other
Short pause. Henning takes his arm back. Pause

Henning
So here we are

Johannes
Should we call

Henning
That must be what they want us to do
yah to call them

The Friend
We could call
couldn't we

Karsten
It can't hurt to call
Anything is possible

Henning
I just don't know
Short pause
But what I do know
is that I will find something to drink

Johannes
Yah thanks that sounds great

The Friend
Thank you
Henning goes out. Karsten looks out the window. Johannes goes and sits down next to The Friend.
Pause

The Oldest Daughter
Mom
you have to answer me
please
Short pause
say something to me
don't just lie there
somewhat short pause
say something to me

The Youngest Daughter
Ola
do you know when he's coming

The Oldest Daughter
No
Pause
But I'm sure he will come as fast as he can
that's what he said

The Youngest Daughter
Sure
Short pause

The Oldest Daughter
Of course he will

The Youngest Daughter
Yah

Pause

The Oldest Daughter
to Mom
And Ola will be here soon
Somewhat short pause
Everyone's coming
everyone's coming to see you
Henning
and Johannes
Ola's coming
he'll be here soon
right

The Youngest Daughter
If only Johannes would get here

The Oldest Daughter
puts down Mom's hands, stands up
But
yah

The Youngest Daughter
Ola
Short pause
what did Ola say
yah when you called

The Oldest Daughter
No
Short pause
yah well I guess he asked what it was
how it happened
who had found her
if there was anything that could be done
somewhat short pause
and then he said he'd come
that's all
yah

MOM
a
a
somewhat short pause
a

THE OLDEST DAUGHTER
Mom

MOM
a
somewhat short pause
la
sa
ka
la
a
a
somewhat short pause
a

THE OLDEST DAUGHTER
Mom
oh Mom
THE YOUNGEST DAUGHTER goes over to the bed
Towards THE YOUNGEST DAUGHTER
Isn't there anything we can do
somewhat short pause
yah but
yah
yah she's just lying there
so

THE YOUNGEST DAUGHTER
We just have to stay here

THE OLDEST DAUGHTER
Yah
Pause
I think she fell asleep

The Youngest Daughter
Yah
yah I guess she's asleep
that's good

The Oldest Daughter
Yah
somewhat short pause
but

The Youngest Daughter
Yah
she's so peaceful lying there
so
somewhat short pause
and so lovely
she is yah
yah beautiful
isn't she
somewhat short pause
and now she's sleeping
sleeping soundly
tucked in her bed
like a little kid
she lies there sleeping

The Oldest Daughter
She's breathing isn't she
Take her pulse
The Youngest Daughter stays standing there
You don't want to
No I'll do it
myself
then

The Youngest Daughter
Yes but
cuts herself off
yah

The Oldest Daughter
You think it's gross

The Youngest Daughter
No
but
cuts herself off. The Oldest Daughter takes Mom's hands, and Mom opens her eyes

The Oldest Daughter
But Mom
I'm here now
Hilde is here
And Nora is here
I just got here
just now
do you recognize me
I am here

The Youngest Daughter
Mom
can you hear

The Oldest Daughter
I am here
can you hear me
Mom
can you hear me
Towards The Youngest Daughter
She's not hearing me
Do you think she can hear

The Youngest Daughter
Of course she can hear
Short pause
Mom
Now
yah both
Hilde
and
I
are

here
Mom

The Oldest Daughter
I am here
It's me
Hilde
I'm here
Mom
I am here
right Mom
And Ola's coming soon
And everybody else is coming
Henning's coming
And Johannes
Everyone will be with you
everyone's coming
We are with you
We'll take care of you
Pause
We'll be here with you
we will

The Youngest Daughter
We'll take care of you
don't be scared ok
Pause. Mom closes her eyes, and The Youngest Daughter goes and stands in front of the window. The Oldest Daughter gets up, stands next to the bed and looks down. Pause. Henning comes in with a bottle and four glasses

Henning
Here we are
yah it's about time
but finally
Henning hands a glass to Johannes and pours, then he pours another glass, hands it to The Friend

The Friend
Thank you
Henning pours again and hands a glass to Karsten

KARSTEN
Thank you very much

HENNING
holds his glass out
Yah let's toast
a toast to the birthday girl
to our extremely dearly beloved Mom
Everyone lifts their glasses, drinks. Short pause. HENNING *shoots his chest forward, wobbles a bit, spreads out his little finger*
Imitates
Thank you
thank you all very much
and you have organized
yah such a gorgeous party
HENNING drinks a sip
Gorgeous
divine
yah it's truly incredible
Pause

JOHANNES
towards THE FRIEND
Yah a toast
a toast to Mom
JOHANNES and THE FRIEND toast together, drink. Pause

HENNING
But where are they
I don't understand it

JOHANNES
No me neither
Short pause
Maybe we
should
call

HENNING
Yah we should
I'll do it

Johannes
Yah
Henning goes out, taking his glass with him. Johannes stretches his arm along the back of the sofa. Karsten looks out the window again. Pause

The Oldest Daughter
Let's hope Ola gets here soon

The Youngest Daughter
And Johannes

The Oldest Daughter
Ola and Mom
they have never
really gotten along
somewhat short pause
they've always
argued about everything
And now he'll regret it
but he
he's not even coming is he
he doesn't care
he never cared
it's
cuts herself off

The Youngest Daughter
He is coming
of course he's coming
and of course he cares

The Oldest Daughter
Sometimes they didn't speak to each other
for long stretches at a time
once it went on for years

The Youngest Daughter
And he didn't say anything when you called

The Oldest Daughter
He did
yah I told you

he said
yah that he'd come

THE YOUNGEST DAUGHTER
That's all
KARSTEN goes and sits down on the sofa

THE OLDEST DAUGHTER
Yah what did you want him to say

THE YOUNGEST DAUGHTER
For years
they didn't speak
they didn't see each other
had nothing to do with each other
somewhat short pause
it went on like that for years
not a single word to each other
never spoke
not a single word
but then
there's a soft knock at the door
they almost never spoke
the only son
they never speak
but now
yah now she can't speak
she's never liked me
he says
she's hated me
always hated me
I never want to speak to her again
he said
Never speak to her again
somewhat short pause, a soft knock at the door again
they didn't get along
in a way
they didn't fit together
too different
maybe

Ola comes in, he stops, stays standing there

Mom
loudly
a
la
ma
complaining
ma
a
m
a
a
aa
maa
somewhat short pause
aa
ma
a
ma
somewhat short pause
ma

The Brother
Yah I
cuts himself off. Pause

Mom
ma
a
a
Short pause
a
Short pause
a
Short pause
ma
Short pause
sa

a
a

THE BROTHER
Yah

THE YOUNGEST DAUGHTER
But
Short pause

THE OLDEST DAUGHTER
This is sad
really awful

THE BROTHER
Yah
But
yah
yah it was a stroke

THE OLDEST DAUGHTER
Yah

THE BROTHER
And nothing can be done

THE OLDEST DAUGHTER
No
I guess not
Pause

THE BROTHER
Yah
To THE YOUNGEST DAUGHTER
You were the one who found her
Short pause
She was lying on the floor
Short pause
Can she speak

THE YOUNGEST DAUGHTER
Yah she was lying on the floor

Pause

THE BROTHER

And there's nothing that can be done

Pause

Nothing

THE OLDEST DAUGHTER

She can't speak

just

somewhat short pause

yah you heard it yourself

THE BROTHER

Yah

Pause

THE OLDEST DAUGHTER

It's too awful

Yah

Yah really way too awful

I have to

yah

towards THE YOUNGEST DAUGHTER

yah can I

yah go out for a bit

I need some air

yah

Pause

THE YOUNGEST DAUGHTER

I should

cuts herself off

THE BROTHER

I can stay here

I can

you two go

THE YOUNGEST DAUGHTER hands the bowl and sponge to THE BROTHER, he takes it, looks at it inquisitively, she walks away from him, stops and stands there

THE YOUNGEST DAUGHTER
No I can't

THE OLDEST DAUGHTER
I'll stay
I can stay

THE BROTHER
No now it's my turn
you two go ahead
THE YOUNGEST DAUGHTER goes out

THE OLDEST DAUGHTER
I don't know
somewhat short pause
yah if I can take any more of this
I
no

THE BROTHER
Go on you too
get some air
yah
yah I can stay here
THE OLDEST DAUGHTER goes out. The Brother looks towards the bed. Pause

MOM
a

THE BROTHER looks at MOM
a
Pause
a
MOM sits up in her bed, opens her eyes, looks at THE BROTHER
a
a
ma
ma
somewhat short pause
ma
ma

THE BROTHER
Mom
How are you Mom

MOM
ma
a

THE BROTHER
Are you better Mom
MOM lies down again

MOM
a
somewhat short pause
a
sa
somewhat short pause
ka
somewhat short pause
sa
ka
la

THE BROTHER
And you

MOM
a
a
a
j
Pause. THE BROTHER goes over to the window, stands there and looks out. THE FRIEND goes over to the window and looks out. Both JOHANNES and KARSTEN walk out into the space, they stop and stand there. Pause. THE NURSE comes in, she goes over to MOM, takes her pulse, then places her hands folded in her lap, closes her eyelids

THE NURSE
So it's over
Long pause

The Brother
But hey

The Nurse
Yah

The Brother
Just now

The Nurse
Yah

The Brother
Just now
while I was standing here
while I was standing here looking out the window
yah
yah
hey
do you know
yah
yah I was standing there
and I was thinking that I didn't feel grief
didn't feel anything
and I thought it was because Mom and I
yah we weren't very close
not always

The Nurse
No

The Brother
Or maybe
in a way we were very close
in another way
but I
yah I wasn't sad
or anything
and
yah
yah just empty
like emptied out

like nothing
that's how I was
and
yah
somewhat short pause

The Nurse
But hey
yah I think I should
yah get the doctor

The Brother
But hey

The Nurse

Yah

The Brother
Yah while I was standing there just now
thinking nothing
feeling nothing
just empty
I looked out the window

The Nurse
It's routine
so I
cuts herself off

The Brother
But
yah
yah I stood there
and then
and then quiet
it became quiet
everything became quiet
and there
Short pause
there
Short pause

there
in the sky there
he points
and through me
through me
he looks towards THE NURSE
yah like this yellow
and quivering
kind of
came through me
you know
points toward the bed
from that bed over there
towards me
through me
somewhat short pause
and up into the sky
KARSTEN goes over and stands next to THE FRIEND, he looks out the window

THE NURSE
Yah
yah I'm listening

THE BROTHER
there was
there was a light
an ordinary light
and then a kind of light that couldn't be seen
it could be seen
and not seen at the same time
and it was yellow
yellow and white at the same time
if that's possible
that light
that light
the light up there in the sky
that light went through me

THE NURSE
Yah

The Brother
and there
in the sky over there
I don't understand it
because the light goes through me
and the light expands
golden light
first wide
and then light as the wind
and at first it's dense
and then airy
and then it spreads out
golden
across the sky
everywhere
vanishing
vanishing out into the sky
And everything feels good
And everything is golden
And everything is quiet
everything is golden silence
And then
cuts himself off

The Nurse
Maybe that's how it is to die
Pause. The Brother stands there and looks into the sky and then he turns towards Mom
Here
I can take that
The Brother hands the bowl and sponge to The Nurse, who takes them. The Youngest Daughter comes in.
Towards The Youngest Daughter
It's over now

The Youngest Daughter
Mom is dead

The Nurse
Now she can rest
Pause

And now we'll
yah prepare her
Long pause. The Oldest Daughter comes in

The Youngest Daughter
towards The Oldest Daughter
Mom is dead
She died while
cuts herself off. The Nurse goes out and The Oldest Daughter and The Youngest Daughter hold each other, stay standing there holding each other. The Friend goes and sits down on the sofa. The Brother walks over and strokes Mom's hair, then he goes out. The sisters let go of each other, they walk over and stand next to the bed. The Nurse comes in again, and she walks over to the bed. Pause

The Oldest Daughter
I have to call Henning
Yah

The Youngest Daughter
Go ahead
call
The Oldest Daughter goes out

The Nurse
Well it's over
now she can rest

The Youngest Daughter

Yah
Pause

The Nurse
It went fast

The Youngest Daughter
I wasn't there

The Nurse
But your brother was
she wasn't alone

The Youngest Daughter
I should have been there

Short pause

THE NURSE
Now we'll
somewhat short pause
yah prepare her

THE YOUNGEST DAUGHTER
Yah

THE NURSE
You can see her again later

THE YOUNGEST DAUGHTER
But I should have been there
I was outside
she was alone

THE NURSE
He was there
THE YOUNGEST DAUGHTER
She was alone
I wasn't there
Pause. THE NURSE begins to wheel out the bed
No don't
Don't do that

THE NURSE
You can see her again later

THE YOUNGEST DAUGHTER
Mom died alone
THE NURSE wheels the bed out. Pause. THE YOUNGEST DAUGHTER goes out. Very long pause. HENNING comes in

HENNING
They
yah
yah she is
Short pause
yah
Short pause

dead
somewhat short pause
yah
yah Mom

THE FRIEND
Mom is dead
Pause

HENNING
Yah she
cuts himself off. Pause. KARSTEN walks over and sits down on the sofa, puts his arm around THE FRIEND's shoulders
I just talked to Hilde
She had called
yah left a message
Short pause
yah on the voicemail
Short pause
yah
yah I didn't hear the phone
somewhat short pause
I'd left it in the hallway by the door
it was a stroke
that's what she said in the message
but now
somewhat short pause
yah I was trying to call her
but then she called
just now
I stood there with the phone in my hand
somewhat short pause
trying to call her
one more time
and then
short pause
yah Mom had just died
Short pause
it went fast

a stroke
Short pause
yah

JOHANNES
Mom is dead
Pause. THE FRIEND and KARSTEN stand up, put down their drinks, go out slowly

HENNING
Yah it's awful
She
somewhat short pause
Hilde
didn't sound like herself at all
Pause

JOHANNES
I guess we have to
yah
cuts himself off

HENNING
Mom is
cuts himself off

JOHANNES
They were there
somewhat short pause
yah when she died

HENNING
Apparently they were outside right at that moment
Ola was there
somewhat short pause
and Hilde
somewhat short pause
yah she said
yah that Mom couldn't stand being alone with him
that it killed her
he came in
and then she died

JOHANNES
Yah

HENNING
It was too much for Mom
somewhat short pause

JOHANNES
Yah

HENNING
That's what she said

JOHANNES
I guess we should
cuts himself off. Pause

HENNING
This turned into
cuts himself off. Pause. JOHANNES goes out, he takes his glass with him, and HENNING goes out after him. Very long pause. THE NURSE wheels in the hospital bed again, it's empty now, she goes out
The lights go down, black.

Biographical Notes

Authors

Igor Bauersima (b. 1964) is an author, architect, musician, designer, and theatre and film director. In 1993 he helped to found the OFF OFF Bühne, an alternative theatre group, for which he has written and staged many productions, such as *Plane Thoughts*, *Tourist Saga*, and *Snobs*. His films include *Terminal Diner*, *Bowling*, and *Making Off*. He received a prize for the best alternative theatre production at the 1998 Impulse Festival in North Rhine-Westphalia for *Forever Godard* and, in 2003, the Young Directors prize at Salzburg. Bauersima has directed at important theatres such as Wiener Burgtheater, Schauspiel Hannover, Schauspielhaus Zürich, and Schauspielhaus Hamburg. Born in Prague, he now lives in Zürich and Paris.

Jon Fosse (b. 1959) is the author of over thirty plays, as well as novels, poetry, essays, and children's books. His work has been translated into more than forty languages. Among his many plays are *The Name*, *Dream of Autumn*, *Winter*, *Mother and Child*, *Afternoon*, *Beautiful*, *Visits*, *Night Sings Its Songs*, and *Meanwhile the lights go down and everything becomes black*. They have been performed on major stages across Europe and around the world, including Japan, Australia, Malawi, and Chile. Fosse is the recipient of numerous international awards and honors. In 2003 he became the youngest person ever to win Norway's highest cultural honor, the Norsk Kulturråd Ærespris; more recently, the French government made him a Chevalier of Ordre National du Mérite. He lives in Bergen.

Juan Mayorga (b. 1965) is a playwright and essayist whose plays include *Road to Heaven*, *The Scorched Garden*, *Nocturnal*, and *Love Letters to Stalin*. He has also created new versions of plays by Shakespeare, Calderón, Chekhov, Durrenmatt, and Ibsen. He has taught playwriting at the Royal Academy of Drama (Madrid) and served as an editor of *Primer Acto*. Mayorga's plays have been produced in many European languages, and in Latin America, England, Ireland, and the U.S. He has been awarded several prizes for his work, including the Valle-Inclán Prize and the National Theatre Prize. He lives in Madrid.

Roland Schimmelpfennig (b. 1967) has worked for a time as a journalist in Istanbul, as a translator in the United States, and as dramaturg for the Schaubühne in Berlin. He has been a freelance author since 1996. He has written over thirty stage and radio plays, which have been produced in the major German-language theatres and across Europe. He is also a Professor of Theatre at the School of Art and Design Berlin Weissensee. *Frankfurter Rundschau* has called Schimmelpfennig "the leading German dramatist." Two of his plays are regularly produced in the U. S., *Push Up 1–3* and *The Arabian Night*. He lives in Berlin.

Małgorzata Sikorska-Miszczuk (b. 1964) has written film and TV scripts, short stories, and radio plays, in addition to dramatic works for the stage. *The Death of the Squirrel-Man* received the first prize in a competition for a play about Ulrike Meinhof held by Teatr Usta Usta, Poznań and Teatr Rozmaitości, Warsaw. The performance was invited to represent new Polish drama at the 2008 "New Plays from Europe" biennale in Wiesbaden, Germany. It has also been translated into German. Sikorska-Miszczuk is the author of the new play *Madness*, and the radio play *The Suitcase*, which has received several awards at playwriting competitions in Poland. She lives in Warsaw.

Goran Stefanovski (b.1952) is a dramatist and essayist whose writings have been translated and published in numerous languages. Among his many plays are *Sarajevo*, *The Demon of Debarmaalo*, *Landscape X: Euralien*, and *Everyman*. A recent lecture, entitled "What Future for the Balkans and the EU?", was given at the European Cultural Foundation Conference, The Hague. He is a recipient of the Vilenica Literary Prize, awarded by an international jury to an author from Central Europe for outstanding achievement in the field of literary creativity and essay writing. One of the former Yugoslavia's prominent theatre professionals before leaving Macedonia in the late-1990s, he founded the playwriting course at the Faculty of Dramatic Arts in Skopje. He now lives in Canterbury, England, and teaches at the Canterbury Christ Church University.

Petr Zelenka (b. 1967) is a playwright, theatre and film director, and a screenwriter. His films have won several awards, including the Czech Lion, first prize at the Karlovy Vary and the Moscow International Film Festivals, and his latest film—an adaptation of Dostoyevsky's *Brothers Karamazov*—was the official Czech entry for the 2009 Academy Awards. The films *Buttoners* and *Year of the Devil* have been widely distributed in Europe and abroad. His first play, *Tales of Ordinary Madness*, which he also directed as a film, received the 2002 Alfréd Radok Prize for Production of the Year under his direction, and his latest play, *Coming Clean*, was commissioned by the Narodowy Stary Teatr in Cracow, Poland. Zelenka is also the author of the play *Theremin*. He lives in Prague.

Translators

Melanie Dreyer specializes in international collaboration, and is Co-Artistic Director of International Culture Lab, based in New York City. Her translations have been produced across the country and in Canada. She is Assistant Professor of Acting and Directing at Cornell University and also works as a free-lance director.

David Johnston has translated plays by Juan Mayorga, Federico García Lorca, Ramon Valle-Inclán, Calderón, and Lope de Vega, the latter most recently for the Royal Shakespeare Company and the Washington Shakespeare Company. He is Head of the School of Languages, Literatures and Performing Arts at Queen's University Belfast.

Anna Köhler is an actor, translator, and director. She has performed with The Wooster Group, Steve Buscemi, Richard Foreman, Richard Maxwell, John Jesurun, and Fiona Templeton. She has also translated both German and American authors, including René Pollesch and Richard Maxwell.

Jadwiga Kosicka has translated plays by Janusz Głowacki, Hanna Krall, Felicja Kruszewska, and Amelia Hertz, and many essays in Jan Kott's *Gender of Rosalinda, Memory of the Body*, and *Four Decades of Polish Essays.* She is the translator of the letters of Stanisława Przybyszewska, Zygmunt Hübner's *Theater and Politics*, and *Still Alive*, the autobiography of Jan Kott.

Stepan S. Simek is Associate Professor of Theatre at Lewis & Clark College in Portland, Oregon, and a freelance director. He has published articles on contemporary Czech theatre in *Theatreforum* and *Slavic and East European Performance*. His translations from Czech and French have been produced in New York and in regional theatres and universities. He holds an MFA in directing from the University of Washington.

Sarah Cameron Sunde is a director and translator. She has directed U.S. premieres of plays by international playwrights: *The Asphalt Kiss* by Brazil's Nelson Rodrigues, and her own translations of *Night Sings Its Songs*, *deathvariations*, and *Sa ka la* by Jon Fosse. Other directing credits include productions at The Guthrie Theater, Rattlestick Playwrights Theater, and New Georges, where she is the Associate Director. Sunde is co-founder of Oslo Elsewhere and the Translation Think Tank.

Editors

Bonnie Marranca is the publisher and editor of PAJ Publications and *PAJ: A Journal of Performance and Art*. The author of *Performance Histories*, *Ecologies of Theatre*, and *Theatre-writings*, she has also edited several anthologies, including *Conversations on Art and Performance*, *Interculturalism and Performance*, *Plays for the End of the Century*, *Theatre of the Ridiculous*, and *The Theatre of Images*. A Guggenheim Fellow and Fulbright Senior Scholar and the recent recipient of the Leverhulme Trust Visiting Professorship at Queen Mary/University of London and University of the Arts London, she is Professor of Theatre at The New School for Liberal Arts/Eugene Lang College.

Małgorzata Semil is a theatre critic and translator who, since 1966, has been a member of the editorial board and Deputy Editor (1989-2002) of the monthly *DIALOG*, one of Europe's most important theatre journals. Literary manager of Teatr Powszechny (1995-2007) and, since 2007, literary advisor at Teatr Ateneum in Warsaw, she is President of the Polish Center of the International Theatre Institute (ITI). She has translated into Polish over one hundred English, American, Australian, and African plays, by world renowned authors, including Edward Albee, Neil LaBute, David Mamet, Adam Rapp, Sam Shepard, Judith Thompson, Michael Frayn, David Hare, Christopher Hampton, Sarah Kane, Wole Soyinka, Athol Fugard, Brian Friel, and Martin McDonagh.